BLACK AMERICA SERIES

CLEARWATER
FLORIDA

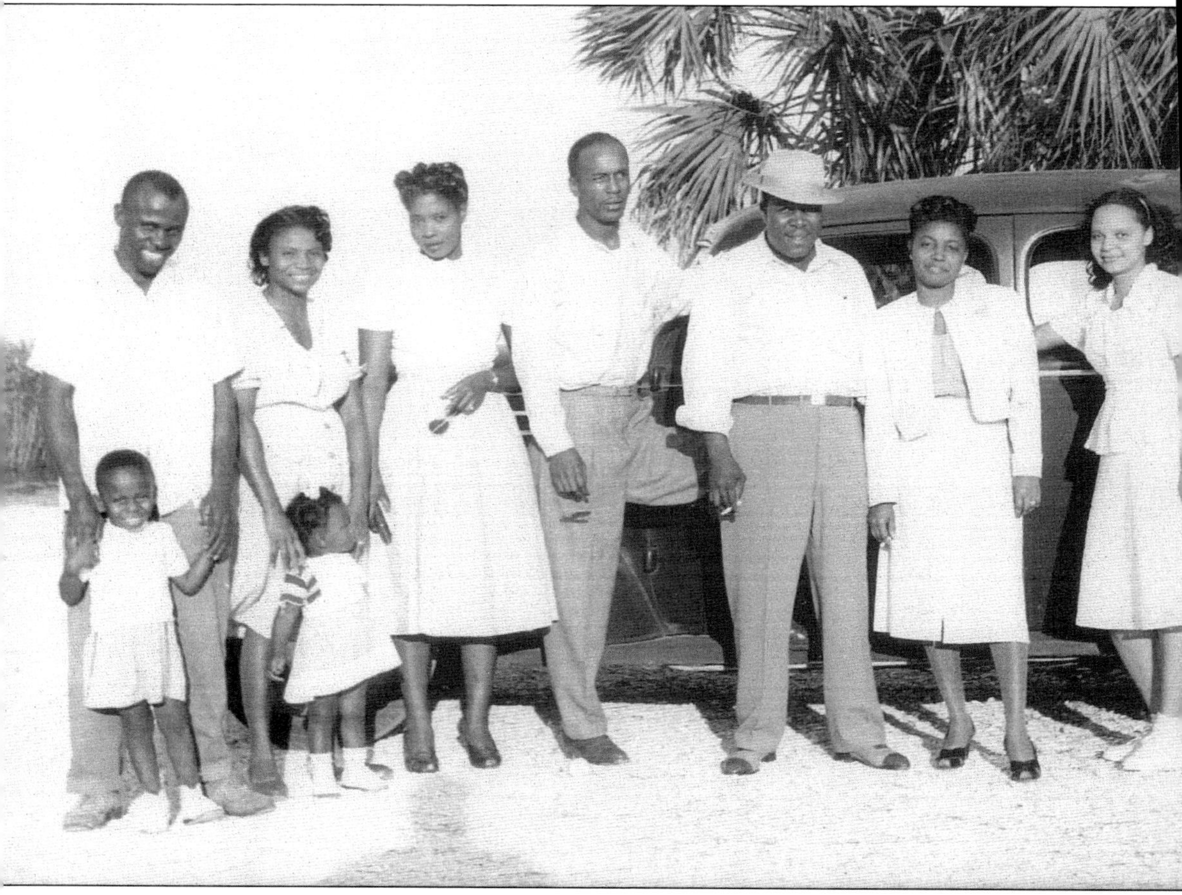

Friends escort Christine Morris, who is returning to college, to a Tamps Bay bus station in the late 1940s. Along the way, they stop on the Clearwater Causeway to take this photo. Pictured from left to right are Mr. and Mrs. Leroy Rhodes and children, Edward and Eleanor; Mr. and Mrs. Lewis Paige; Mr. and Mrs. Jack Morris; and Mrs. Wooding, wife of James Wooding Jr., who is taking the photograph.

BLACK AMERICA SERIES

CLEARWATER
FLORIDA

Sandra W. Rooks and Randolph Lightfoot

ARCADIA
PUBLISHING

ISBN 978-0-7385-1473-4

Published by Arcadia Publishing
Charleston, South Carolina

Printed in the United States of America

Library of Congress Catalog Card Number: 2002109579

For all general information contact Arcadia Publishing at:
Telephone 843-853-2070
Fax 843-853-0044
E-Mail sales@arcadiapublishing.com
For customer service and orders:
Toll-Free 1-888-313-2665

Visit us on the Internet at www.arcadiapublishing.com

We dedicate this book to Christine W. Morris, who not only contributed immensely to the images captured in the book, but who also worked untiringly in assisting us in archiving and selecting the contents for the book. We also dedicate the book to Dorothy M. Thompson for devoting so much of her life to collecting the history of African Americans in Clearwater and for inspiring us to do the same. We pay tribute to the teachers, principals, and staffs of Curtis Elementary, Williams Elementary, and Pinellas High School, who helped shape and mold the lives of many of the subjects depicted in the book. And, finally, we pay tribute to our family members and friends who inspired us, got excited along with us, and urged us on as the book developed. Thank you so much!

Contents

ACKNOWLEDGMENTS

We are truly grateful to the many who have contributed and assisted us in the production of this book. We thank Althemese Barnes for encouraging us to write the book. We acknowledge the board of directors and members of the Pinellas County African American History Museum. We thank Christine Morris, whose 33 years of experience as a librarian for the City of Clearwater taught her to hold on to precious memories of the past, which she graciously shared with us. We thank Rosalie Robinson, who through the inspiration of her history teacher, recognized the importance of saving and collecting historic pieces at an early age. We also thank Milton P. Rooks Jr. for the many pictures he held on to that belonged to his parents. For their volunteer service in helping us put everything together, we thank Donald J. Ivey, curator of collections for the Pinellas County Historical Museum, Sarah N. Musooli, a student volunteer, and Mary P. Haire, a retired English teacher. For the many contributions from their family albums, personal collections, and church archives, we thank Talmadge Rutledge, Donald Keene, Leola B. Washington, Mary Cummins, Margaret Algee, Barbara Williams, and Gloria Jones. For sharing copies of programs from their fraternities, sororities, and other social organizations, we thank Mayme W. Hodges, Lovetta Williams, Stella Bradley, Kimberly Cecil, and Rose Brewton. For the use of office space, we thank the Pinellas County School System, Alpha Kappa Alpha Sorority, Inc., Nu Beta Omega Chapter, and Alpha Phi Alpha Fraternity, Inc., Omicron Beta Lambda Chapter. To those whose names should be included in the list, but were inadvertently omitted, please forgive us for the oversight.

INTRODUCTION

" When an elder dies, it is as if a whole library burned down." — African Proverb

Black America Series: Clearwater, Florida brings to the forefront the lifestyles of people who maintained their pride and dignity despite the obstacles that stood in their way. They took pride in the way they dressed, the way they raised their children, and even in the stern way their parents and teachers disciplined them. When times were tough, these proud people turned to the church for spiritual guidance and to each other for strength and support. In spite of all the indignities and Jim Crow restrictions of the past, they held firmly to their beliefs. They believed in equality of opportunity and the ability to live the "American Dream," regardless of a person's station in life.

The book is not meant to provide the reader with a comprehensive study of the African-American experience in Clearwater, but with a sampling of what life was like, particularly in the years between the early 1900s and the late 1970s. What surprised the authors most was that many of the contributors felt that their pasts had no merit. Often times, old pictures were kept in shoeboxes collecting dust, or in cardboard boxes stored outside, and some were hanging on the walls in plain view but were deemed unimportant.

Step into the history of these proud people when you turn the following pages and see the rare images that have been preserved for future generations. Perhaps you can sense the pride felt by the subjects who are portrayed. We hope you enjoy this pictorial journey.

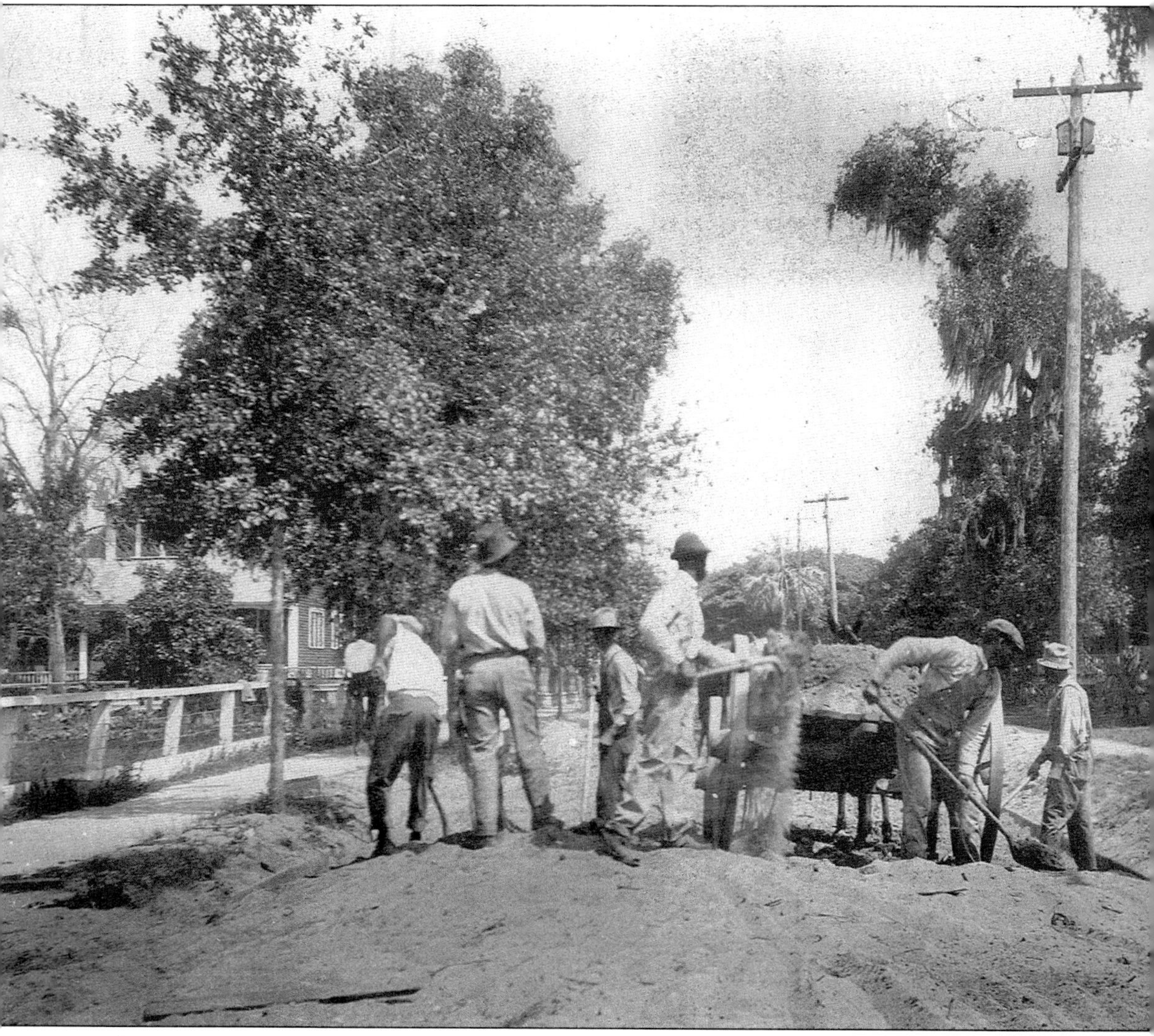

African-American workers made possible the construction of many roads in Clearwater. This photograph was taken during the paving of Osceola Avenue in 1910.

One

Early Settlers and Pioneers

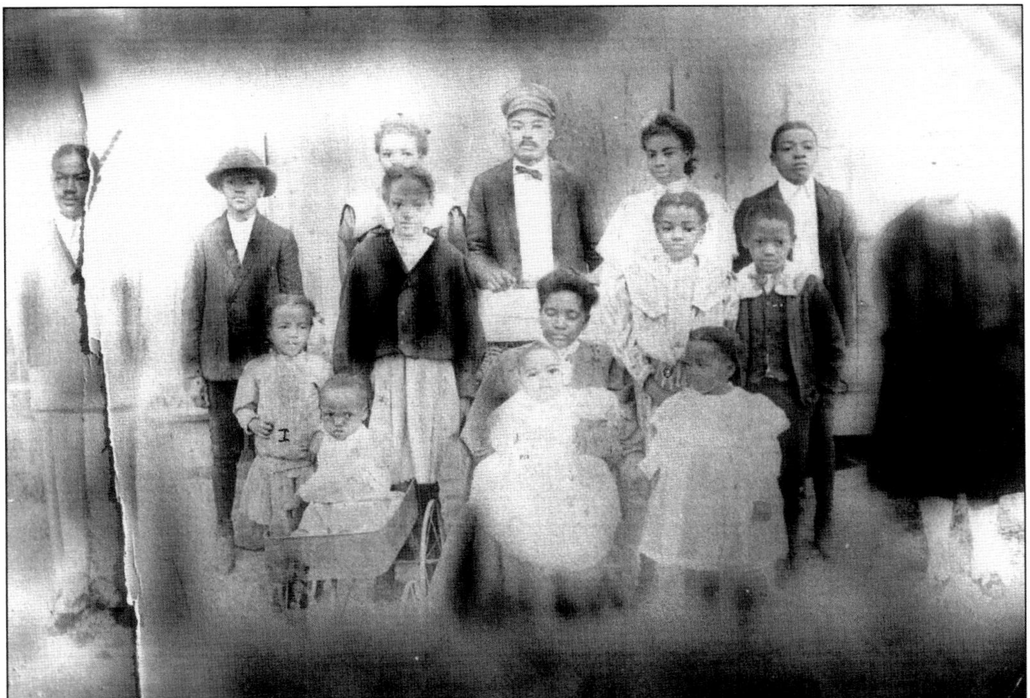

Mack Dixon Sr. is shown here with his wife and 13 of his 15 children in a 1905 photo. The Dixon family moved to Clearwater from Hampton, Florida and settled in "Bobbitt Quarters," an area set aside for African Americans near the railroad tracks. With profits acquired from the sale of property that became the cornerstone of the African-American community, Dixon was able to purchase a large two-story house for his family on Washington Street. He established a legacy of business ownership that has endured for over 100 years.

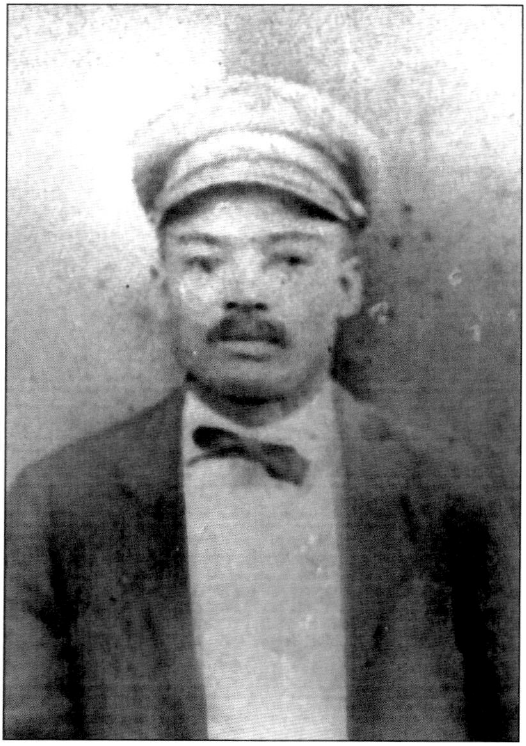

Mack Dixon Sr. is shown in a 1905 photo. He came to Clearwater from the tiny community of Hampton, near Starke, Florida. From the salary he earned as a train conductor, and from additional work he took on at a local lumber mill, he was able to purchase the property between Cleveland and Court Streets and Greenwood Avenue and Myrtle Street, an area that eventually became known as the "Mack Dixon Subdivision." This area became the heart of the African-American community in Clearwater.

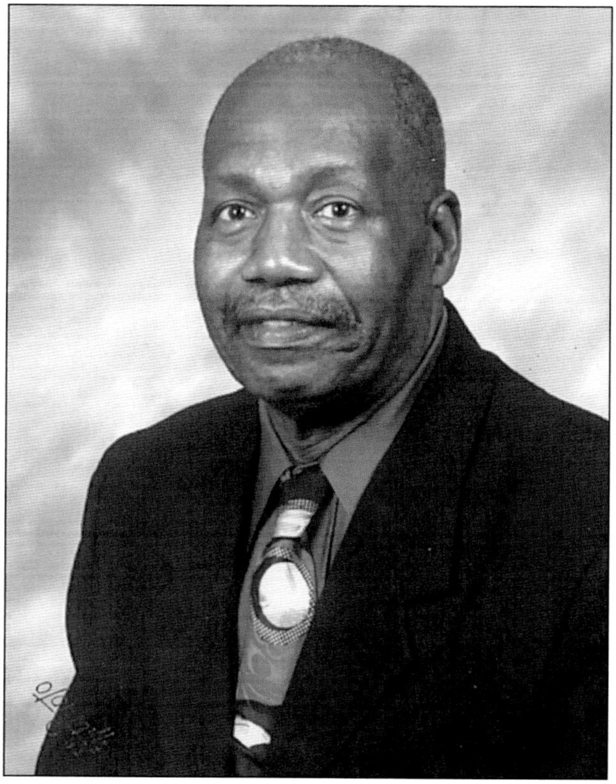

Bernard Dixon, grandson of Mack Dixon Sr., continued the proud tradition of his grandfather by owning and operating B&T Hair and Beauty Supply, a clothing and cosmetics business, which had locations on Greenwood Avenue and Highland Avenue in Clearwater and a later location in Largo.

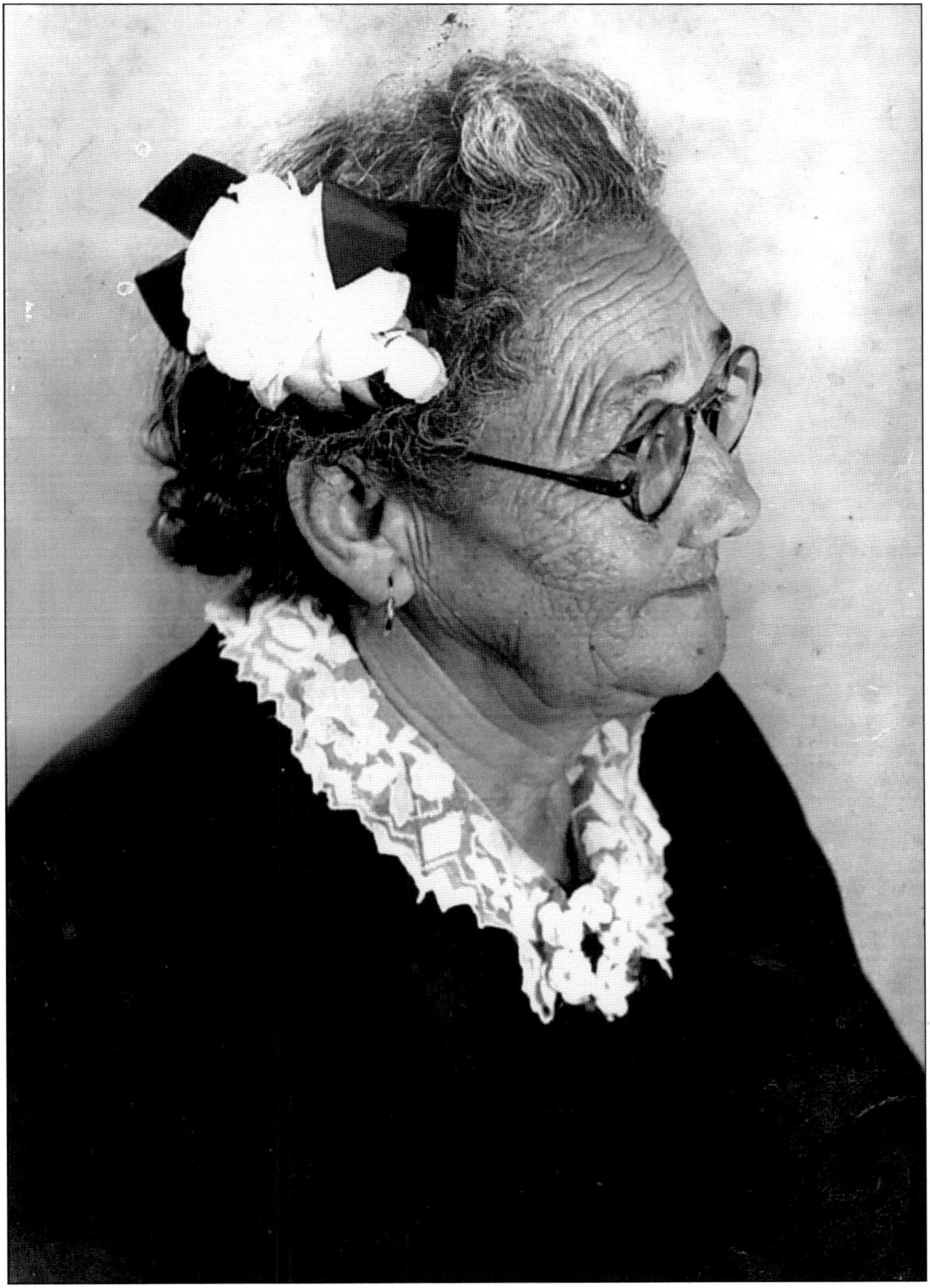

This is a photograph of Blanche Littlejohn, who came to Clearwater in 1913 and lived to be 108. She was in great demand as a speaker because of her sharp knowledge of early Clearwater history. Everyone in Clearwater held Mrs. Littlejohn in high esteem because she served as the link to our heritage.

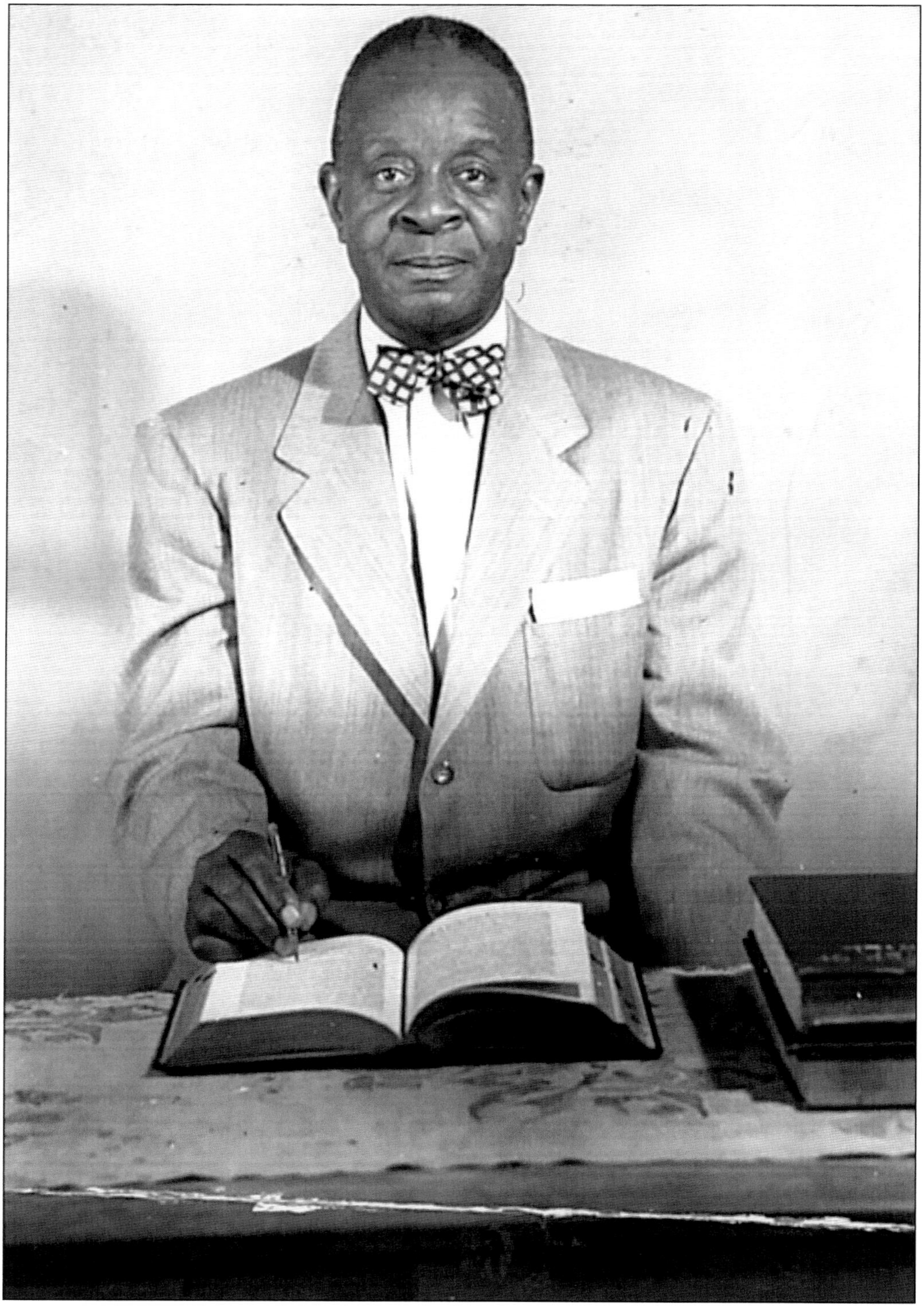

Shirley W. Curtis was a native of High Springs, Florida and came to Clearwater in 1912. In 1924, he was appointed principal of the Pinellas Industrial Institute in Clearwater, which in 1930 became Pinellas High School and was then attended exclusively by African Americans.

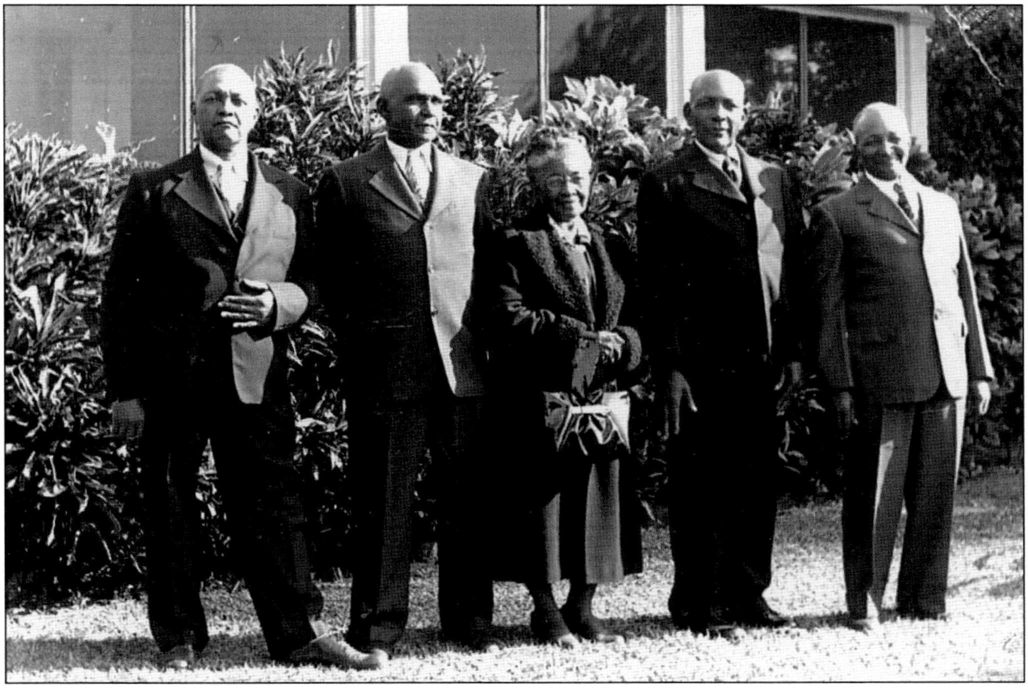

The stalwarts of the Wigfall family are shown in a 1952 photo sporting their Sunday best. Pictured from left to right are Eddie Wigfall Sr., Sidney Wigfall, Adeline Wigfall Johnson, Peter Wigfall, and Thomas Wigfall.

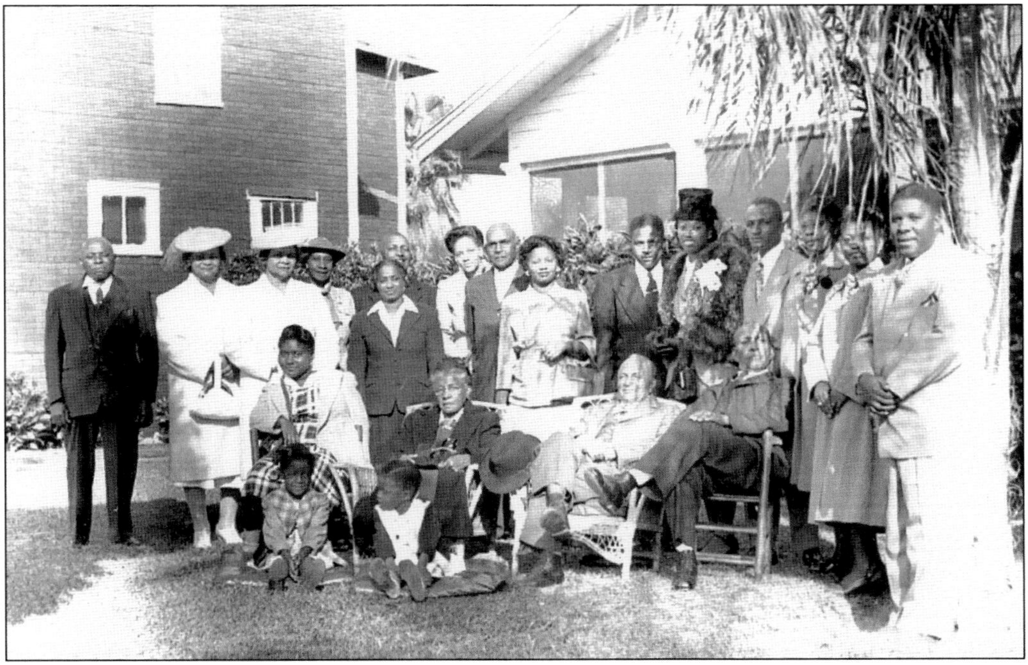

This photograph was taken at the Wigfall family gathering on Christmas Day in 1948 on Railroad Avenue. The Wigfalls owned several businesses in the Clearwater area including a laundry pressing company and a taxicab service.

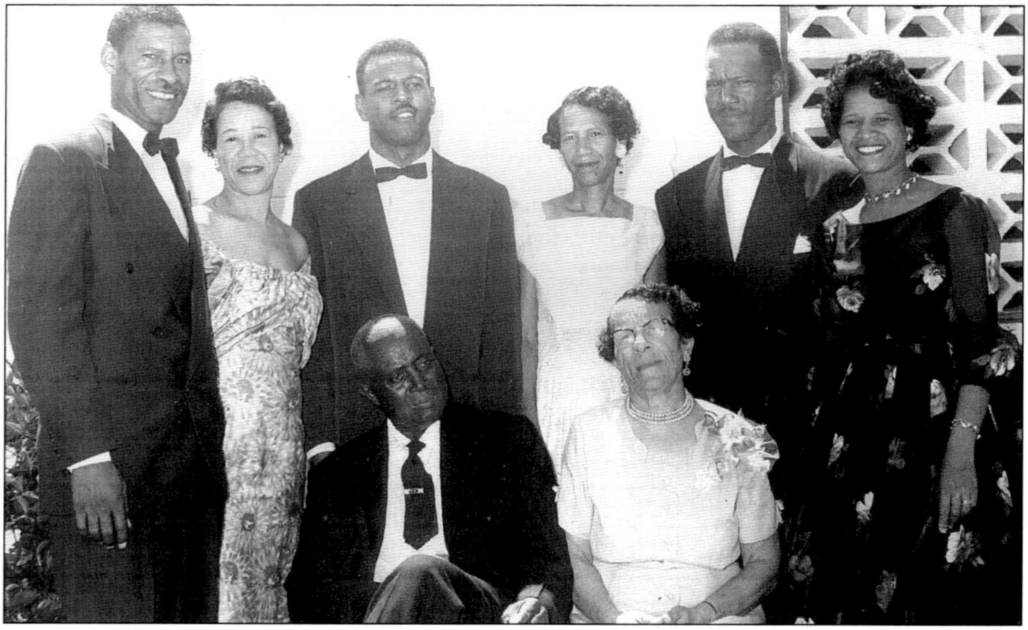

Shown here is homecoming day for the Rutledge family at an Independence Day family reunion at the home of Clearwater pioneer businessman Calvert C. Rutledge in 1959. The reunion attracted all six Rutledge siblings and more than 100 other relatives and friends. The Rutledge family operated several successful businesses in Clearwater including a grocery store, laundry, hair styling, and a dry cleaning establishment. A proud Mr. and Mrs. Rutledge are shown seated, as they pose formally with their children.Standing, from left to right, are Leonard, who owns Clearwater's Palm Launderette; Clearwater hair stylist Lydia Jordan; Clearwater dry cleaning establishment owner Talmadge Rutledge; Marjorie E. Thaxton of Norfolk, Virginia; Clearwater brick mason Charles C. Jr.; and Mrs. Bertram (Ernestine) Williams of Seattle, Washington, a nurses' supervisor. The reunion was the first in 15 years.

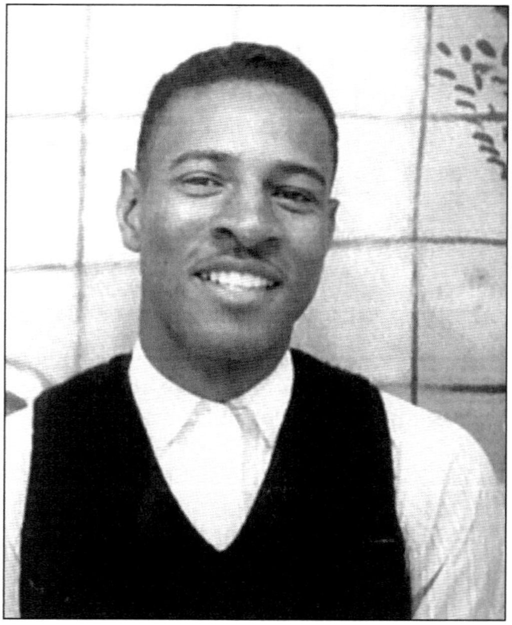

Talmadge Rutledge continues the entrepreneurial spirit started by his pioneer father, Calvert C. Rutledge Sr., with his ownership of a dry cleaner and laundromat. Talmadge was a community activist and staged protests to break the barriers of discrimination in Clearwater.

Rev. Arthur Jackson, co-founder of Mt. Zion Methodist Church, is pictured during the 1920s. In 1918, Reverend Jackson from Archer, Florida, and Rev. J.S. Todd came to Clearwater and found two missions serving without a permanent church home. One was serving in a small house and the other in the Methodist mission. The parent mission had been destroyed by a tropical storm. The members worked together and decided to purchase two lots so that they could be centrally located and worship together. The lots were purchased on September 22, 1920. Reverend Jackson and the trustees of the combined missions built the first church and named it Mt. Zion Methodist Episcopal Church. The pastor and the men of the church did much of the building's construction without pay. The ladies prepared food and served the men during lunchtime.

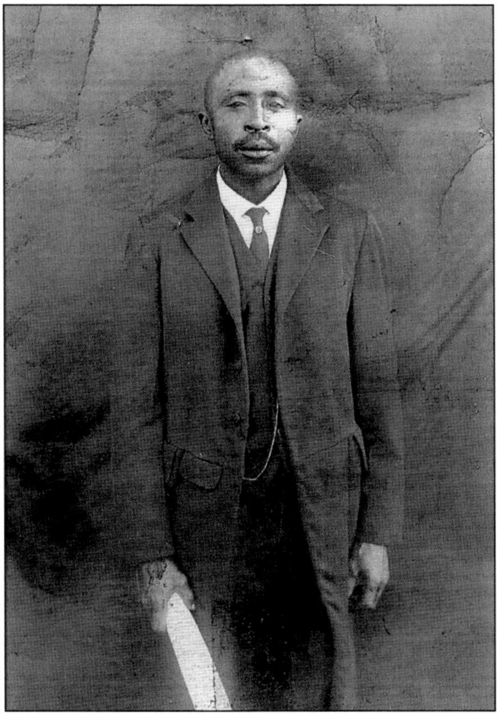

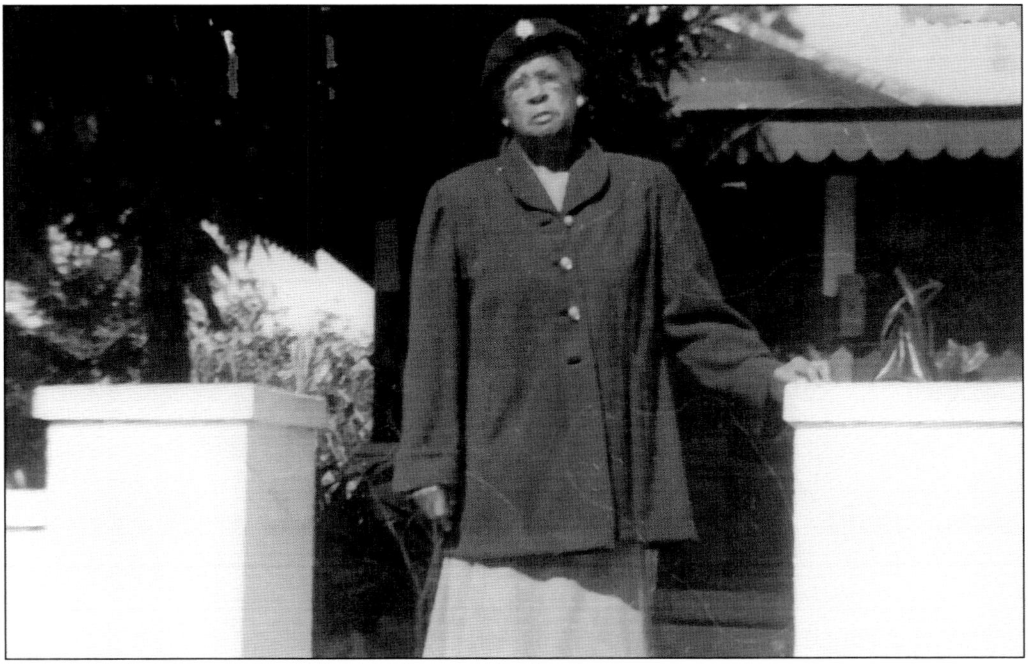

Della Jackson poses in front of her home on Palm Bluff Street in Clearwater. Mrs. Jackson, wife of Rev. Arthur Jackson, who was the co-founder of Mt. Zion Methodist Church, was a certified midwife between the 1930s and the 1950s. Because of Clearwater's Jim Crow laws, African-American babies were delivered in the basement of Morton Plant Hospital. Mrs. Jackson was the first African-American midwife to assist a physician at Morton Plant Hospital.

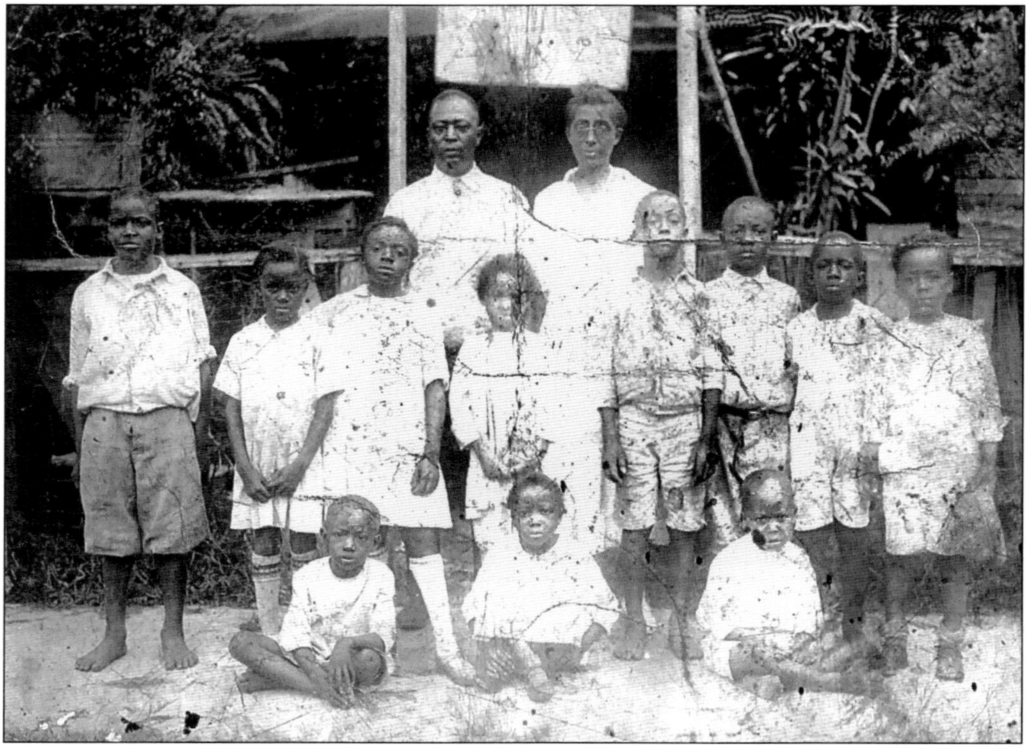

This is an unidentified family in Clearwater in the early 1900s.

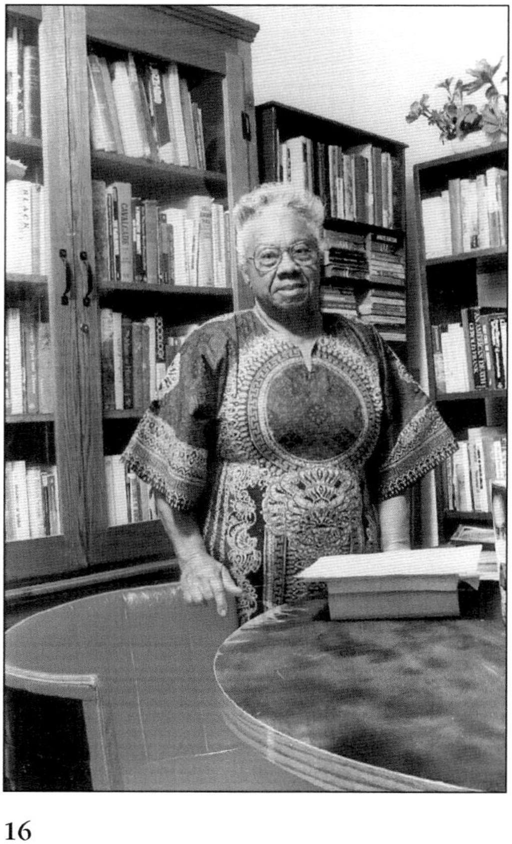

Dorothy M. Thompson, pioneer educator and historian, is pictured in her African-American History Museum. In 1943, Dorothy Thompson became the plaintiff in a salary equalization suit against the Pinellas County School Board. On October 17, 1945, the Pinellas County School Board approved an equal pay plan. Dorothy Thompson's determination and persistence brought retribution from school administrators. She was transferred to Jordan Elementary in St. Petersburg, 22 miles from her Clearwater home, and she remained there for 14 years.

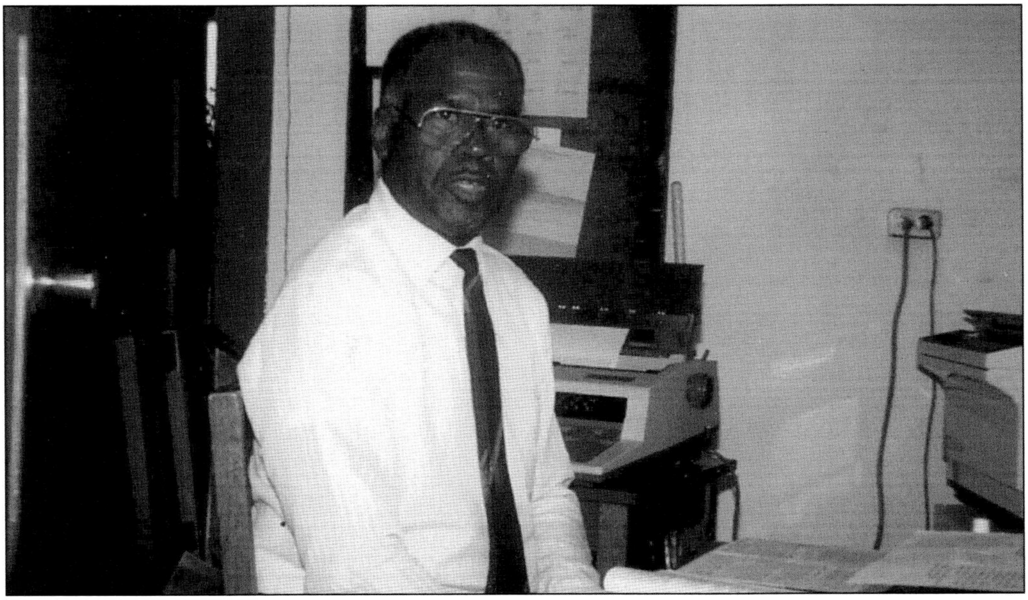

James C. Rembert was the first principal of Ridgecrest Elementary School. In 1957, he was appointed to serve as principal of Ridgecrest, a predominantly African-American school. In 1969, Ridgecrest only served fifth and sixth grade students, as the school was used as the focal point for integration in Pinellas County. Mr. Rembert's leadership was necessary for a smooth transition. Teachers, students, and citizens admired Mr. Rembert for his dedication and devotion to "his children" and to education. Mr. Rembert's parents were pioneer members of Clearwater's historic Mt. Olive A.M.E. Church, in which he was raised and is still a member.

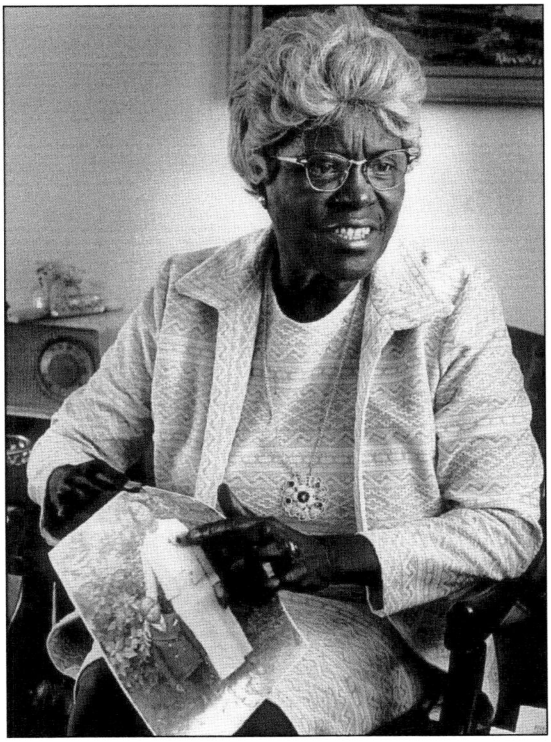

This is a photo of Lula Hatchett, matriarch of a family that produced a son, Paul, who became a Clearwater City Commissioner, and another son, Joseph Jr., who became the first African-American judge to serve on the Florida State Supreme Court and later the first to serve on a Federal District Court in the South.

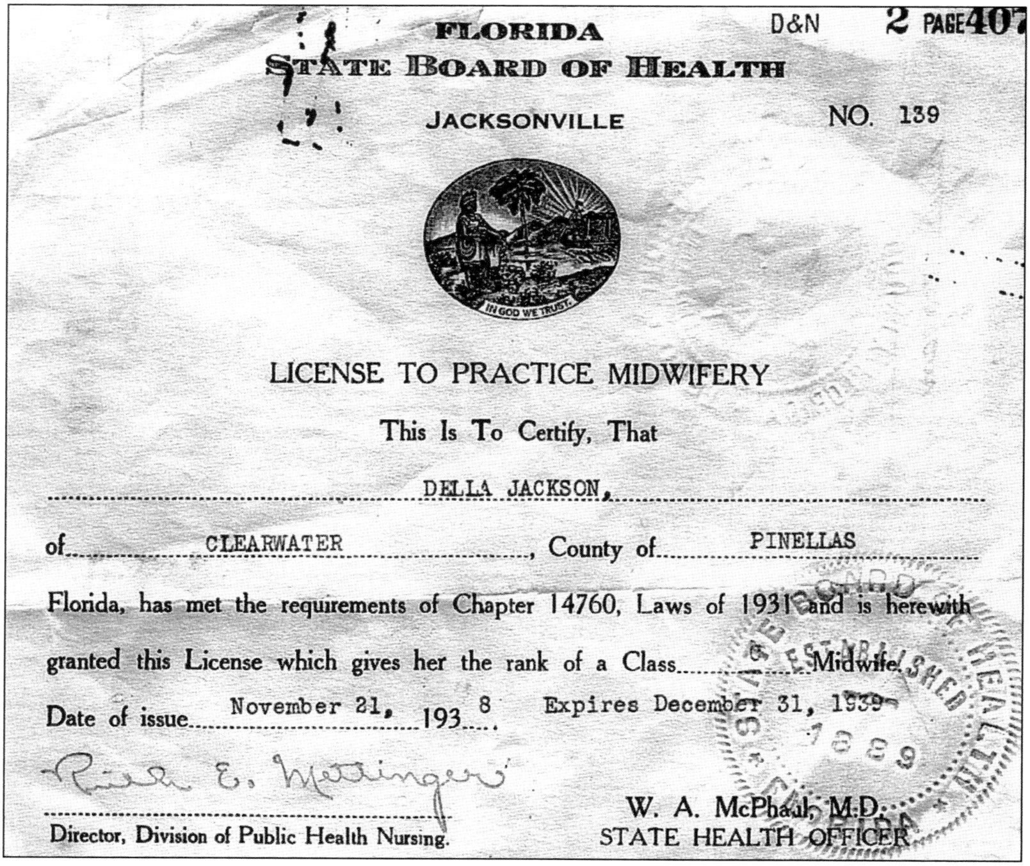
FLORIDA
STATE BOARD OF HEALTH
D&N 2 PAGE 407
JACKSONVILLE
NO. 139
IN GOD WE TRUST
LICENSE TO PRACTICE MIDWIFERY
This Is To Certify, That
DELLA JACKSON,
of CLEARWATER, County of PINELLAS
Florida, has met the requirements of Chapter 14760, Laws of 1931 and is herewith granted this License which gives her the rank of a Class Midwife.
Date of issue November 21, 1938 Expires December 31, 1939
Ruth E. Mettinger
Director, Division of Public Health Nursing.
W. A. McPhaul, M.D.
STATE HEALTH OFFICER

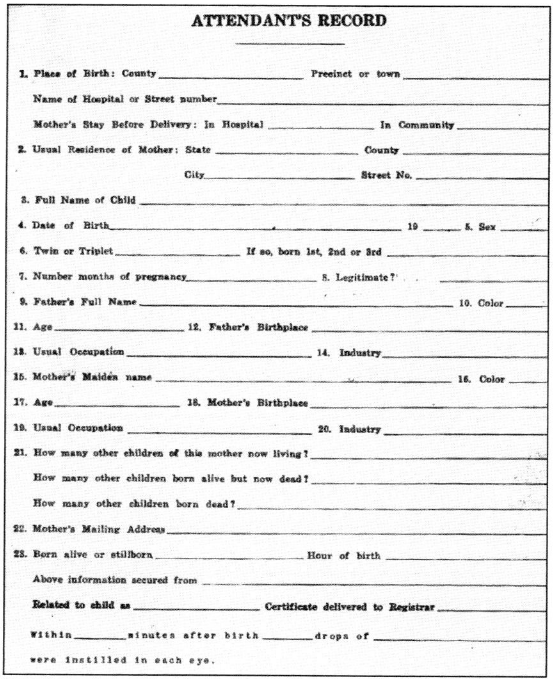
ATTENDANT'S RECORD

1. Place of Birth: County ____ Precinct or town ____
Name of Hospital or Street number ____
Mother's Stay Before Delivery: In Hospital ____ In Community ____
2. Usual Residence of Mother: State ____ County ____
City ____ Street No. ____
3. Full Name of Child ____
4. Date of Birth ____ 19 ____ 5. Sex ____
6. Twin or Triplet ____ If so, born 1st, 2nd or 3rd ____
7. Number months of pregnancy ____ 8. Legitimate? ____
9. Father's Full Name ____ 10. Color ____
11. Age ____ 12. Father's Birthplace ____
13. Usual Occupation ____ 14. Industry ____
15. Mother's Maiden name ____ 16. Color ____
17. Age ____ 18. Mother's Birthplace ____
19. Usual Occupation ____ 20. Industry ____
21. How many other children of this mother now living? ____
How many other children born alive but now dead? ____
How many other children born dead? ____
22. Mother's Mailing Address ____
23. Born alive or stillborn ____ Hour of birth ____
Above information secured from ____
Related to child as ____ Certificate delivered to Registrar ____
Within ____ minutes after birth ____ drops of ____
were instilled in each eye.

Here is a copy of the official license issued to Della Jackson to practice midwifery. The Florida State Board of Health in Jacksonville certified Jackson on November 21, 1938. Jackson delivered more than 300 babies between 1930s and the 1950s.

Pictured at left is a blank copy of the attendant's record to be filled out by Della Jackson shortly after the delivery of a child and then filed with the state. Jackson was required to deliver the certificate to the registrar and within 20 minutes of the birth place two drops of silver nitrate in each eye of the newborn to prevent blindness.

Two

Churches and Religion

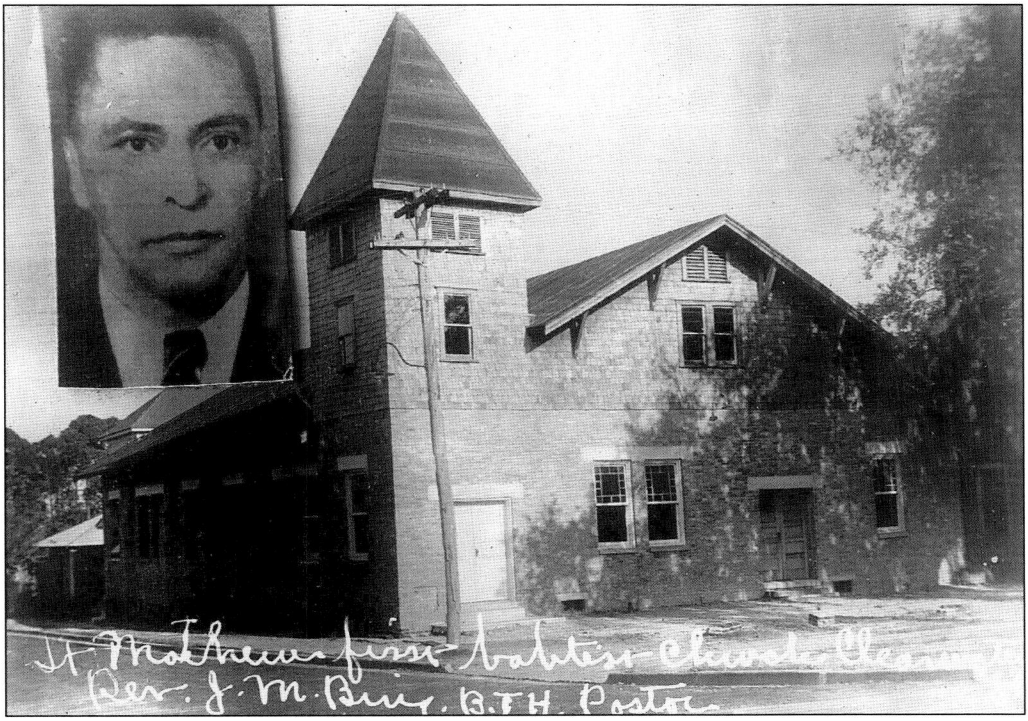

Pictured above is St. Matthew First Baptist Church, which is located at 703 Seminole Street and was completed in the mid-1940s. An earlier church building was located in the 500 block of what is now called the Blanche Littlejohn Trail. Rev. L.N. Anderson was called as pastor in 1912. In 1918, when he was called to minister elsewhere, Rev. M L. Cherry stepped in. Then, in 1923, the church split. Some members went with Reverend Cherry and formed Mt. Carmel Baptist Church. When Reverend Anderson returned in 1927 to St. Matthew, members reunited and the congregation grew to become the largest congregation of any black church in Clearwater. (*Clearwater Sun*, August 2, 1980.)

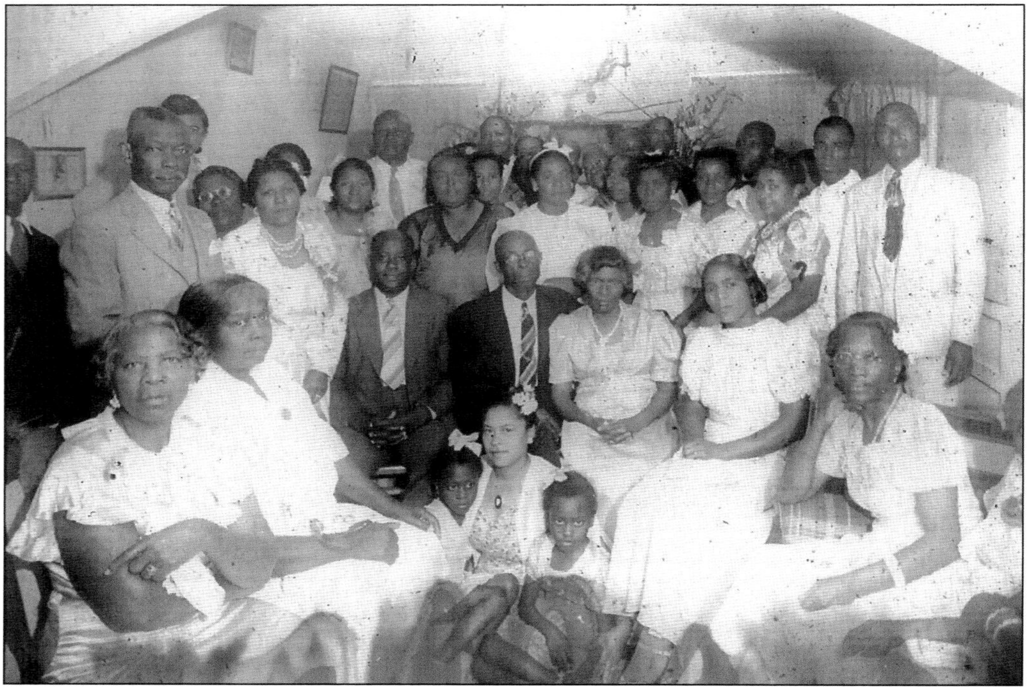

Shown here is a St. Matthew Church party in the early 1900s.

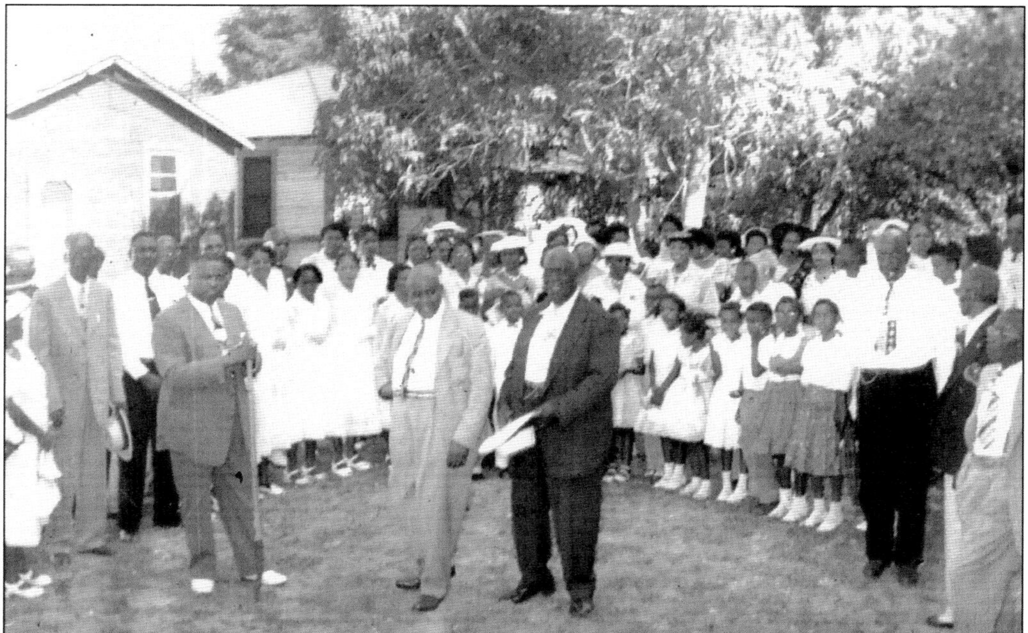

Below is a groundbreaking ceremony for the educational building. This took place in the 1940s when the church was located on Seminole Street and Railroad Avenue.

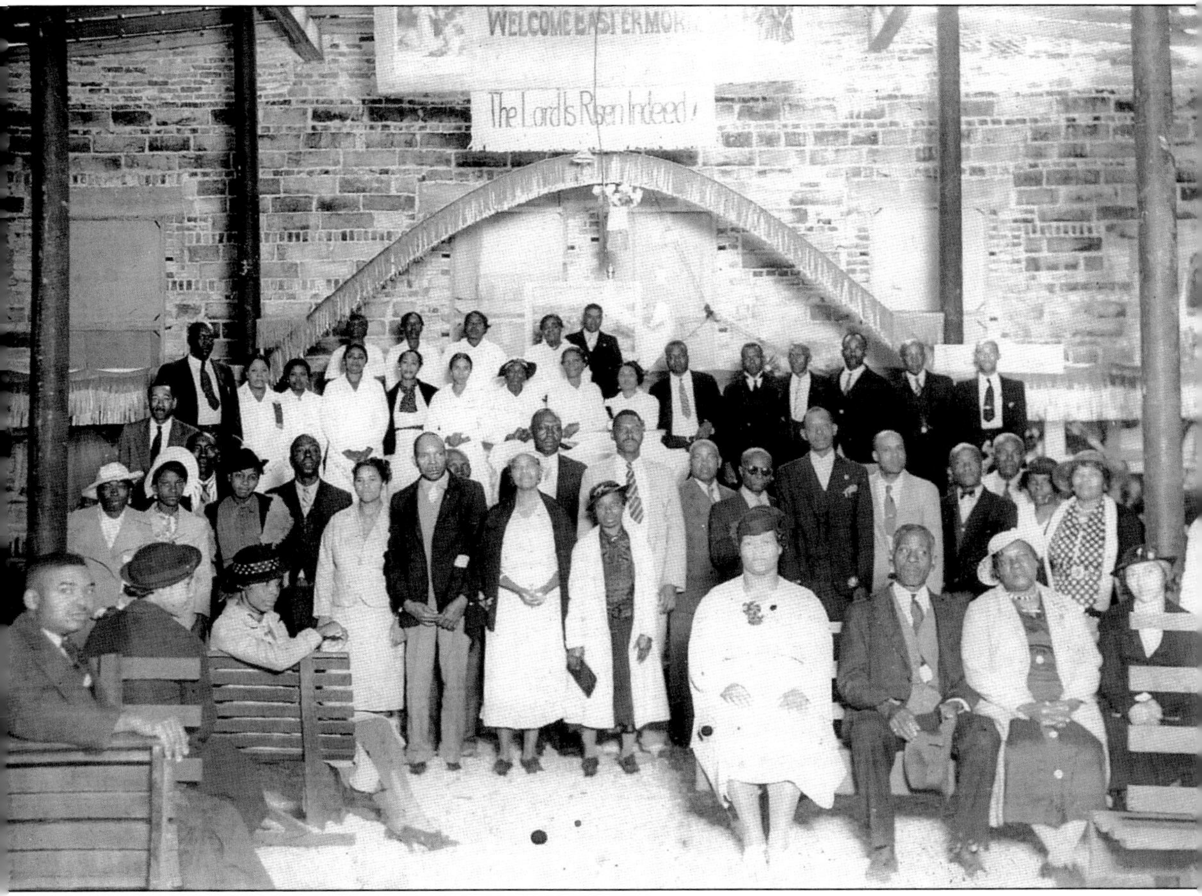

Depicted above is the interior of St. Matthew in its early days. Note that the floors are covered with sawdust.

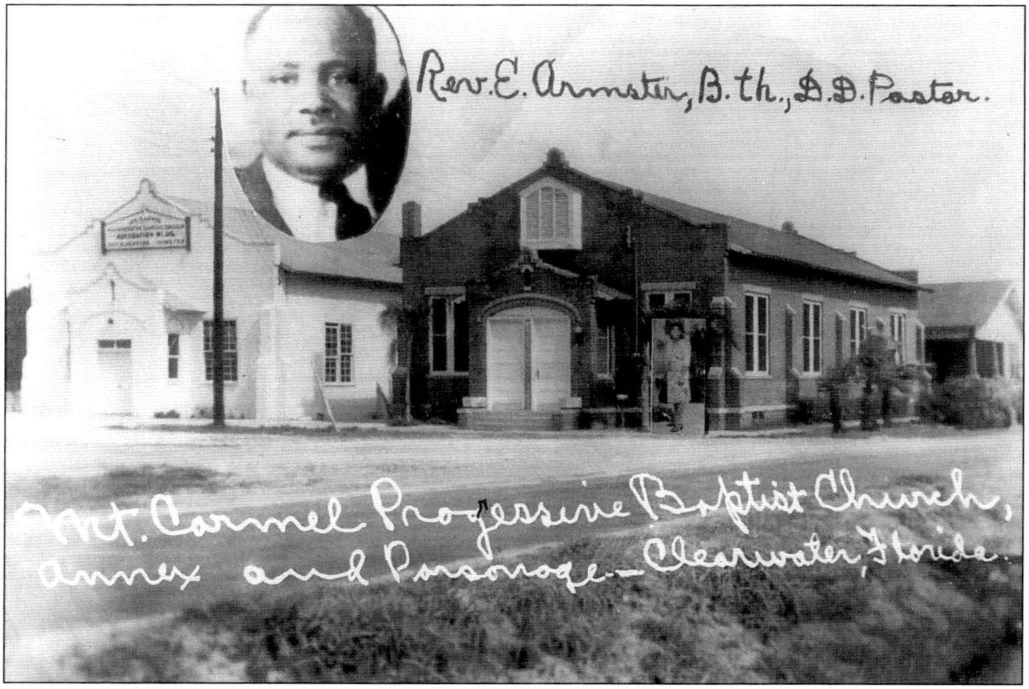

This picture is of Mt. Carmel Progressive Baptist Church, which was founded in 1923 with Rev. M.L. Cherry as its pastor. Shown in the picture is the church, annex, and the parsonage. Shown in the inset is Rev. E. Armster, one of the church's former pastors.

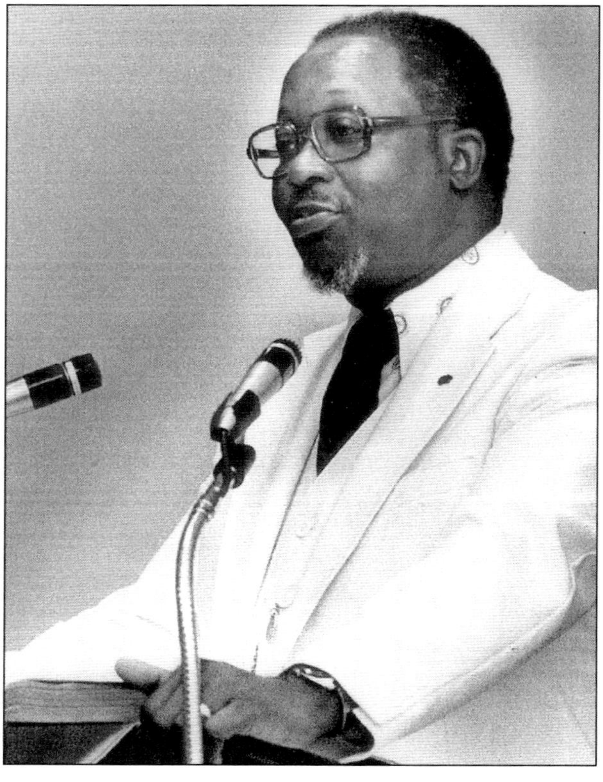

This is Rev. Mac Williams, pastor of Mt. Carmel in 1969. He also served as the president of the local NAACP. The picture illustrates the minister making his point clear as he speaks.

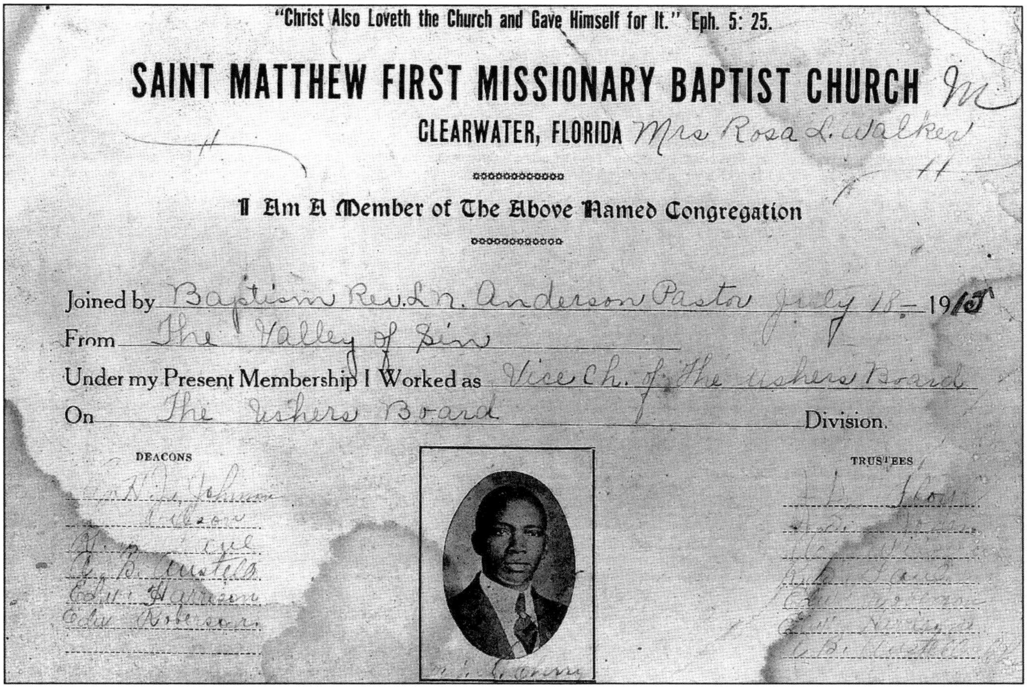

"Christ Also Loveth the Church and Gave Himself for It." Eph. 5: 25.

SAINT MATTHEW FIRST MISSIONARY BAPTIST CHURCH

CLEARWATER, FLORIDA Mrs Rosa L. Walker

I Am A Member of The Above Named Congregation

Joined by Baptism Rev. L.N. Anderson Pastor July 18 — 1915

From The Valley of Sin

Under my Present Membership I Worked as Vice Ch. of the Ushers Board

On The Ushers Board Division.

DEACONS

TRUSTEES

This baptismal certificate for Rosa Walker is dated July 18, 1915. It was signed by Rev. M.L. Cherry, who was called to Mt. Carmel Progressive Baptist church. Rev. L.N. Anderson remained as pastor of St. Matthew

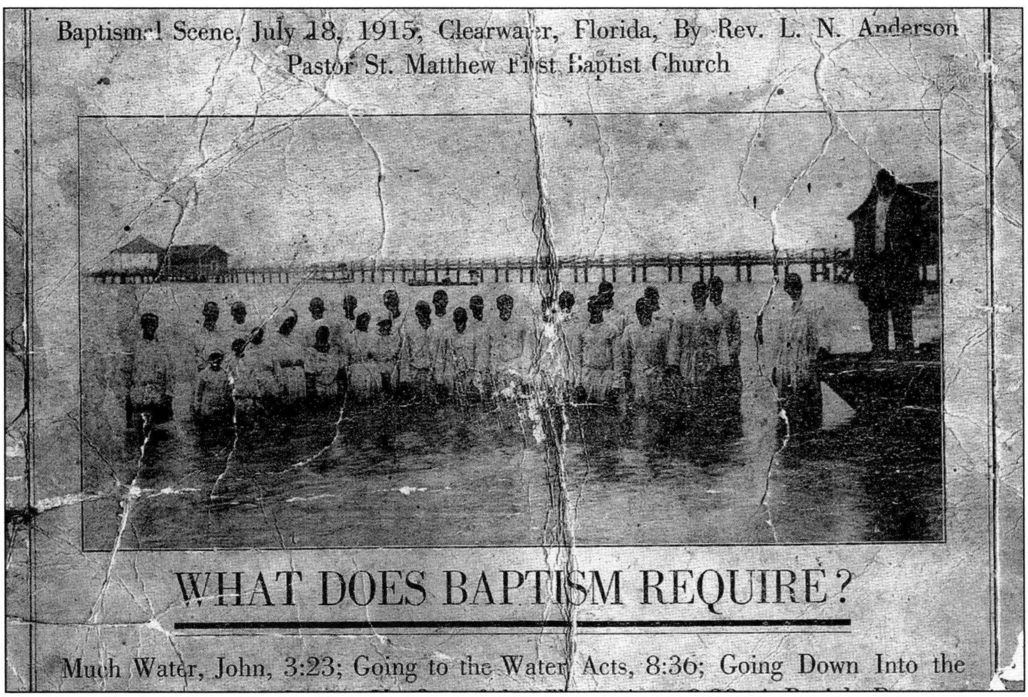

This document displays a baptism on July 18, 1915. Rev. L.N. Anderson was then the pastor of St. Matthew First Baptist.

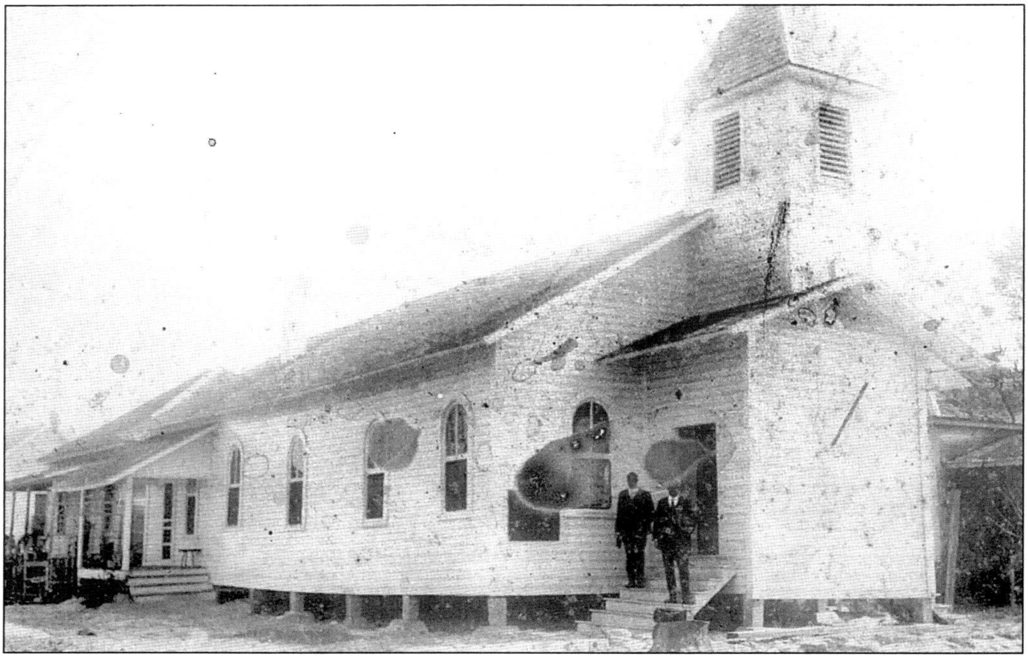

Pictured here is Bethany C.M.E Church. In 1891, the church was built on Cleveland Street where the downtown post office stands today. Later, in 1923, a new church was constructed at Pierce and Madison.

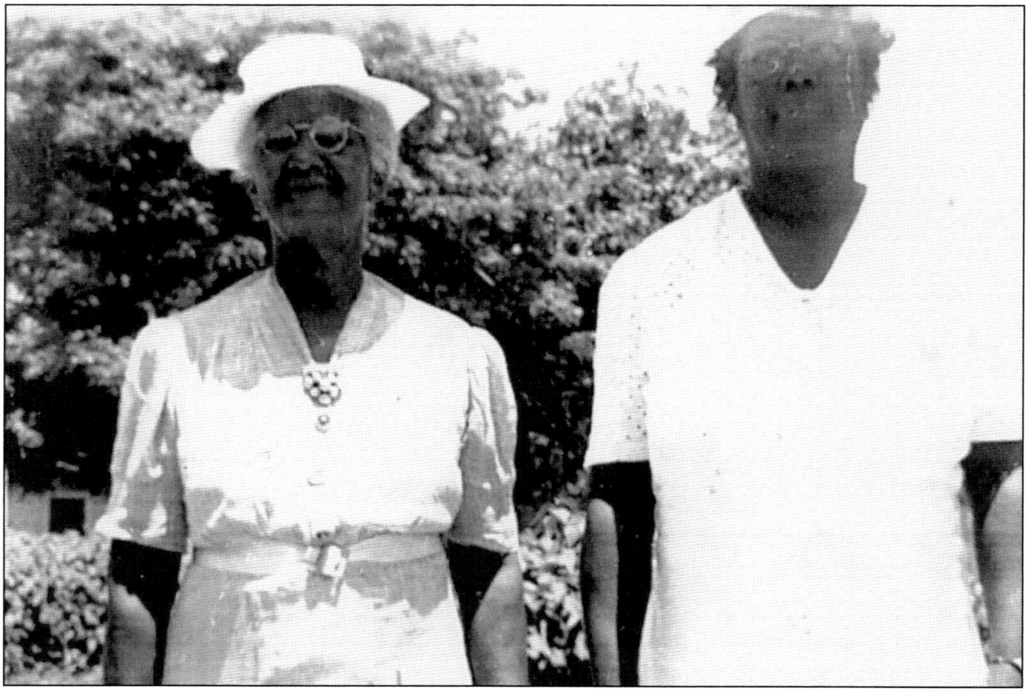

Pictured here are stewardesses of Bethany C.M.E. Church—Chanie Dixon and Annie Coar. C.M.E. originally stood for Colored Methodist Episcopal but was changed to Christian Methodist Episcopal in 1961.

To the right is a picture of the Church of the Reconciler at 915 Drew Street. In the early 1960s, Thomas Johnston recruited members in the surrounding neighborhoods by going door to door. The church was chartered as a multiracial church in November 1968.

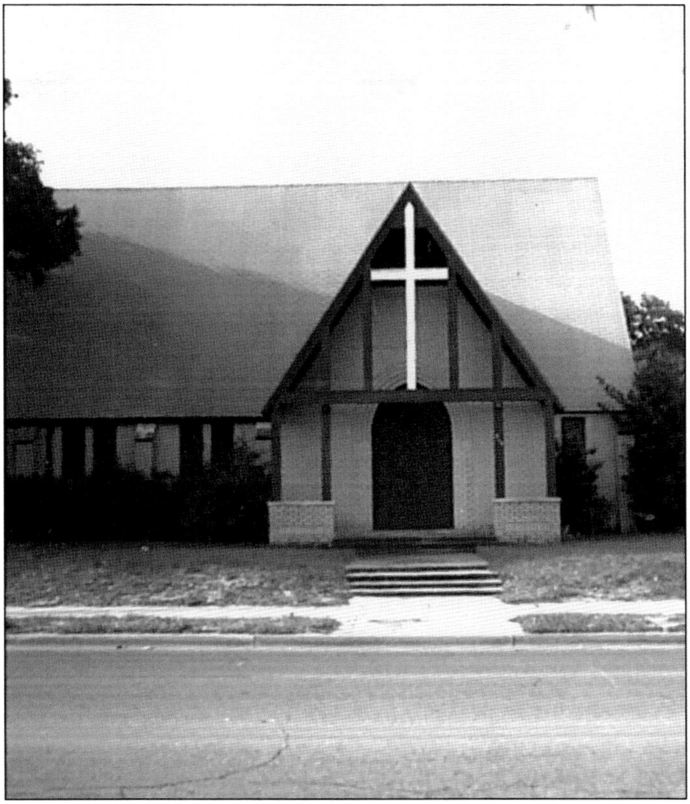

These are three former ministers of the Church of the Reconciler. From left to right are Thomas Johnston, Haimdat Sawh, and Bing Kong Han.

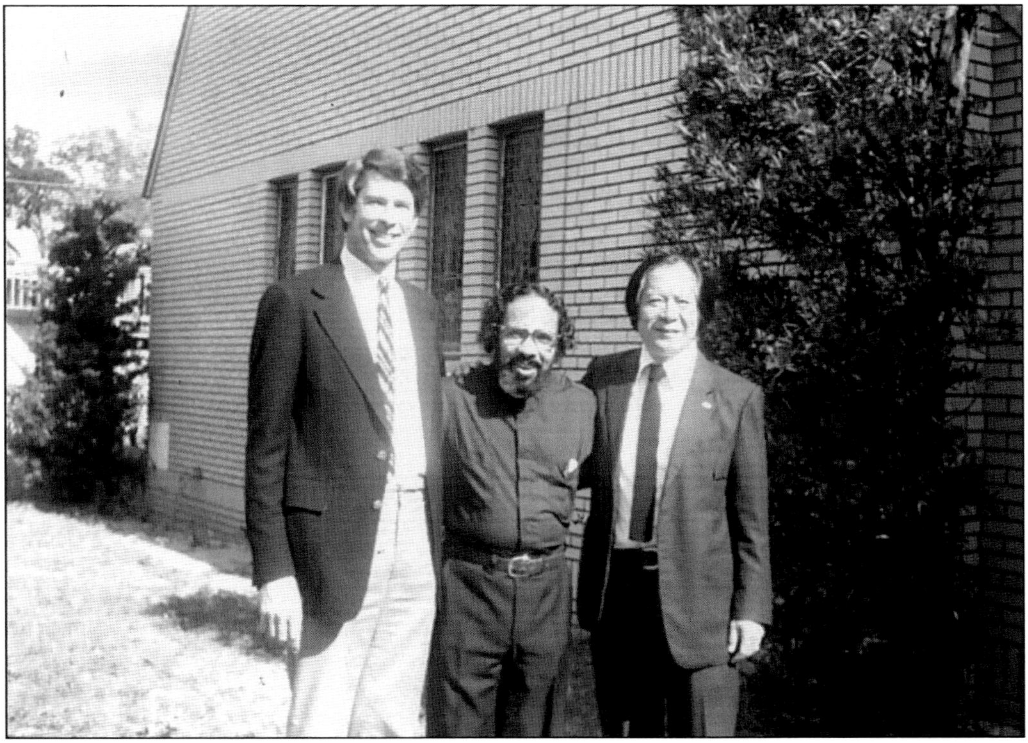

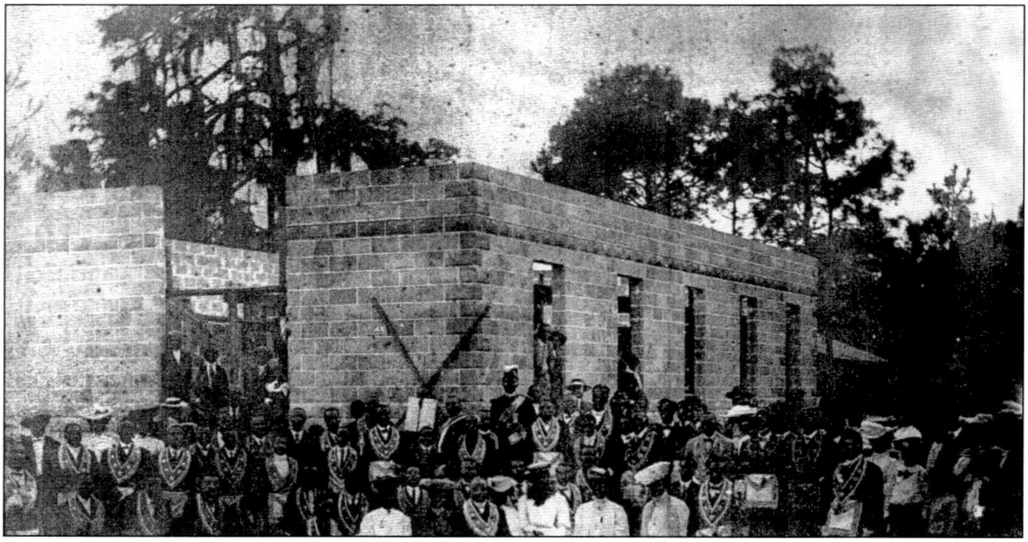

Hope Henry A.M.E. Church served as one of only two black churches in Clearwater. This picture was taken at the laying of the cornerstone on December 16, 1906. Later, Hope Henry became historic Mt. Olive A.M.E. Church.

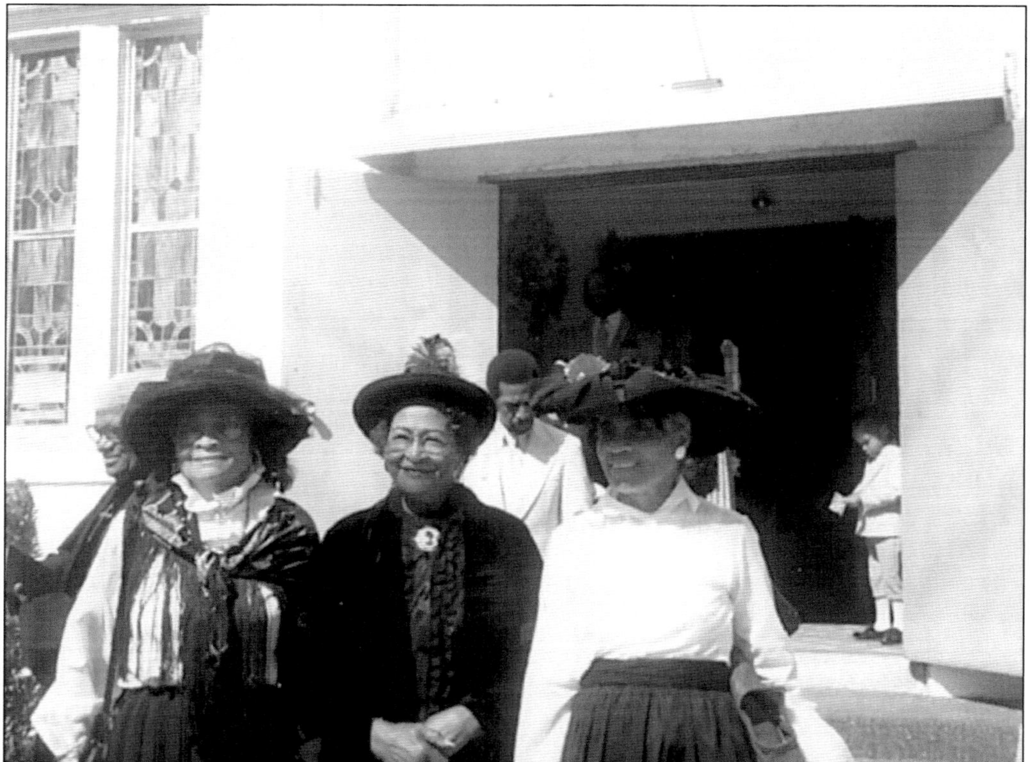

Depicted above are Gertrude Clarke, Clealia Jackson, and Ruth Mills. They are celebrating Founder's Day at Mt. Olive A.M.E. Church. The members were asked to wear pioneer clothing on that day.

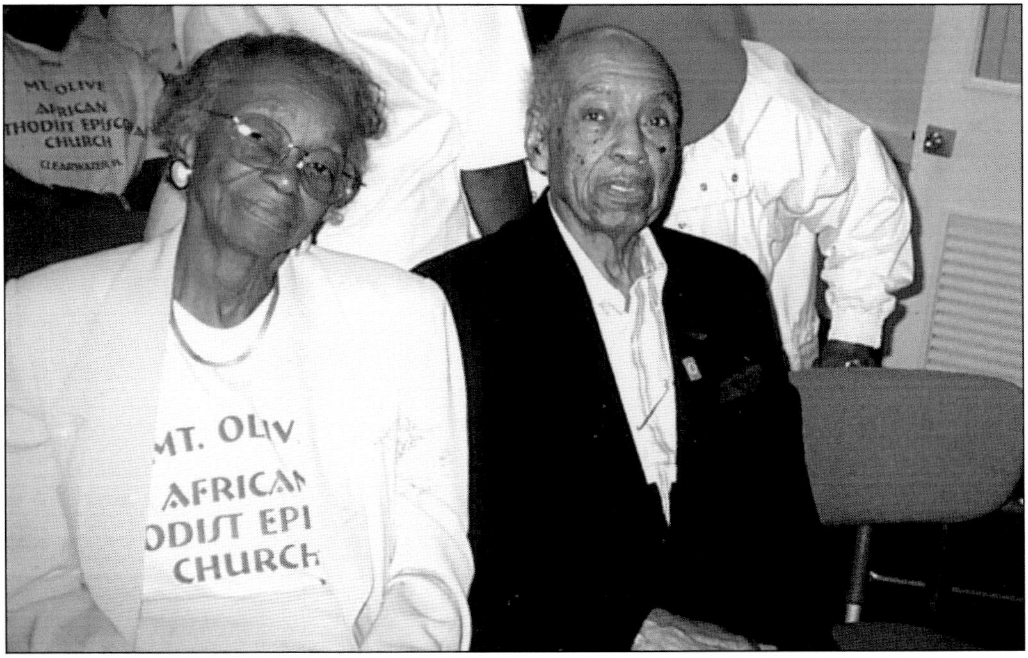

Mr. and Mrs. Edward Henry, long-standing members of Mt. Olive, are depicted as part of a group of church members that traveled to Deland, Florida in 1999 for a hearing on their church being designated as a landmark and placed on the National Register.

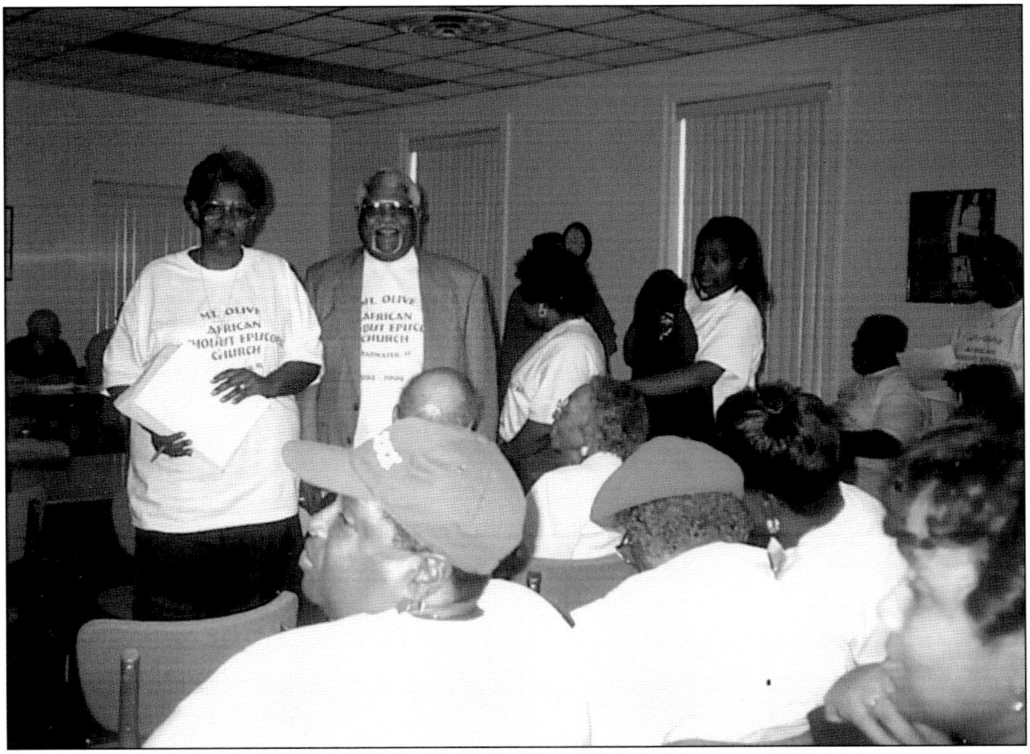

Pictured above is the delegation led by Helen Hargray and Rev. Jimmie B. Keel.

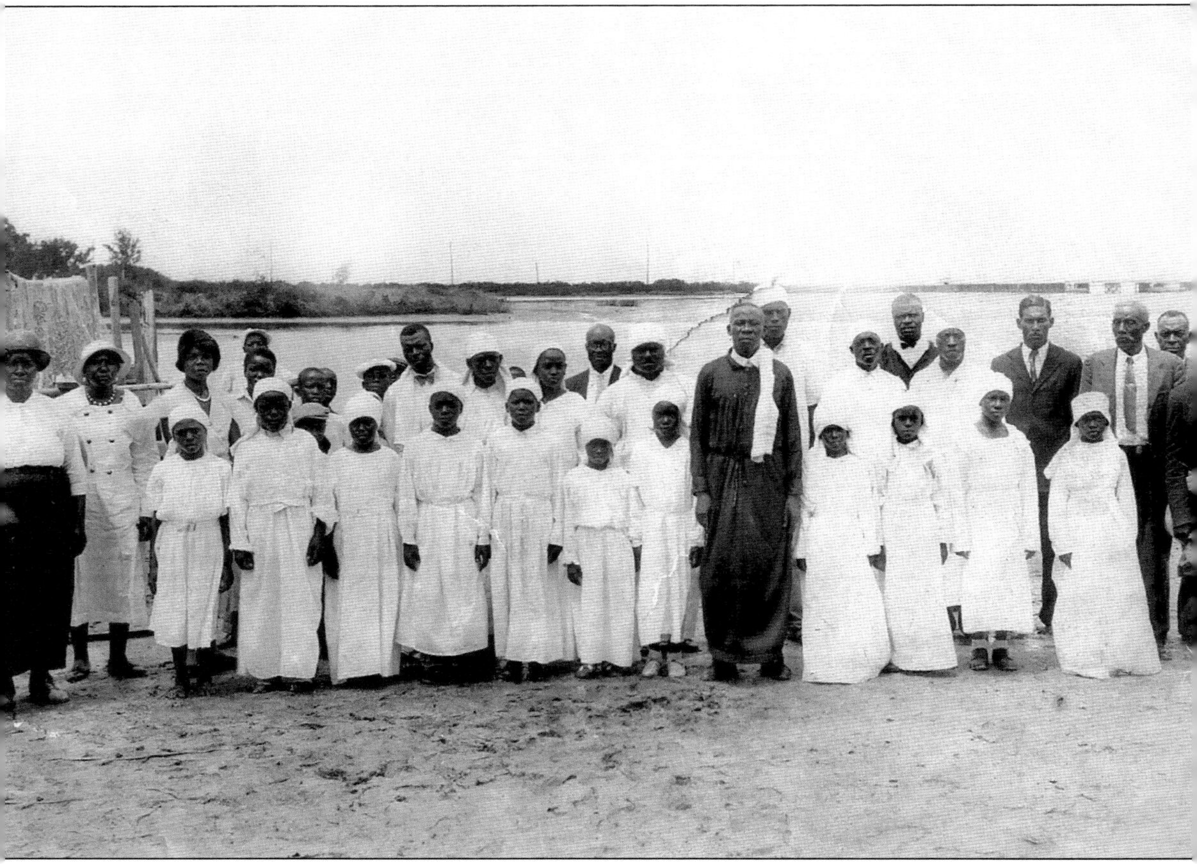

This photograph was taken at a 1934 baptism at Stevenson Creek. Rev. Joseph Hines, in the black robe, was the first permanent minister of St. John Missionary Baptist Church.

Shown here is Ollie Asia, fondly known as "Aunt Ollie." She was a faithful member of Mt. Olive Missionary Baptist Church for over 25 years. Mrs. Asia lived to be 94 years old and was a pillar of the community.

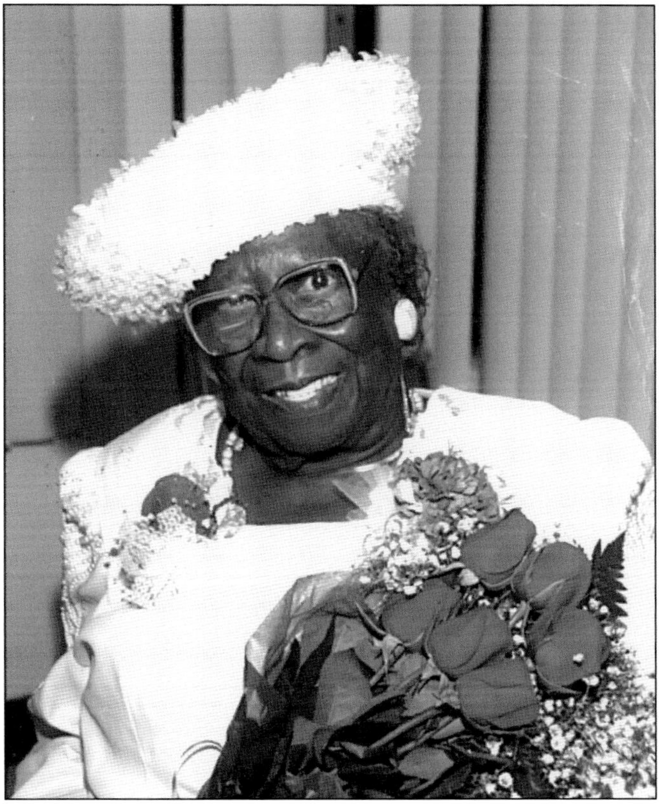

Pictured below is Mt. Olive Missionary Baptist Church. It was originally built in the 1920s, and it was later renovated in 1980. It is located on Harvey's Lane.

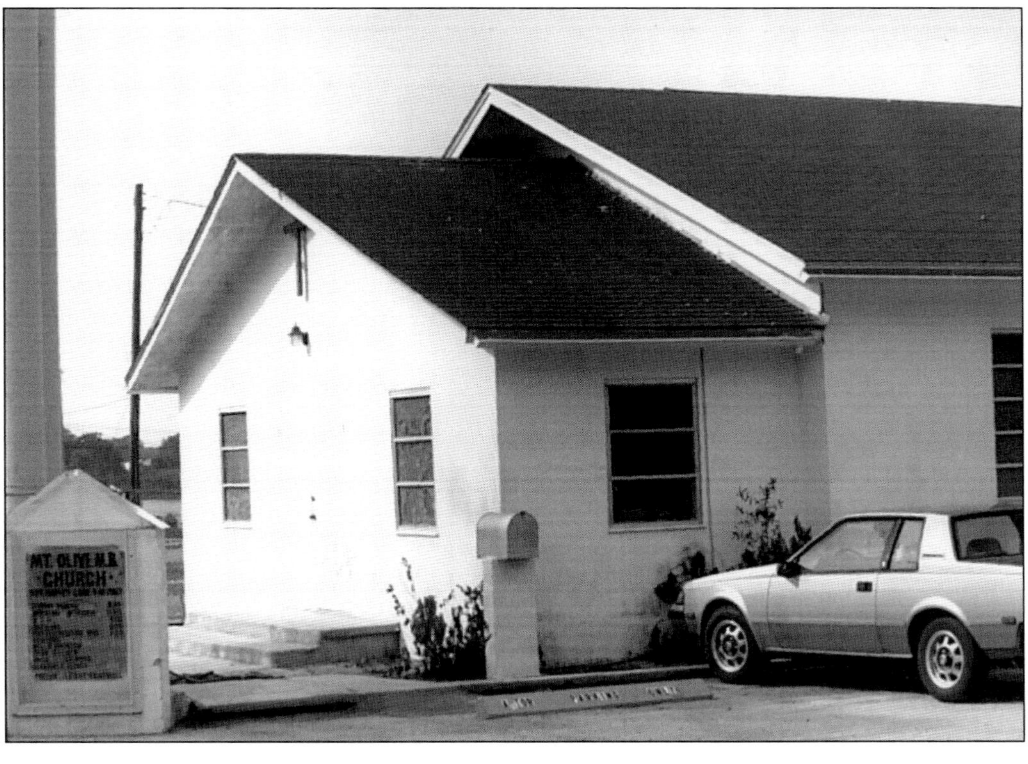

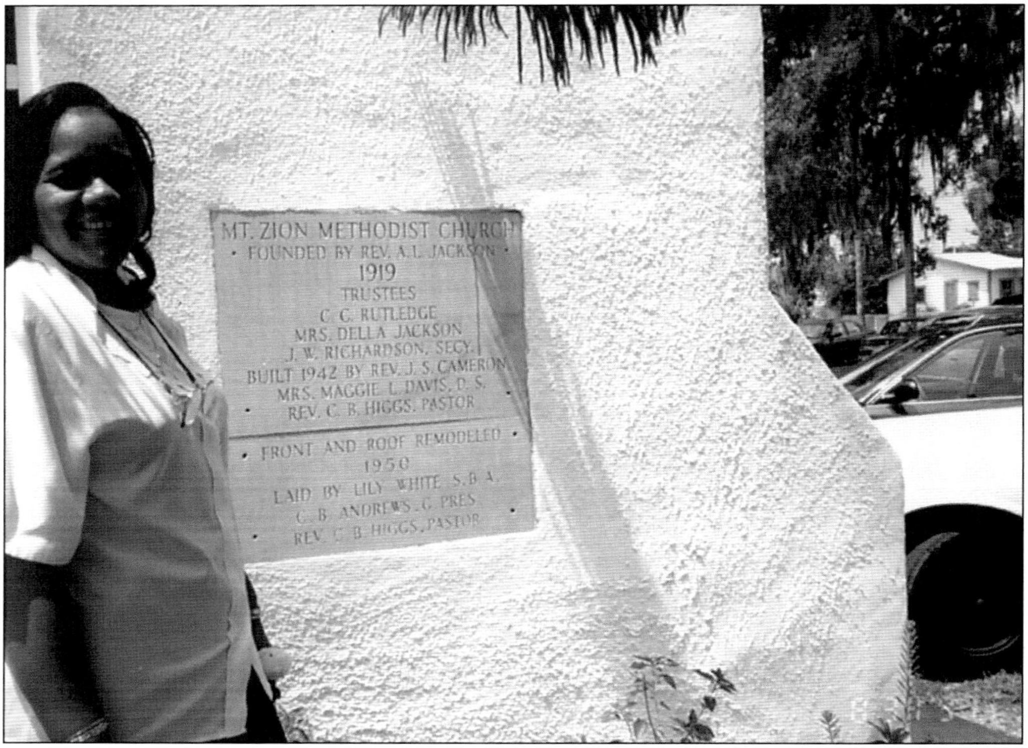

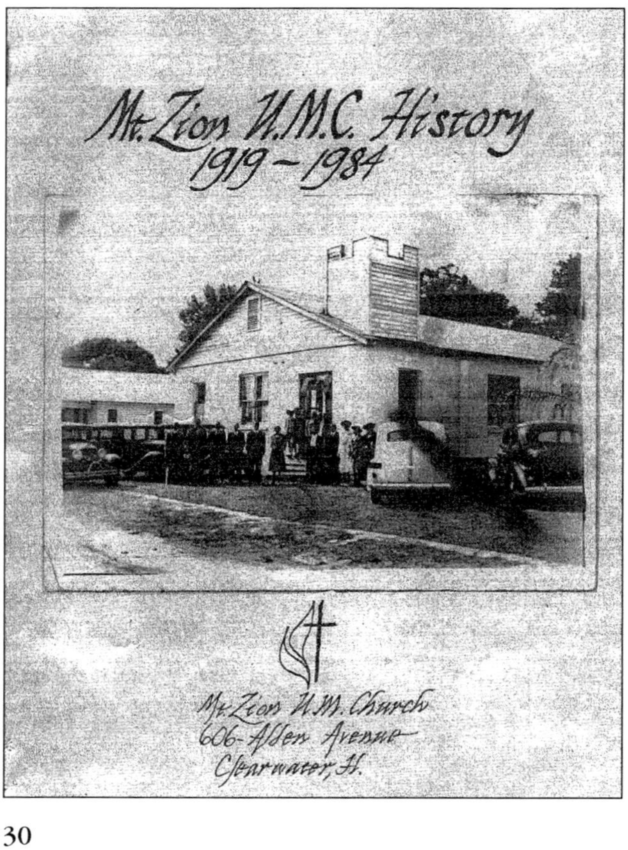

Above is Faye Rutledge Mobley posing in front of a cornerstone for Mt. Zion United Methodist Church, which was founded by Rev. A.L. Jackson in 1919. In 1997 the church relocated to Howard Street.

This is a cover of an anniversary program for Mt. Zion United Methodist Church in its early beginnings. The first structure was built in 1920 and utilized until 1927 when Reverend Jackson and the congregation erected a larger building.

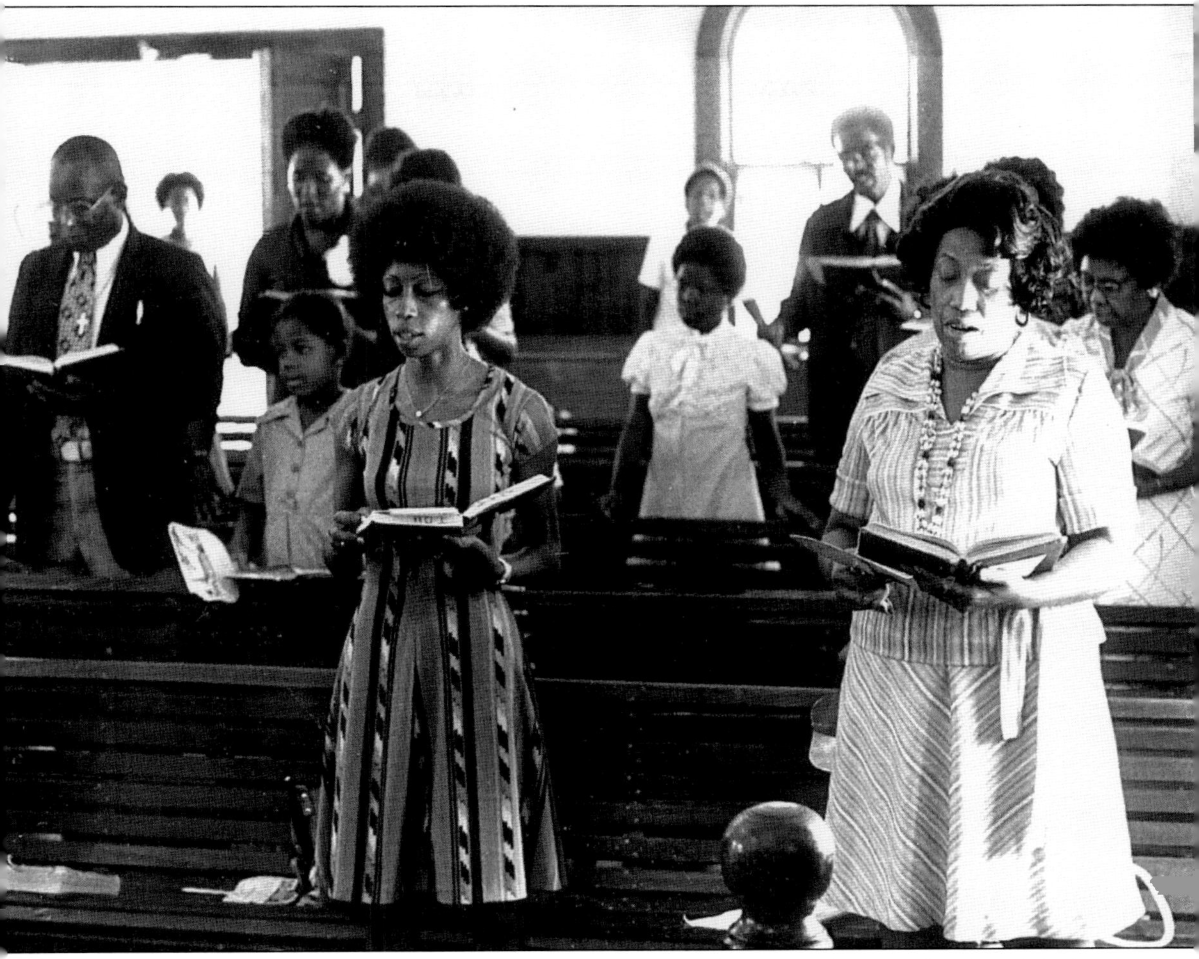

Pictured here is the congregation at Bethany C.M.E Church singing hymns. On the right is Margaret Algee, granddaughter of Mack Dixon Sr. Pictured on the left is Janice Isaac.

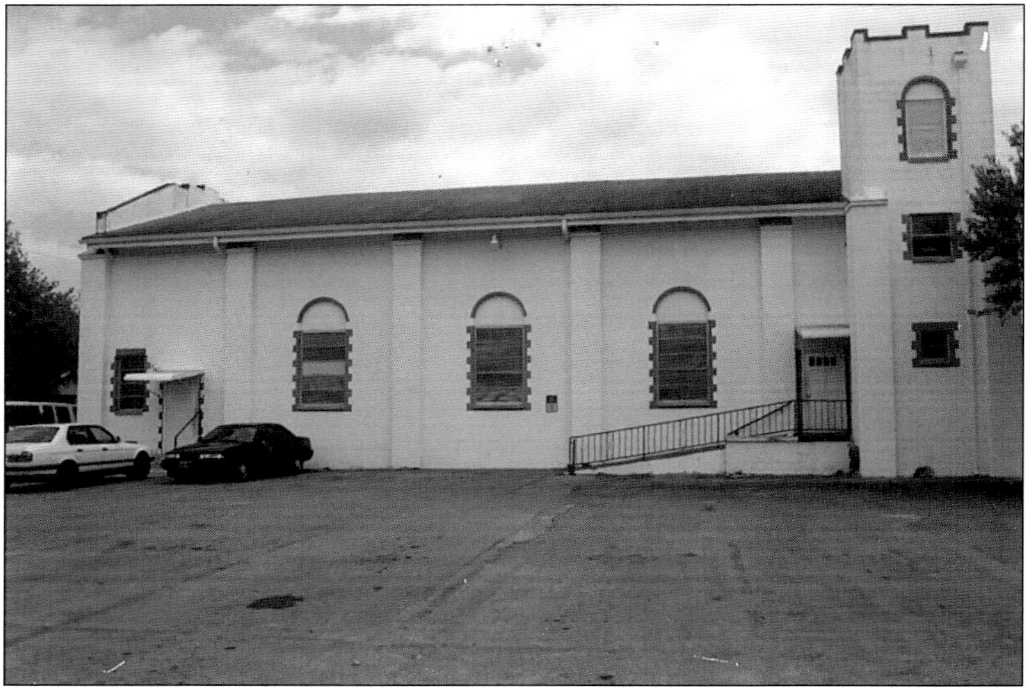

Above is a picture of St. John Primitive Baptist Church. The church was located on the corner of Engman Street and Roosevelt Avenue in 1913. In 1915, a church was built at 1012 Palmetto Street.

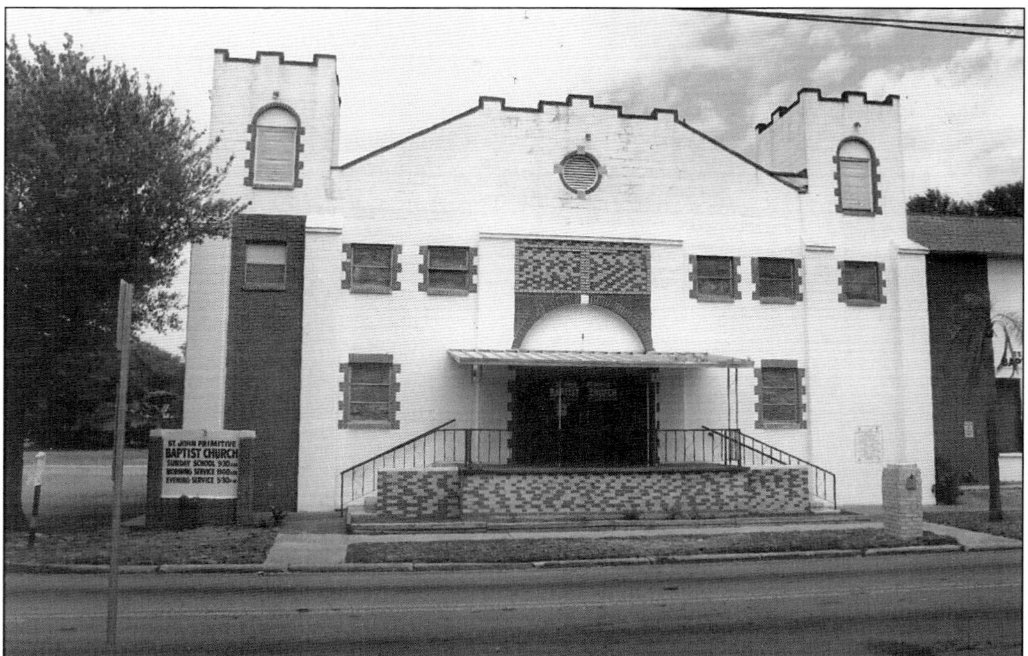

Shown here is a front view of St. John Primitive Baptist Church at its present location on Palmetto Street.

Three

BUSINESSES

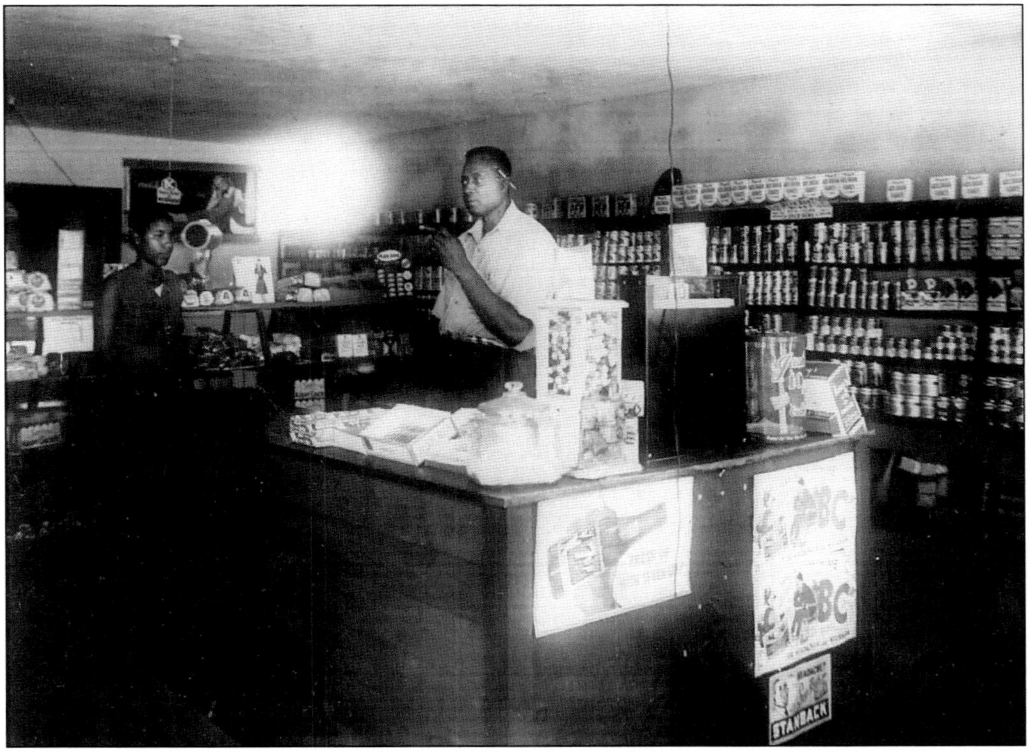

In a 1940s photo, Calvert Charles Rutledge Sr. poses inside his grocery store located at 1115 North Greenwood Avenue. The store was built in the mid-1940s.

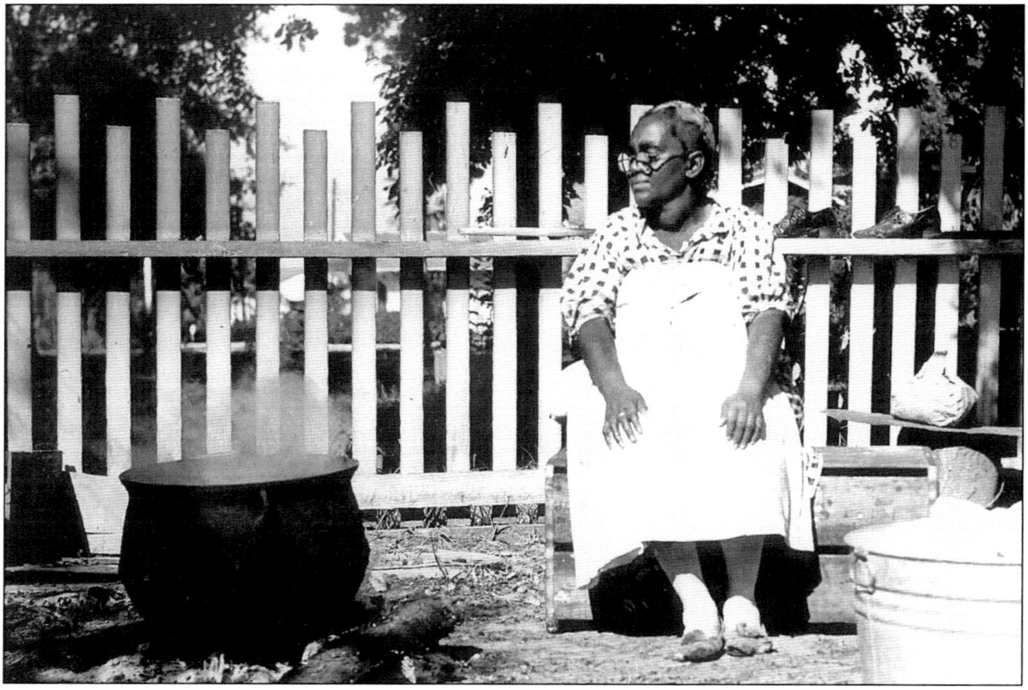

Gertie Ryans keeps a watchful eye on the clothes in the pot in this early 1900s photo. Mrs. Ryans did laundry by hand in the backyard of attorney Gus Wilder off Fort Harrison Street in Clearwater.

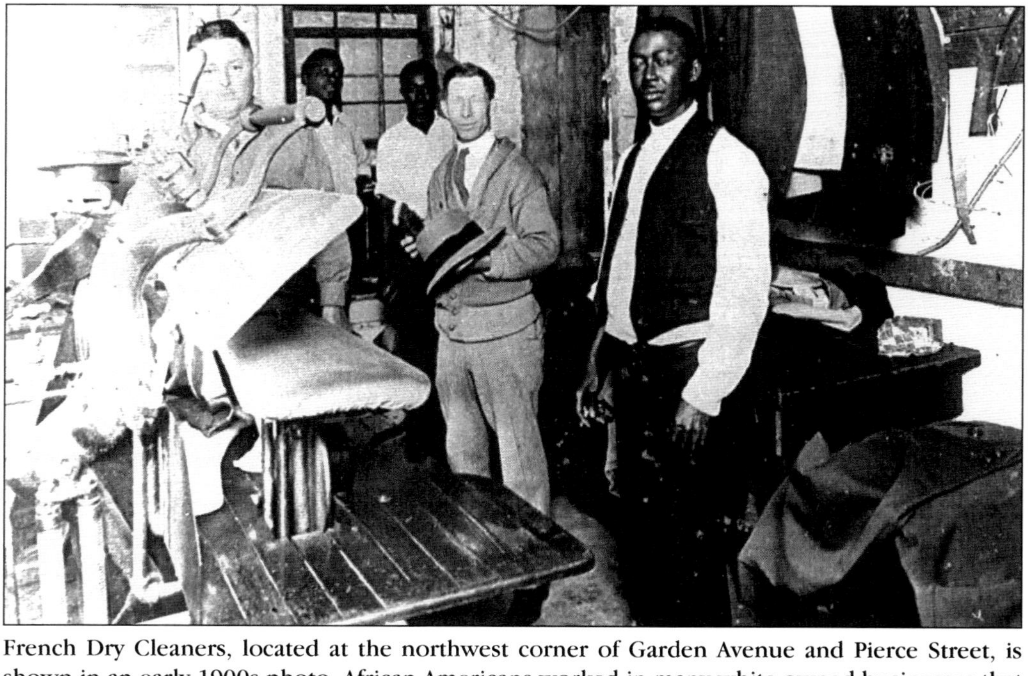

French Dry Cleaners, located at the northwest corner of Garden Avenue and Pierce Street, is shown in an early 1900s photo. African Americans worked in many white-owned businesses that served the community. The African-American workers pictured from left to right are Theodore Jenkins, Ora S. Hart, and Mr. Wallace.

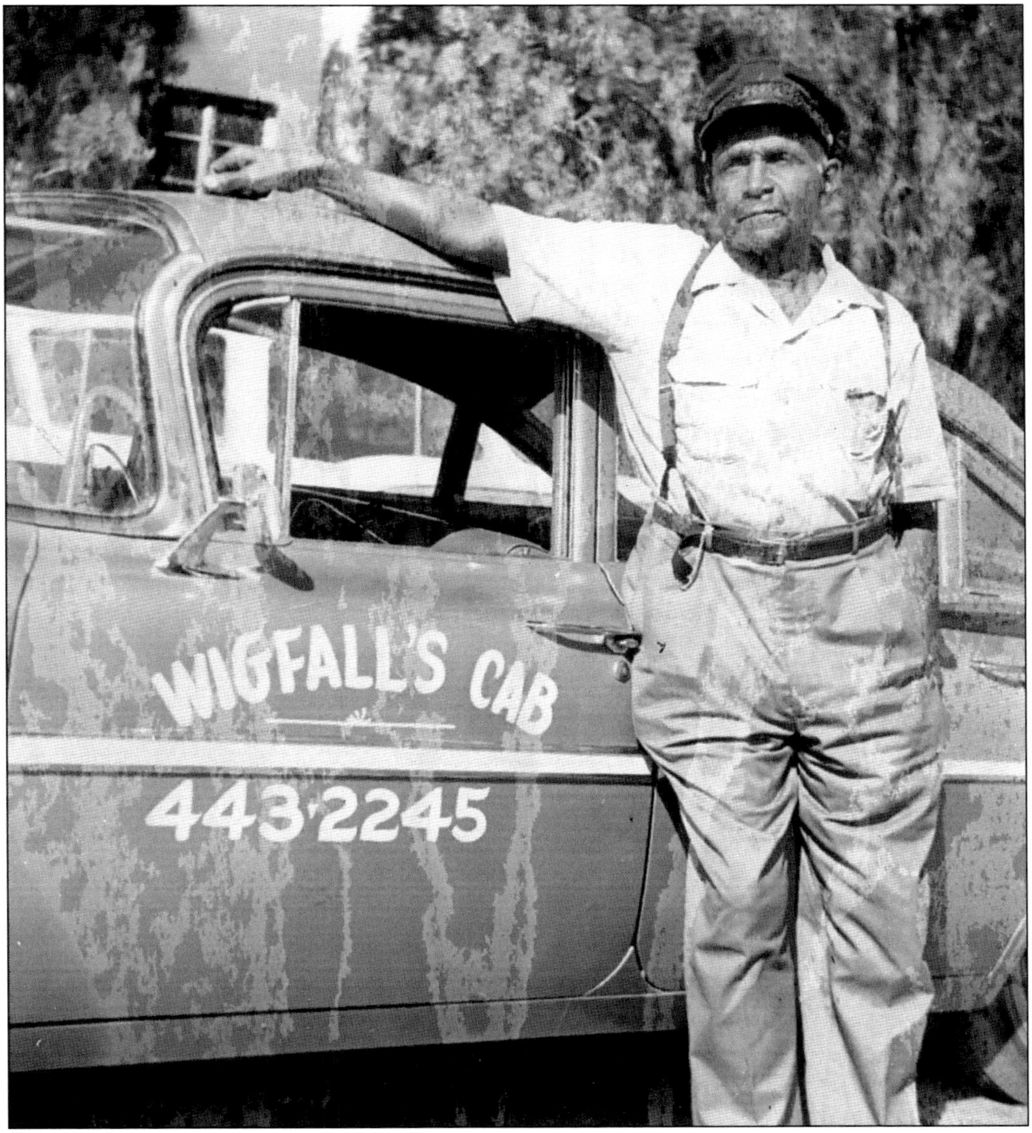

Sidney Wigfall, owner of Wigfall's Cab, stands beside his cab in a 1950s photo. Wigfall started his taxi service in 1921 and served the Clearwater area for 46 years until he retired in 1967. In an interview, Wigfall recalled the 1920s when tourists arrived in Clearwater by rail and the passenger stations were the hub of seasonal activity. Many of the streets were dirt roads and there were no sidewalks, just boards. The Jack Tar Hotel site was a temporary courthouse, and a trip to Clearwater Beach by way of a narrow wooden bridge at the foot of Seminole Street was a precarious journey. Two cars could only pass each other with a bit of scraping. Wigfall was retained by the families of Judge Kenesaw Mountain Landis, commissioner of baseball, and by the Warner Brothers of moviemaking fame, to serve as a personal chauffeur on sightseeing and shopping tours. Driving in the early years required no driver's license, and anyone was in the taxi business if he had a workable car and could drive reasonably well. Wigfall wore out 20 taxis between 1921 and 1967 and was listed in *Ripley's Believe It or Not* for driving 46 years without having an accident or receiving a traffic citation. When he retired in 1967 at the age of 83, Wigfall still had excellent eyesight and required no glasses.

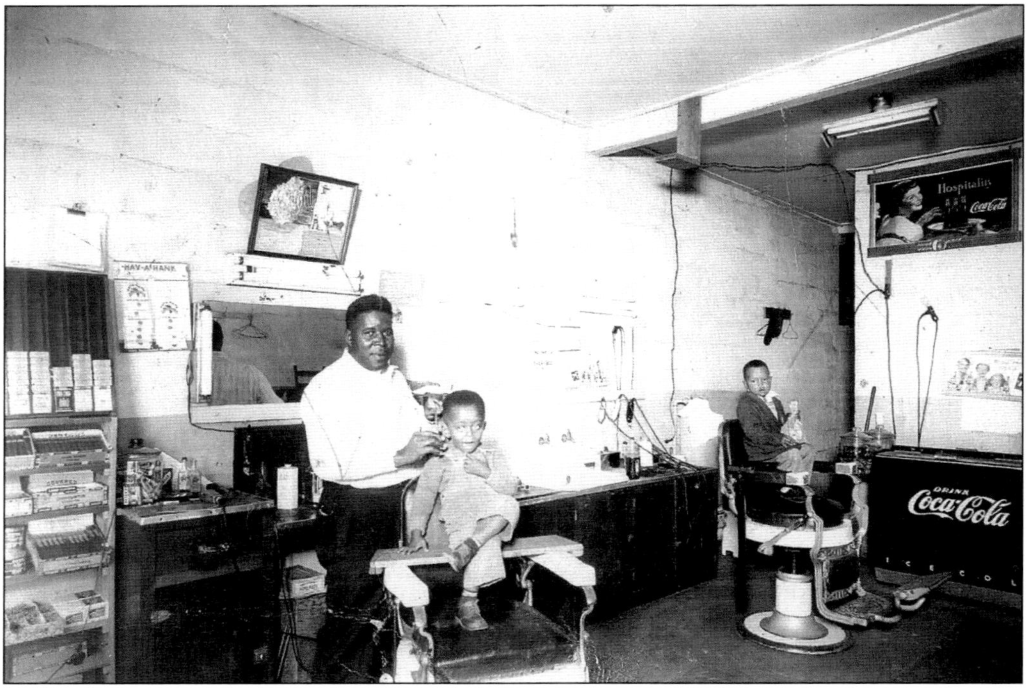

Jack Morris, a local barber, is pictured serving young customers in his barbershop on North Garden Avenue in this 1940s photo.

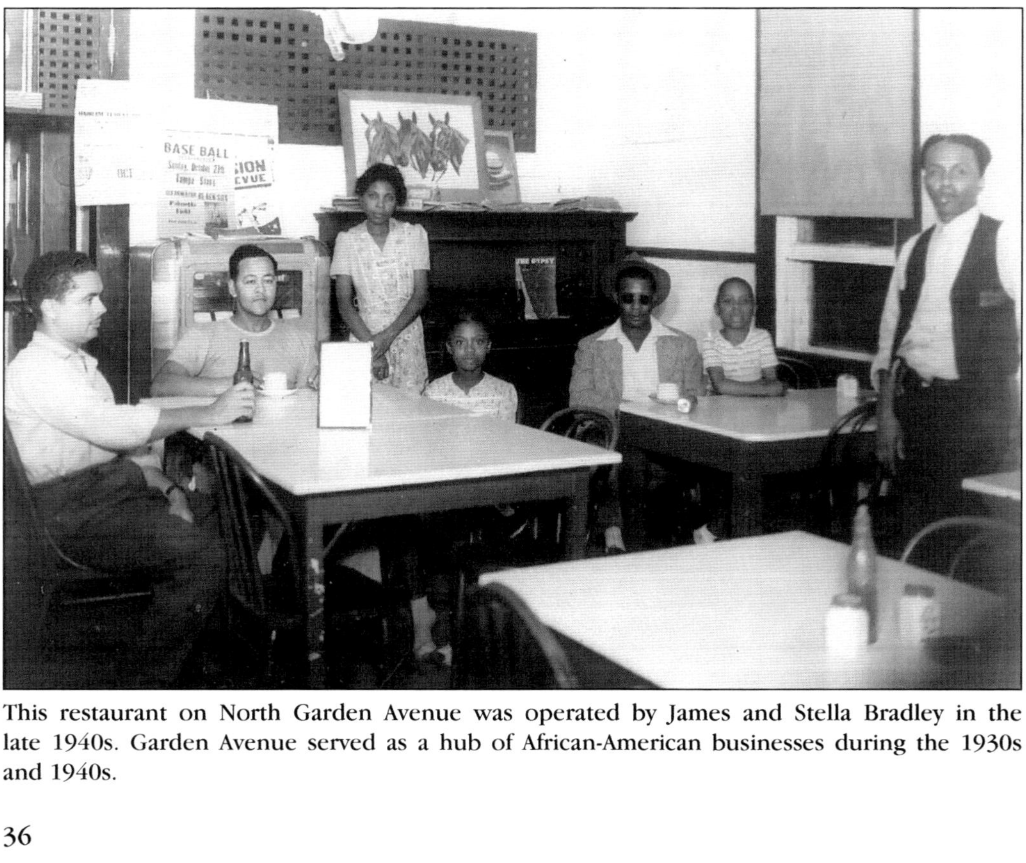

This restaurant on North Garden Avenue was operated by James and Stella Bradley in the late 1940s. Garden Avenue served as a hub of African-American businesses during the 1930s and 1940s.

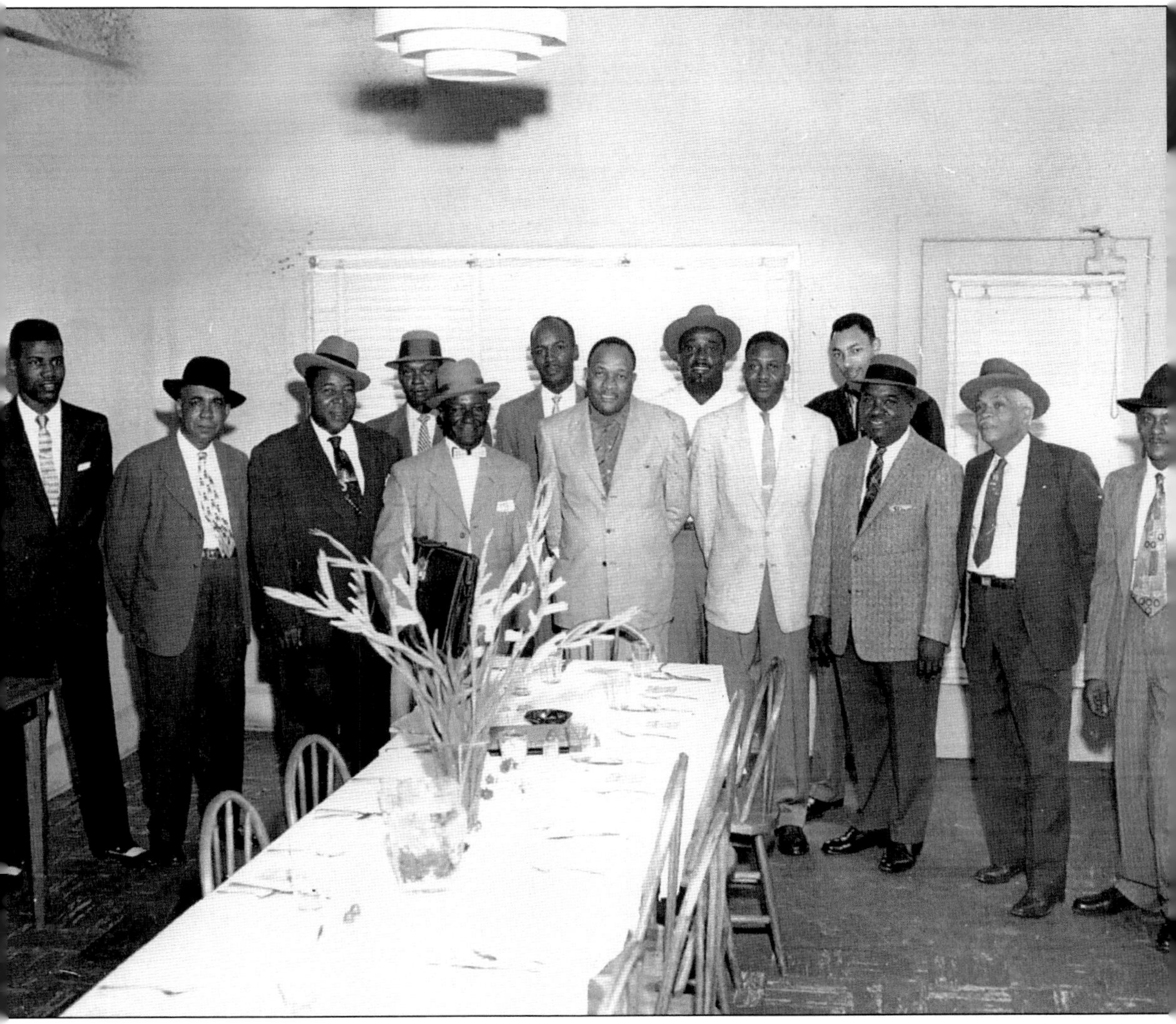

Members of the Suncoast Barbers Association pose for a picture at one of their meetings in the late 1950s. This humanitarian group sponsored community projects and contributed to blood banks, the United Community Fund, the American Legion Hospital for Crippled Children, the Little League, the Holt Street Recreation Center, nursery schools, and various other causes. The group was organized in 1957 and was composed of barbers in the Clearwater-St. Petersburg areas.

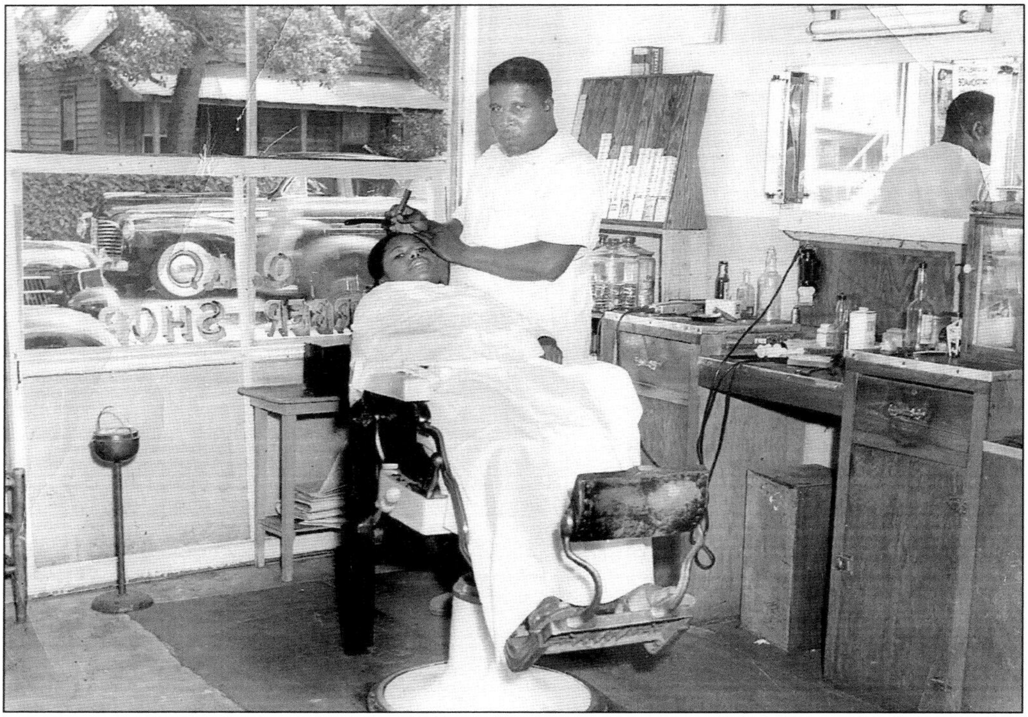

Jack Morris is photographed with a customer in his barbershop in the late 1940s. Jack Morris was married to Christine Morris, the first African-American librarian in Clearwater.

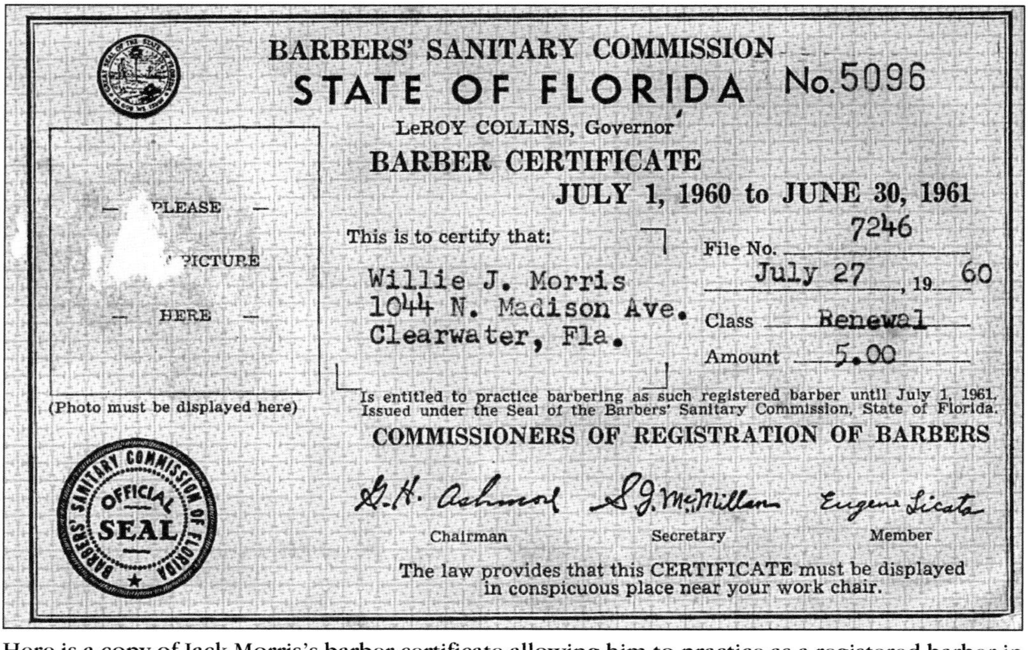

BARBERS' SANITARY COMMISSION

STATE OF FLORIDA No.5096

LeROY COLLINS, Governor

BARBER CERTIFICATE

JULY 1, 1960 to JUNE 30, 1961

— PLEASE —
PICTURE
— HERE —

(Photo must be displayed here)

This is to certify that:

Willie J. Morris
1044 N. Madison Ave.
Clearwater, Fla.

File No. 7246

July 27, 19 60

Class Renewal

Amount 5.00

Is entitled to practice barbering as such registered barber until July 1, 1961.
Issued under the Seal of the Barbers' Sanitary Commission, State of Florida.

COMMISSIONERS OF REGISTRATION OF BARBERS

G.H. Ashmore — Chairman
S.J. McMillan — Secretary
Eugene Licata — Member

BARBERS' SANITARY COMMISSION OF FLORIDA OFFICIAL SEAL

The law provides that this CERTIFICATE must be displayed in conspicuous place near your work chair.

Here is a copy of Jack Morris's barber certificate allowing him to practice as a registered barber in the State of Florida in 1960.

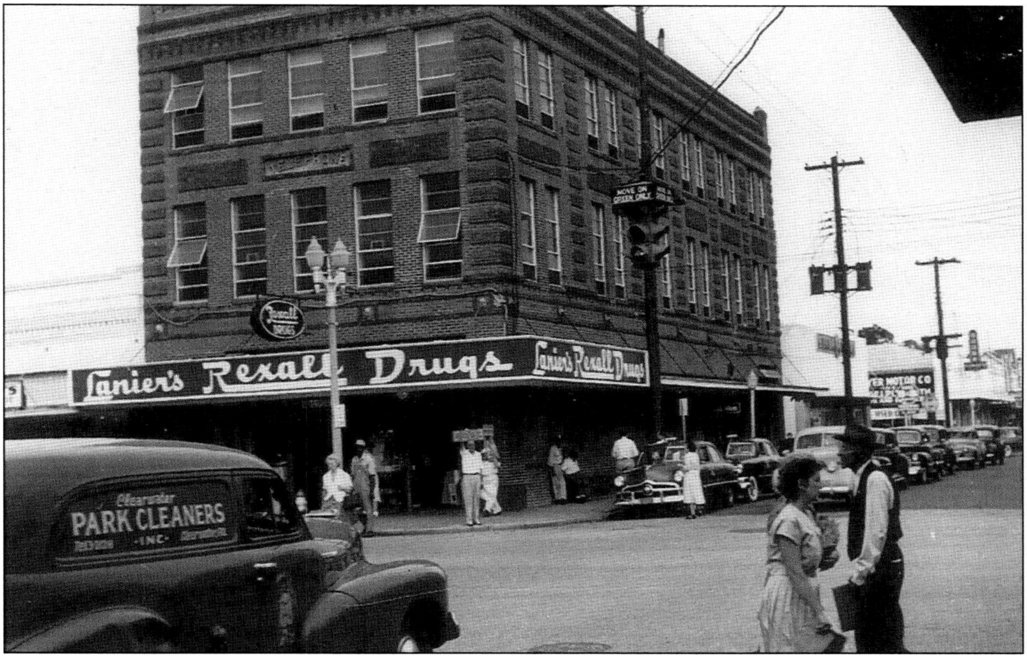

This view shows business establishments in downtown Clearwater at the corner of Cleveland Street and Garden Avenue in the early 1950s. African Americans could get prescription drugs filled at Rexall Drugs but could not make purchases from the soda fountain.

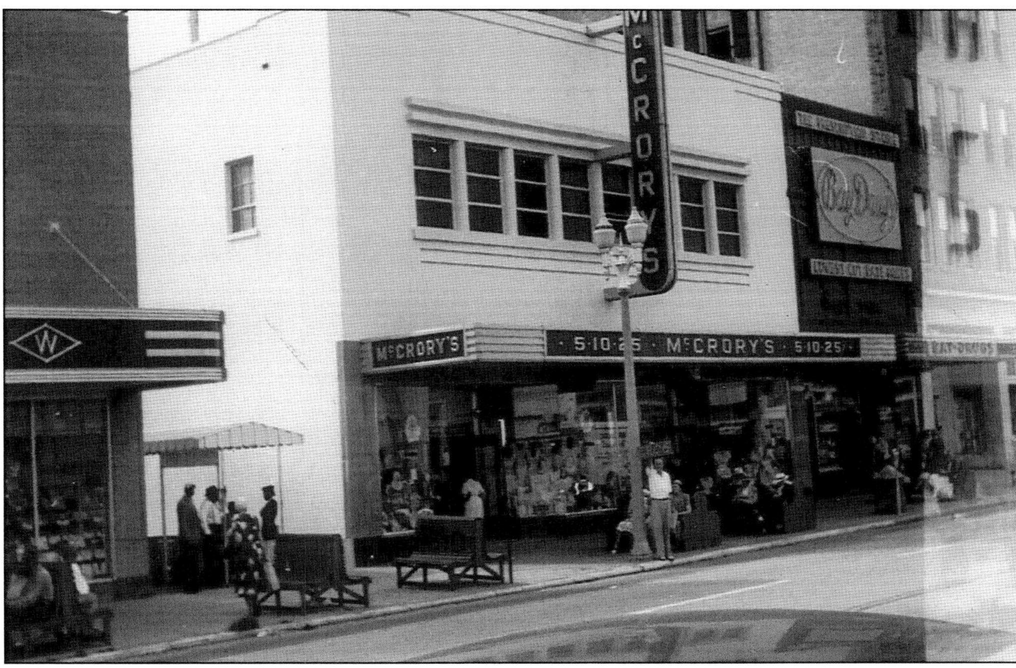

This is McCrory's in downtown Clearwater in the early 1950s. Because of the prevailing Jim Crow laws of the time, African Americans could purchase goods at McCrory's, but they would not be served at the lunch counter. Note Bay Drugs to the right of McCrory's. It became the site of one of the first in a chain of Eckerd Drugs in Florida.

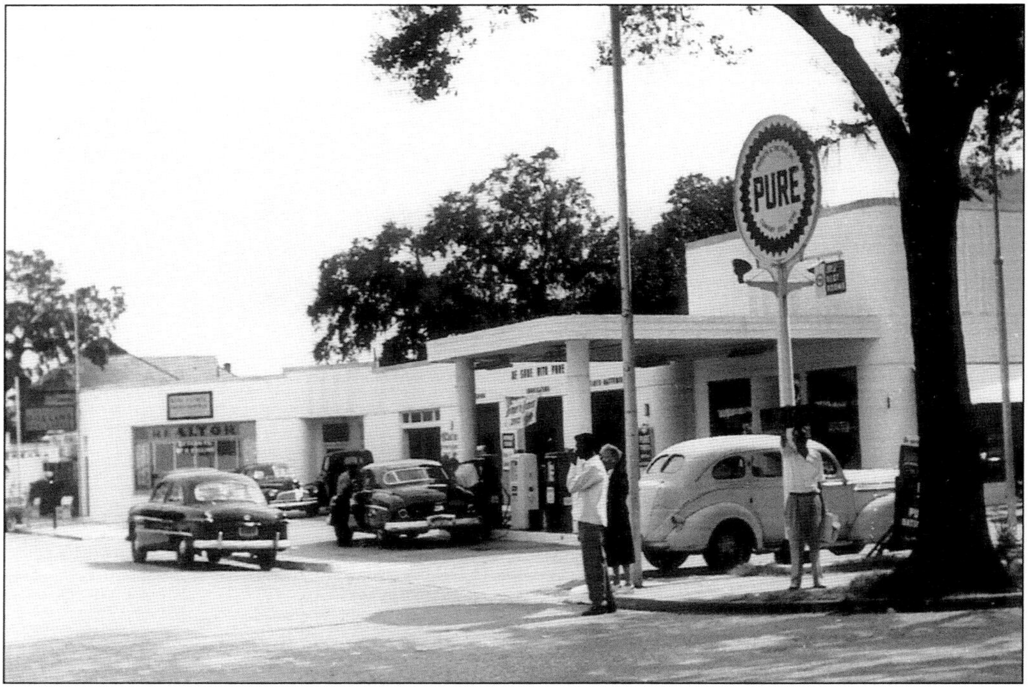

An African-American worker services a 1940s automobile at the Pure Gas Station, which was located at the intersection of Park Street and South Fort Harrison in the early 1950s.

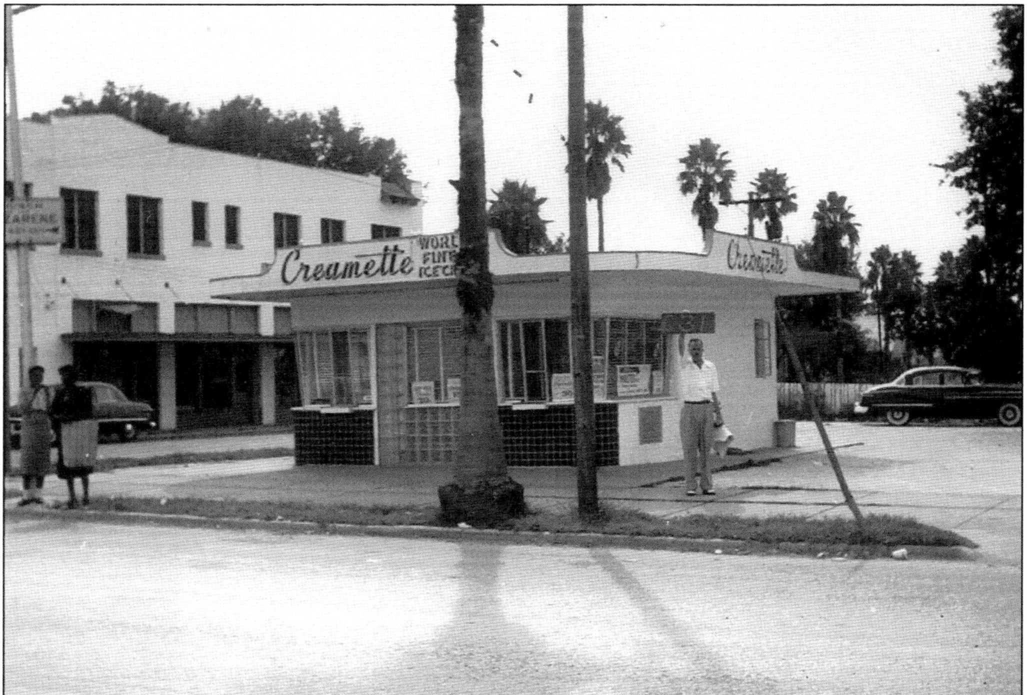

Creamette Ice Cream Parlor was located on Greenwood Avenue in the late 1940s. African Americans frequented this parlor to get a cool, tasty treat from this white-owned establishment.

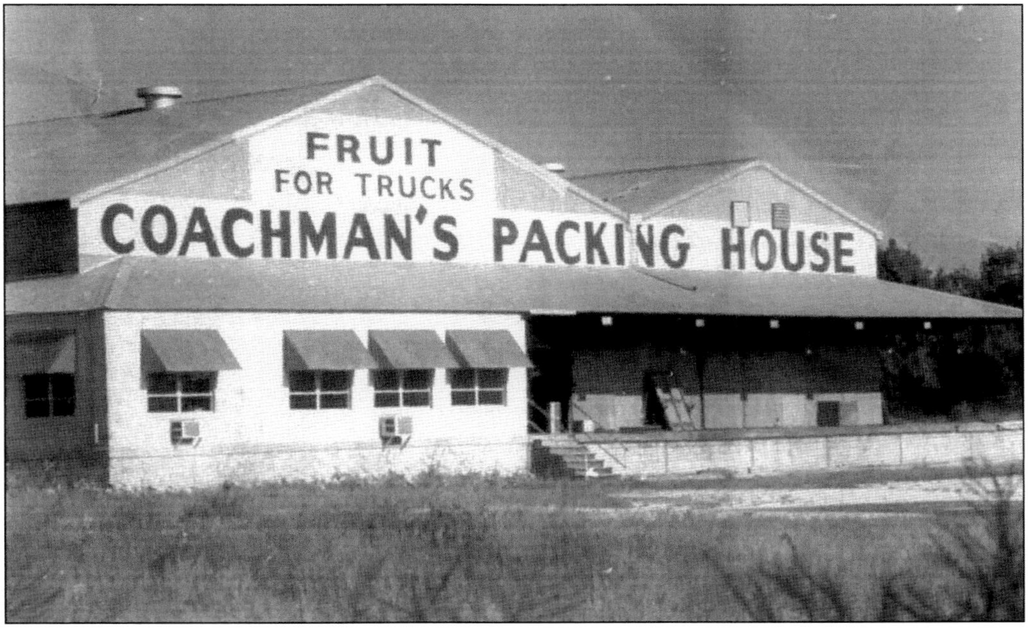

Coachman's Packing House is shown in a late 1950s photo. African Americans were brought into the area to work on the Orange Belt Railroad and in the orange groves in the Clearwater area in the late 1880s. Packing houses, such as Coachman's, distributed fruit picked by African Americans throughout the country.

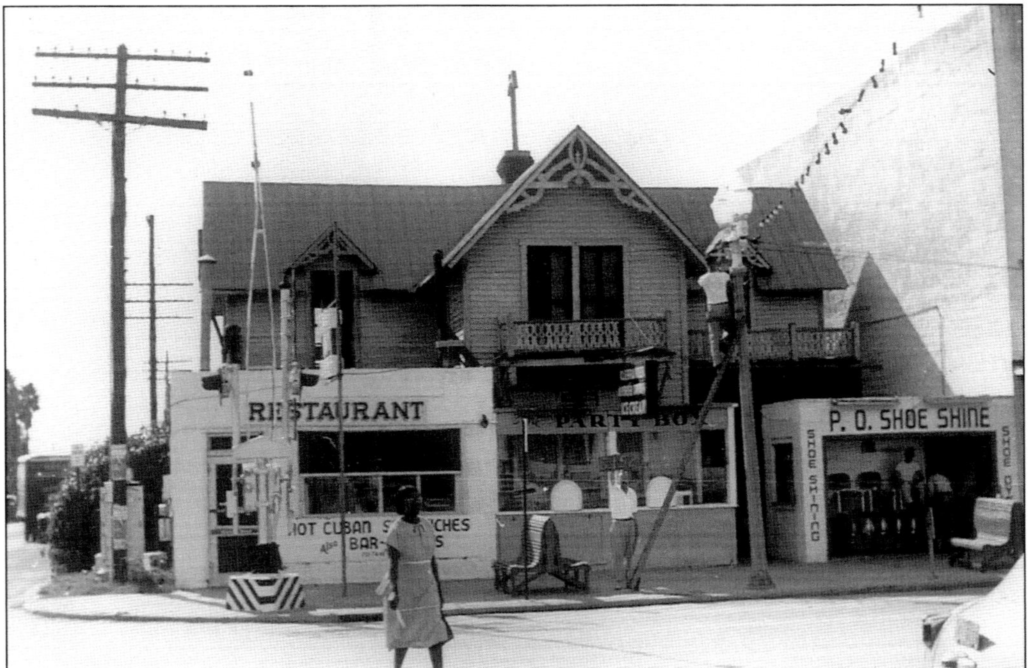

An unidentified African-American woman strolls down Cleveland Street in the early 1940s. Note the shoeshine shop to the right. The shoeshine business was profitable because of the large influx of tourists in the area.

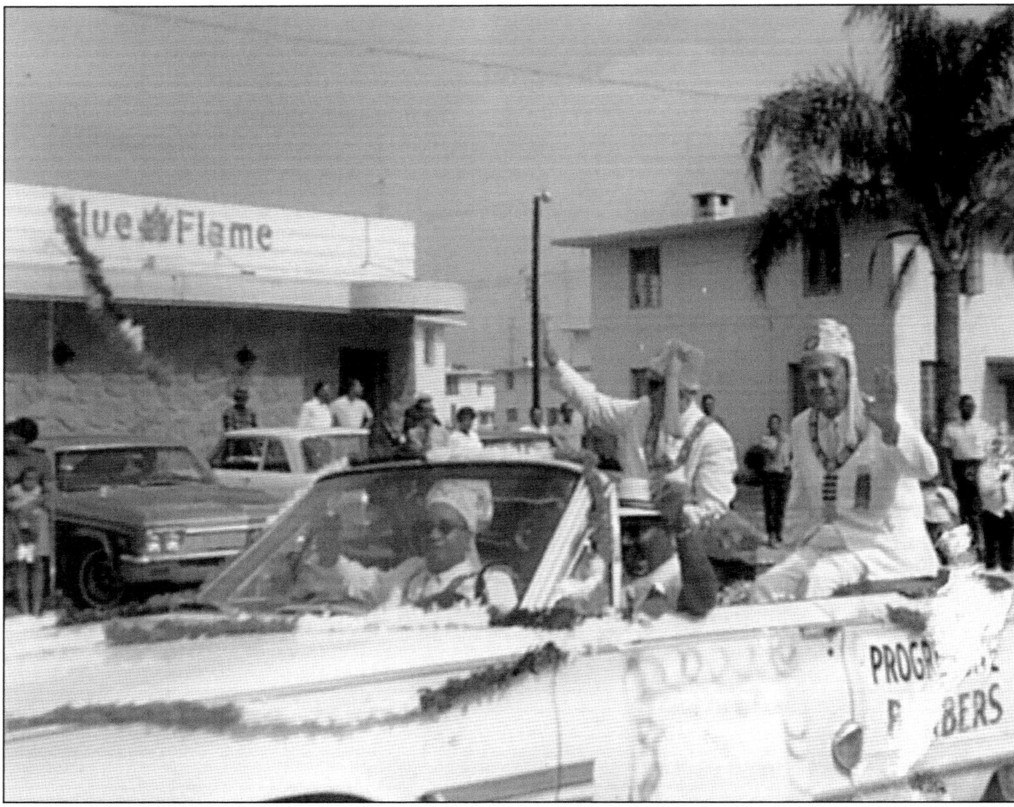

Notice in this photo the Blue Flame Bar and Grill, one of several African-American owned businesses on North Greenwood Avenue. Also captured in the photo is an Elk's parade.

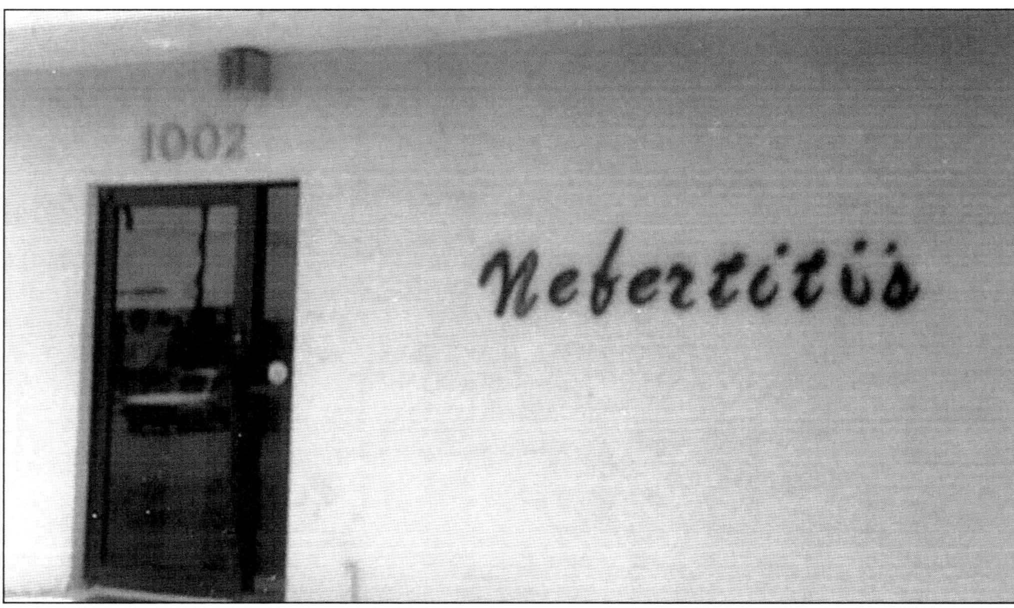

Nefertiti's Salon of Elegance was a beauty shop owned by Ann Biggs. It was located at 1002 North Greenwood Avenue. This photo was taken during the 1970s.

Four

EDUCATION

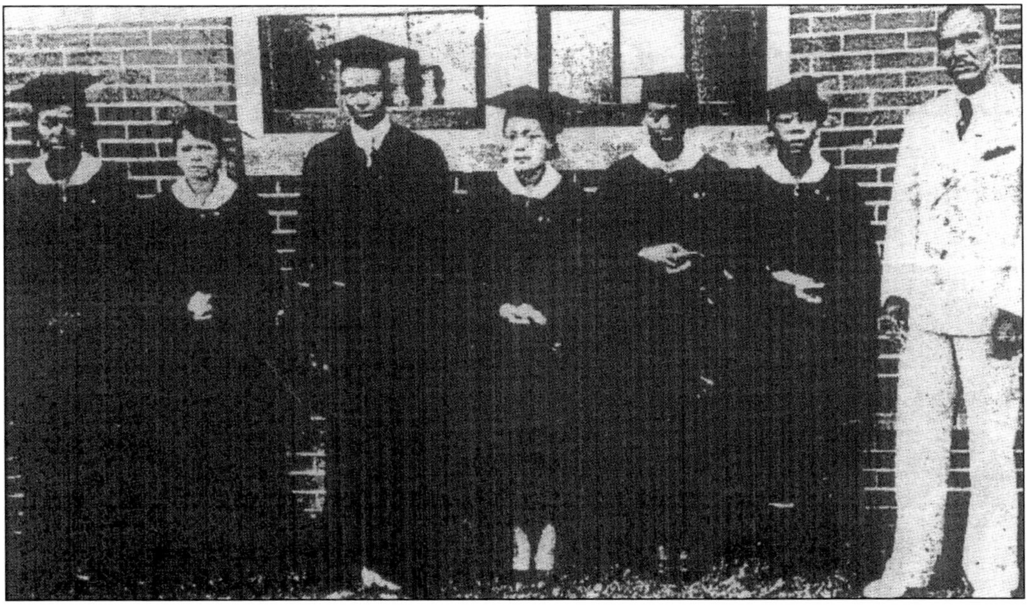

The first graduating class of Pinellas High School was the class of 1934. Pictured from left to right are Mary Young, Cleo Clark, Prince Isaac, Angella Clyvorn, Altamese Ellis, Idella Smith, and sponsor Richard C. Moore. Pinellas High School was originally called the Clearwater Colored School when it was built in 1914 and only went to the eighth grade. In 1931, it became a high school. Later, in 1954, a new school was built at 1220 East Palmetto Street.

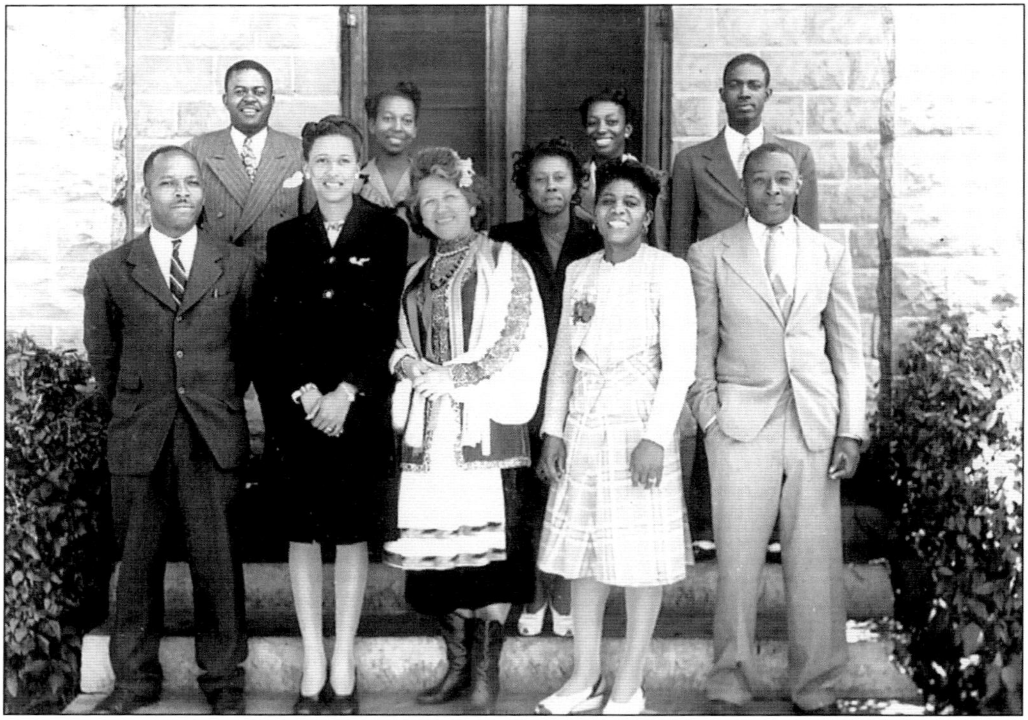

Pictured are early faculty members of Pinellas High in the 1940s. From left to right, they are (front row) Harold Robinson, Francis Thomas, a visiting teacher, Iva Armster, and Milton Rooks Sr.; (back row) Roland Jackson, Portia Jackson, Dorothy Thompson, Vivian Henry, and Leroy Hooks.

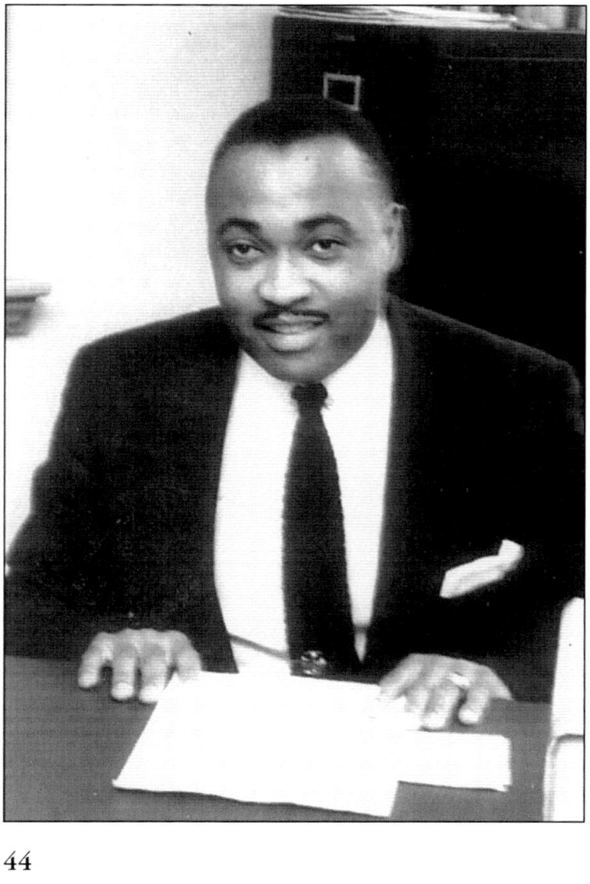

Cecil B. Keene Sr. was principal of Pinellas High School from 1965 to 1968, when Pinellas High was closed as a part of the county's desegregation plan.

Milton P. Rooks Sr. served as principal of Curtis Elementary School from 1931 to 1943. Rooks also taught social studies and speech at Pinellas High School and later taught at Gibbs Junior College.

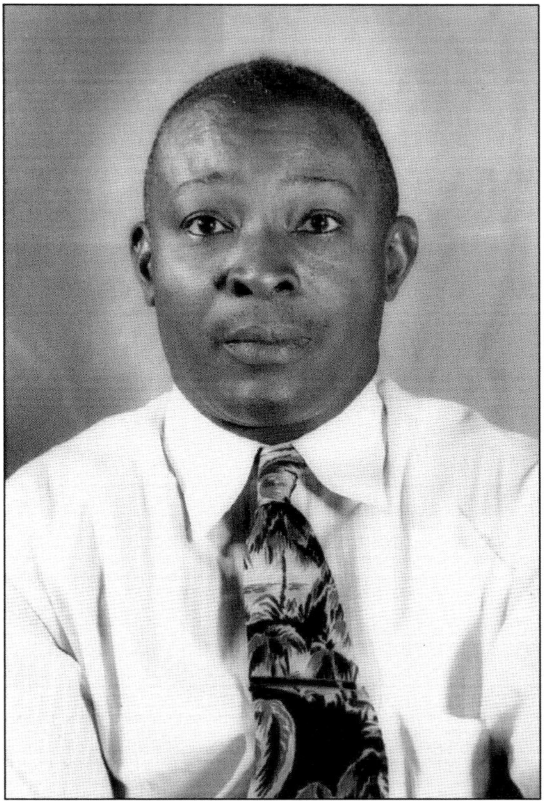

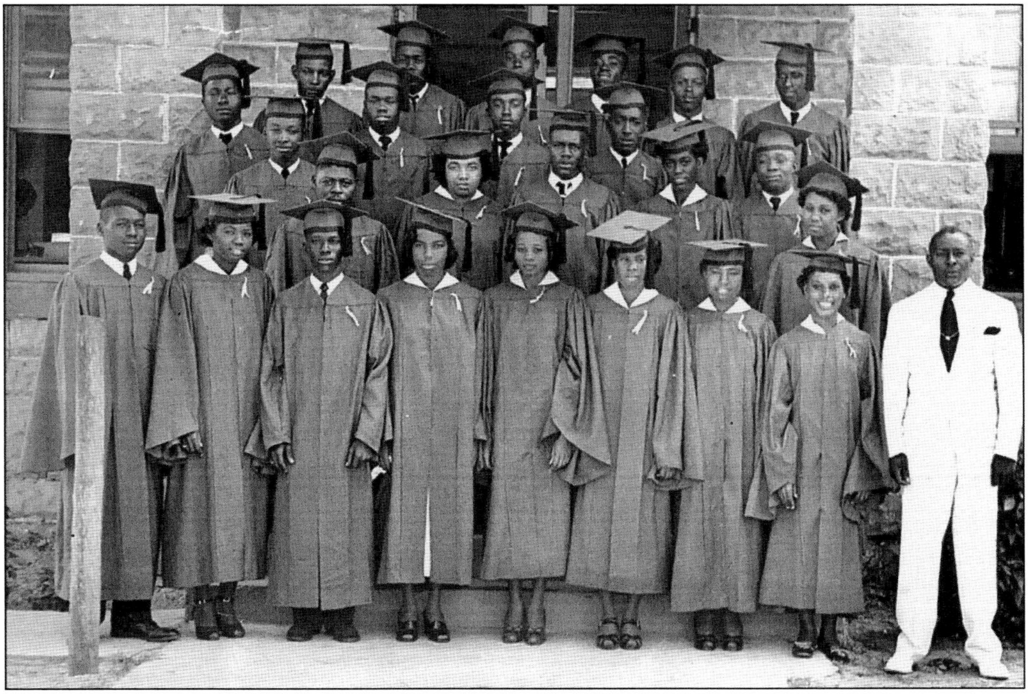

Pictured here is Pinellas High School's class of 1949.

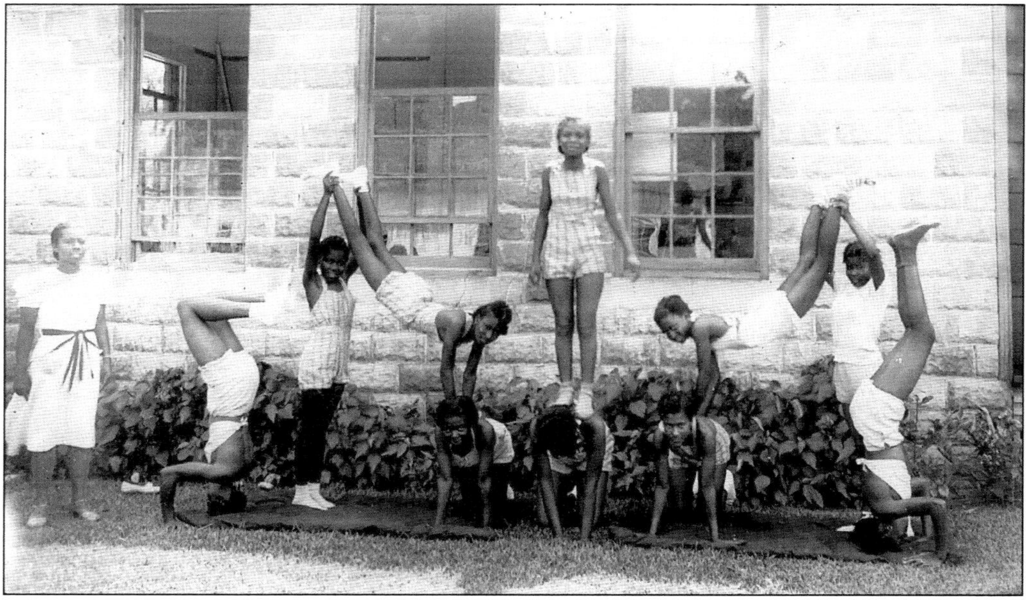

Captured here is a gym class at Pinellas High School during the 1940s. To the left of the group of girls is Dorothy M. Thompson. Standing at the top of the pyramid is Leola Washington, a 1943 graduate of Pinellas High, who returned in 1959 as a teacher at the school.

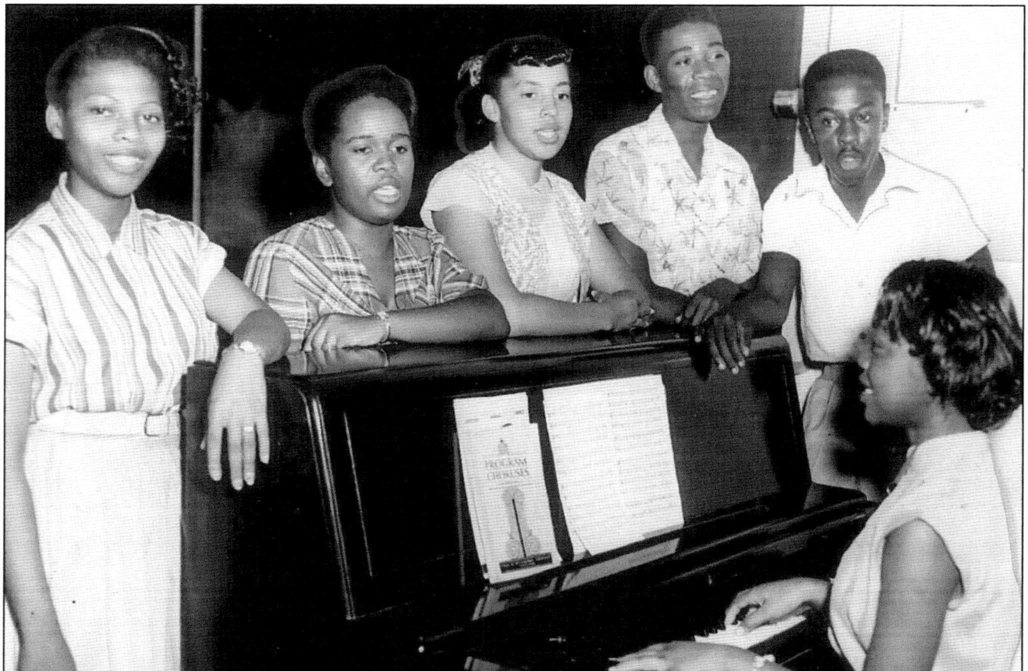

A group of students rehearse for a spring musical given by Pinellas High School on May 4, 1954. Standing from left to right are Idella Miller, Altamese Dorsett, Gertrude Griffin, Roosevelt Freeman, and Rudolph Miller. Dorothy Hooks is the student accompanist, seated at the piano. The performance was directed by Vivian Henry and Herndon Sims.

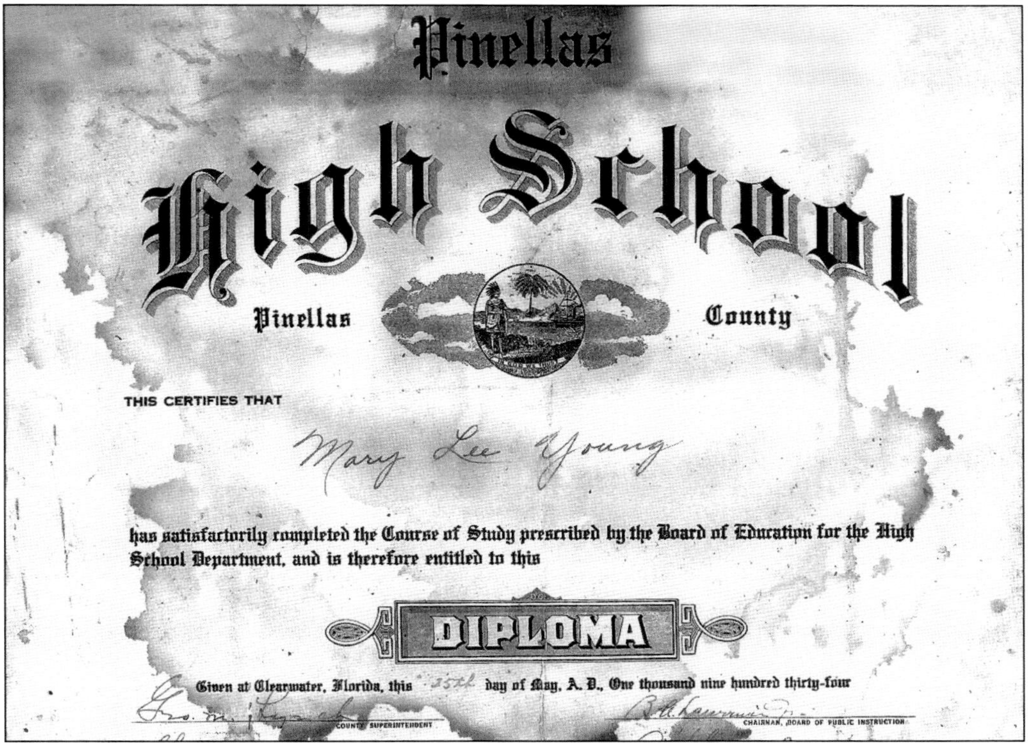

Pinellas
High School
Pinellas County

THIS CERTIFIES THAT

Mary Lee Young

has satisfactorily completed the Course of Study prescribed by the Board of Education for the High School Department, and is therefore entitled to this

DIPLOMA

Given at Clearwater, Florida, this 25th day of May, A. D., One thousand nine hundred thirty-four

COUNTY SUPERINTENDENT

CHAIRMAN, BOARD OF PUBLIC INSTRUCTION

This is the high school diploma for Mary Lee Young, graduate of the class of 1934 at Pinellas High School.

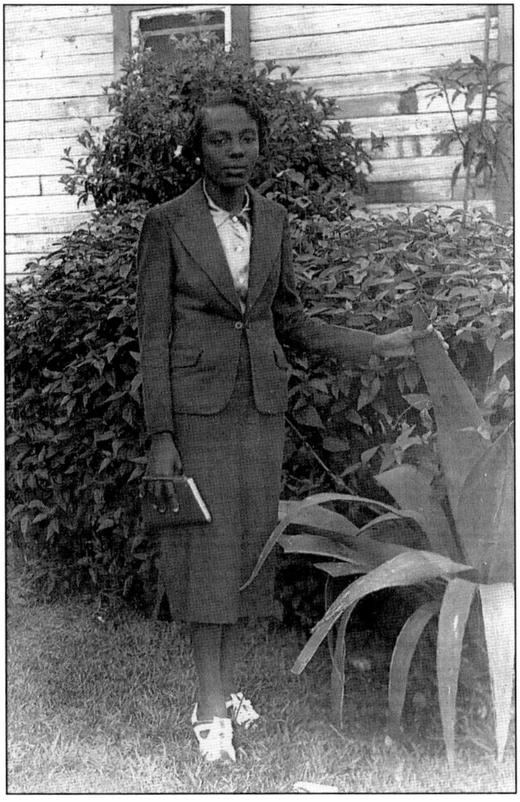

Mary Lee Young Denson is shown here. She was a member of the first graduating class of Pinellas High School.

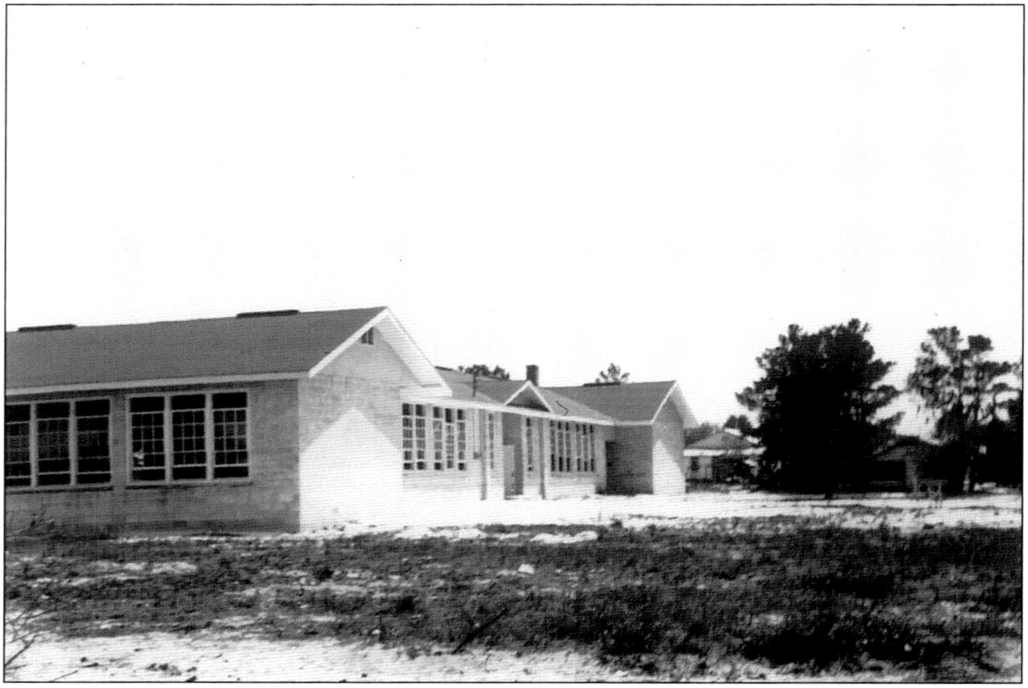

In 1946, a new Williams Elementary School was built. It was the first Pinellas County School built after the war. This school grew from a two-teacher faculty with 40 pupils to a 12-classroom school with as many as 400 pupils.

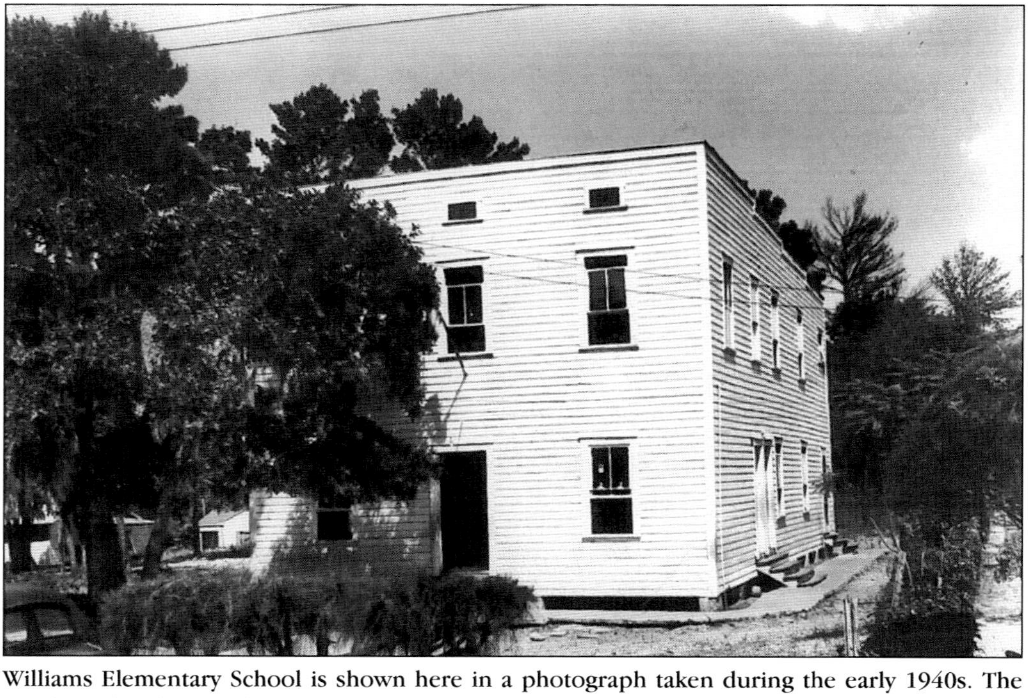

Williams Elementary School is shown here in a photograph taken during the early 1940s. The Knights of Pythias held meetings in an upstairs section of the building, which was located on Brownell Street.

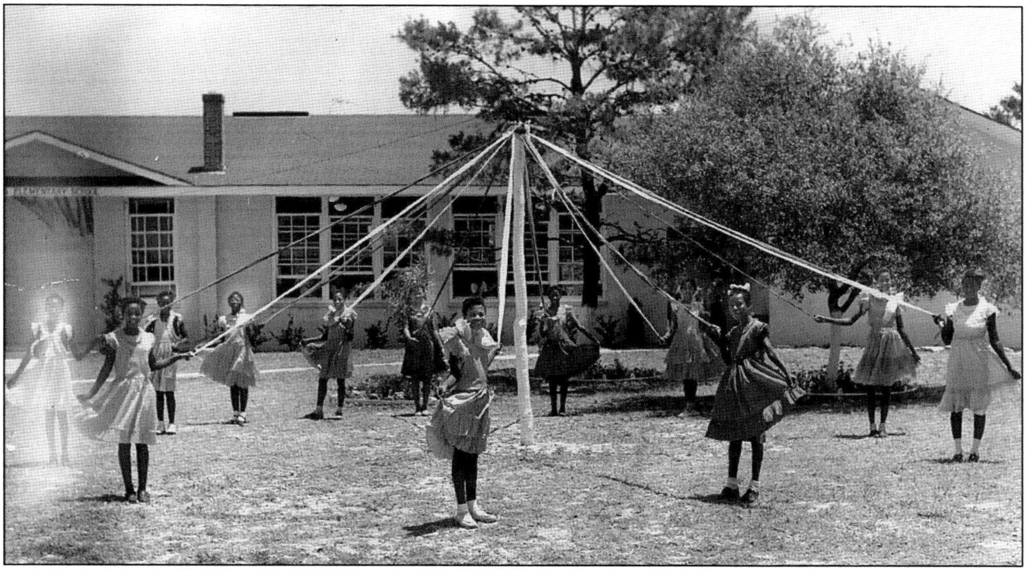
Twelve students from Williams Elementary plait the maypole during a 1950 May Day celebration.

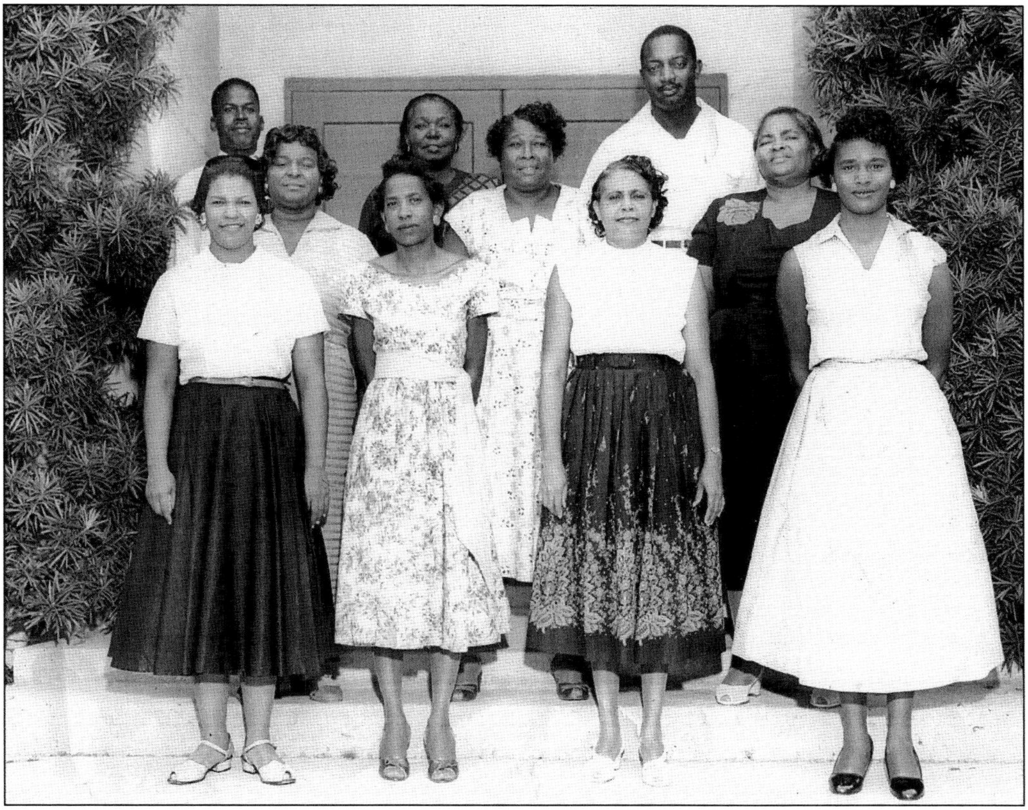
Pictured here is the faculty of Williams Elementary School in the early 1950s. This photo is also featured on the cover of the book. From left to right are (front row) Bennie James, Mayme Hodges, Evelyn Rooks, and Mary Campbell; (middle row) Bessie Gibson, Arabella Faust, and Vivian Nelson; (back row) James Rembert, Mary Smith, and Amos Lewis.

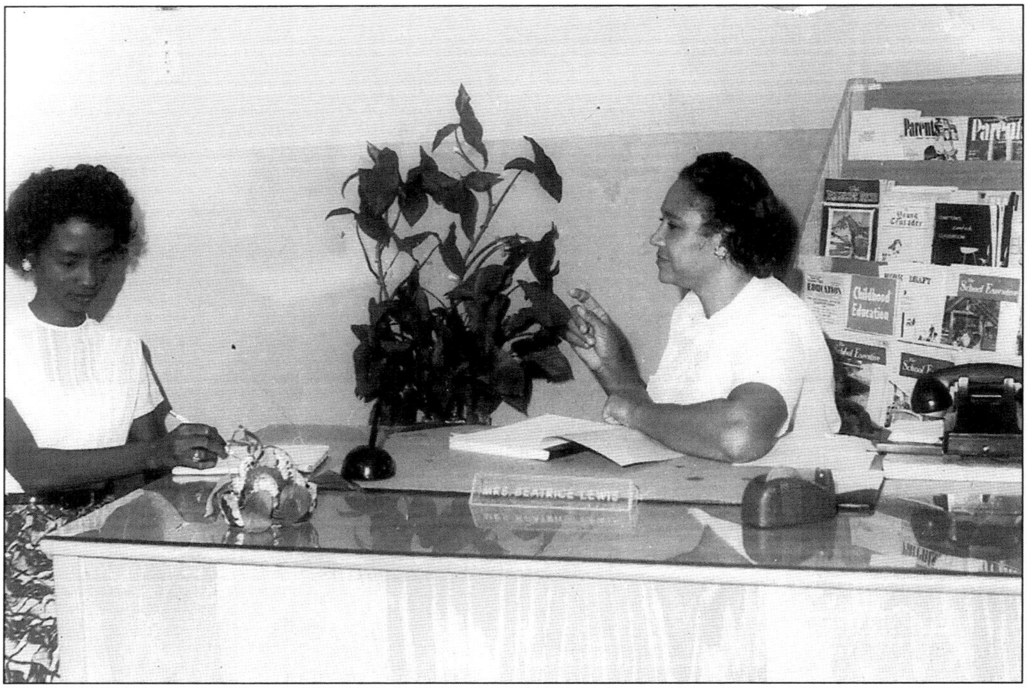

Seated at the desk is Beatrice F. Lewis, principal of Curtis Elementary School, and Lo Anner Rutledge, secretary and bookkeeper. This photo was taken during the 1956–1957 school year.

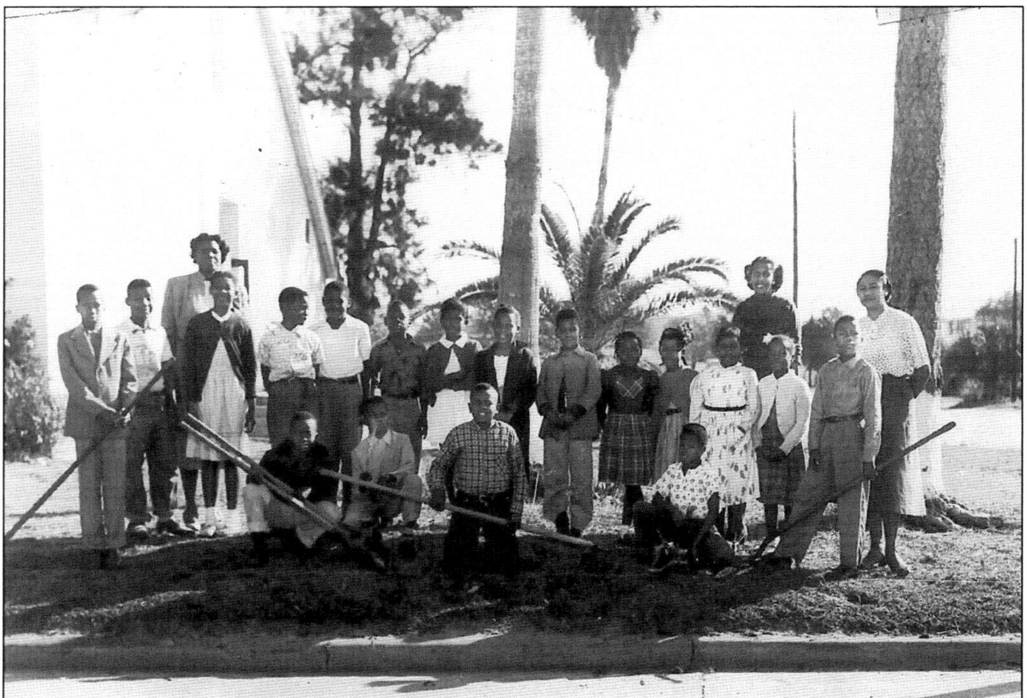

Pictured here is a planting ceremony at Curtis Elementary School in the mid-1950s.

Signed by teacher Altamese D. Ellis and principal Milton P. Rooks, this student report card is from Curtis Elementary School from the 1938–1939 school year.

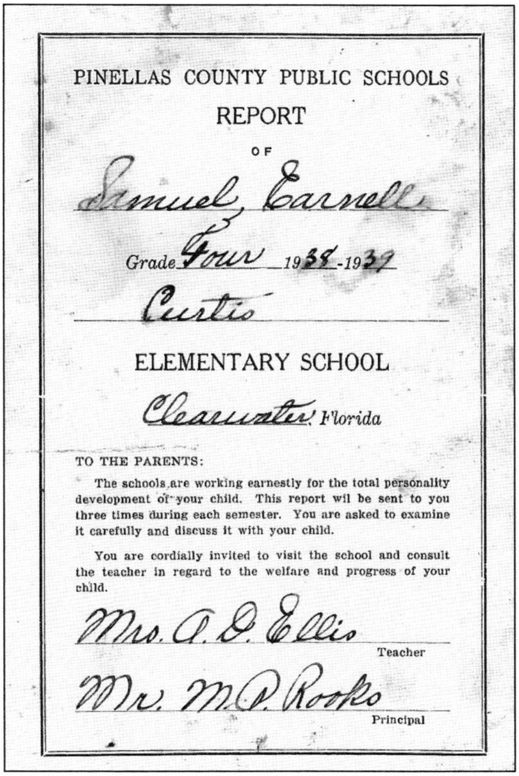
PINELLAS COUNTY PUBLIC SCHOOLS

REPORT

OF

Samuel, Carnell

Grade Four 1938-1939

Curtis

ELEMENTARY SCHOOL

Clearwater, Florida

TO THE PARENTS:

The schools are working earnestly for the total personality development of your child. This report wil be sent to you three times during each semester. You are asked to examine it carefully and discuss it with your child.

You are cordially invited to visit the school and consult the teacher in regard to the welfare and progress of your child.

Mrs. A. D. Ellis Teacher

Mr. M. P. Rooks Principal

The original Curtis Elementary School, shown here in 1948, was built in 1926 at the corner of Greenwood Avenue and Marshall Street. The school was known as Northward Elementary School until it was renamed in honor of Shirley W. Curtis Sr.

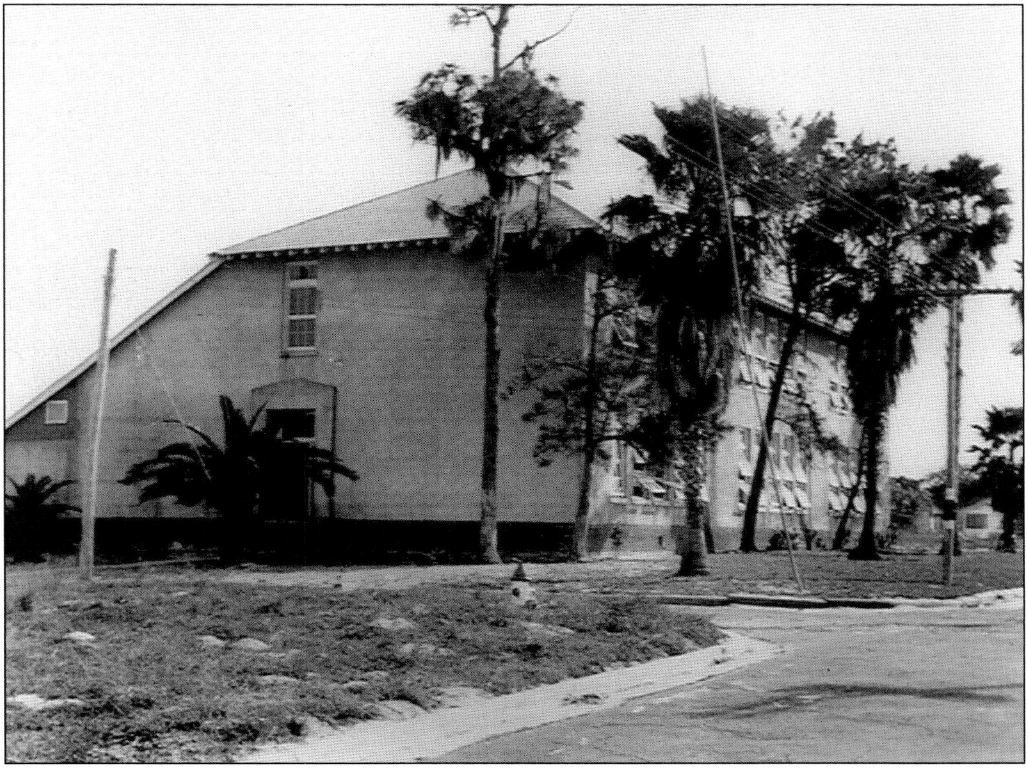

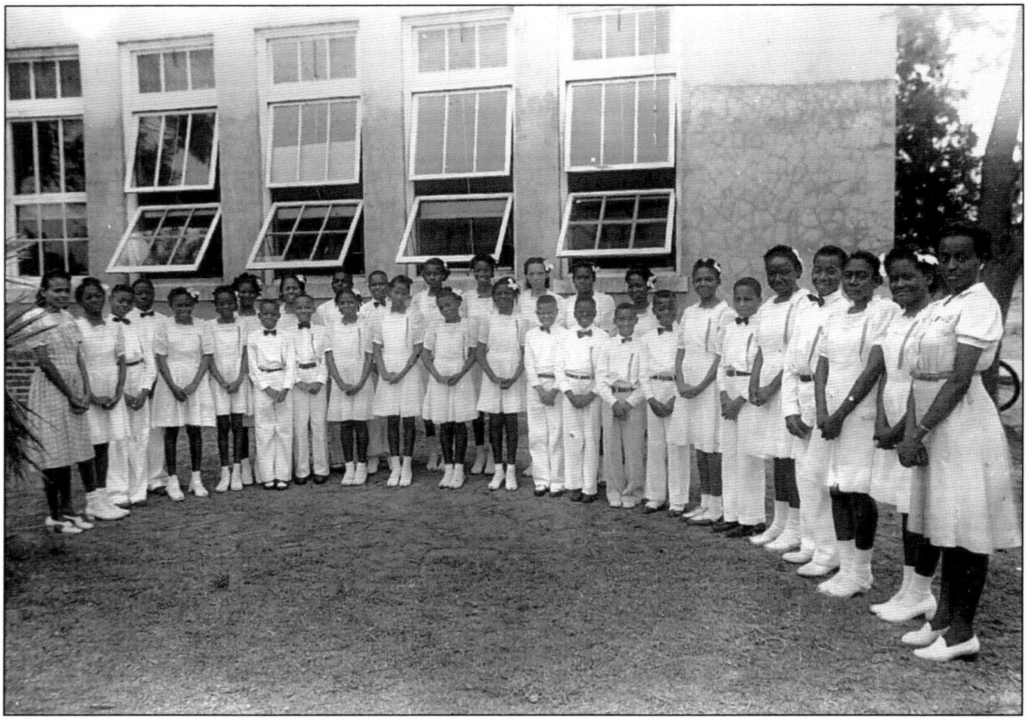

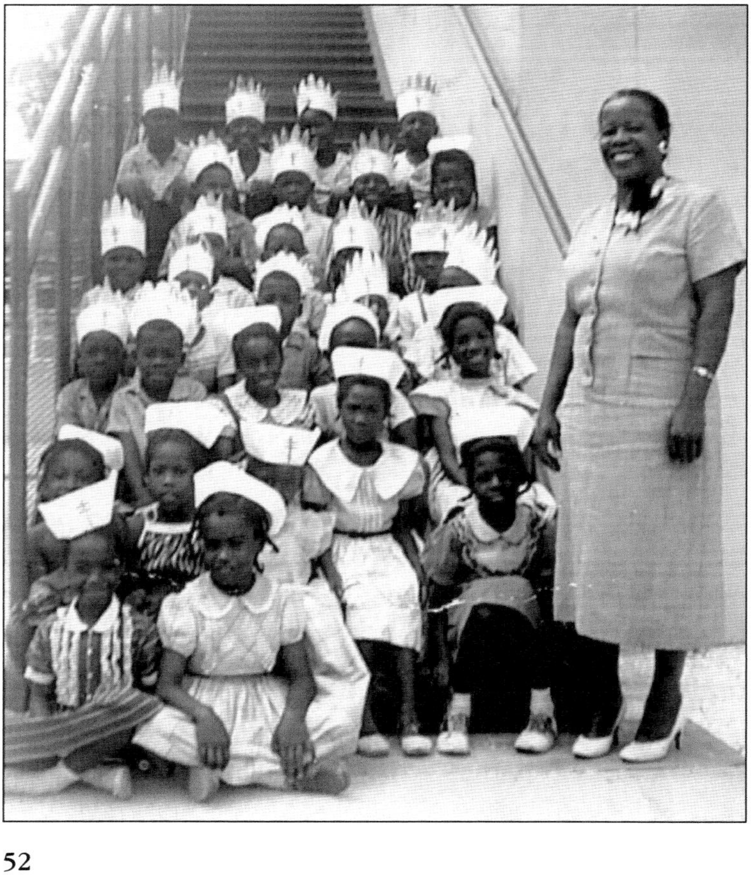

Pictured above are students of Curtis Elementary School flanked by teachers Evelyn Rooks on the left and Altamese Ellis on the right.

Pictured here is a first grade class at Curtis Elementary during the 1957–1958 school year with teacher Idella Smith.

Emma J. Larkins was the teacher of Home Economics at Pinellas High.

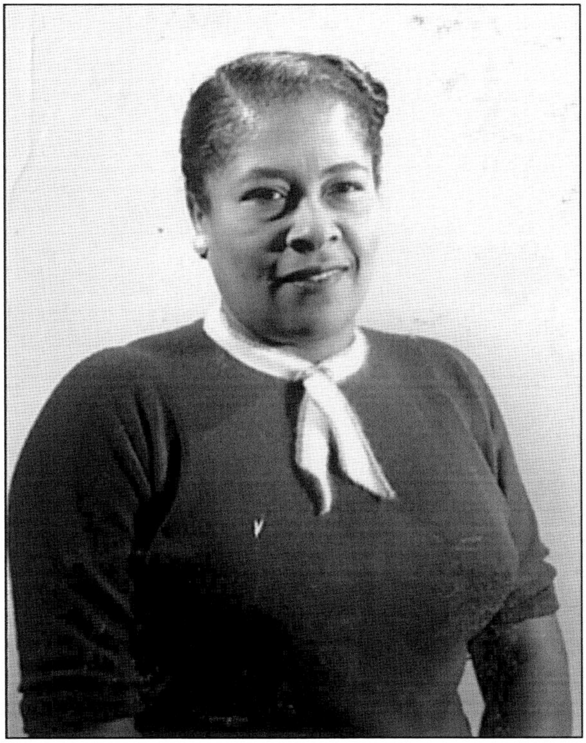

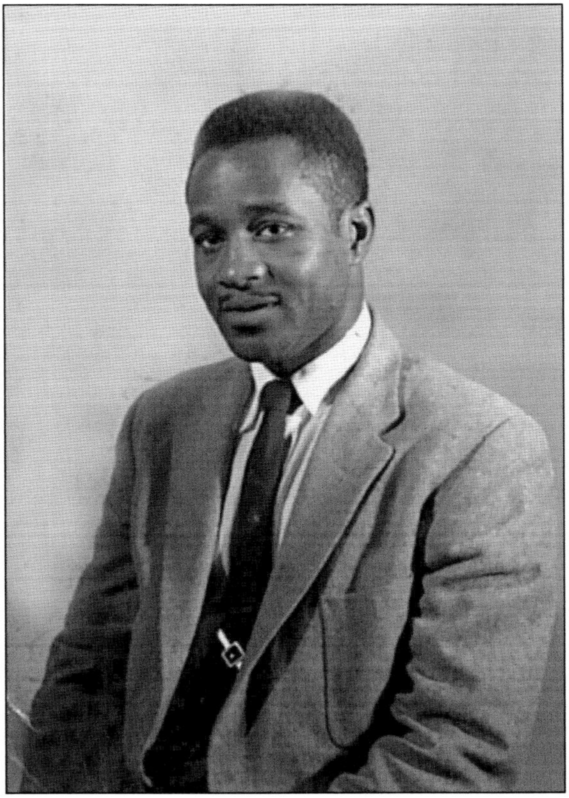

Samuel Hayward, music and band director of Pinellas High School, is shown here.

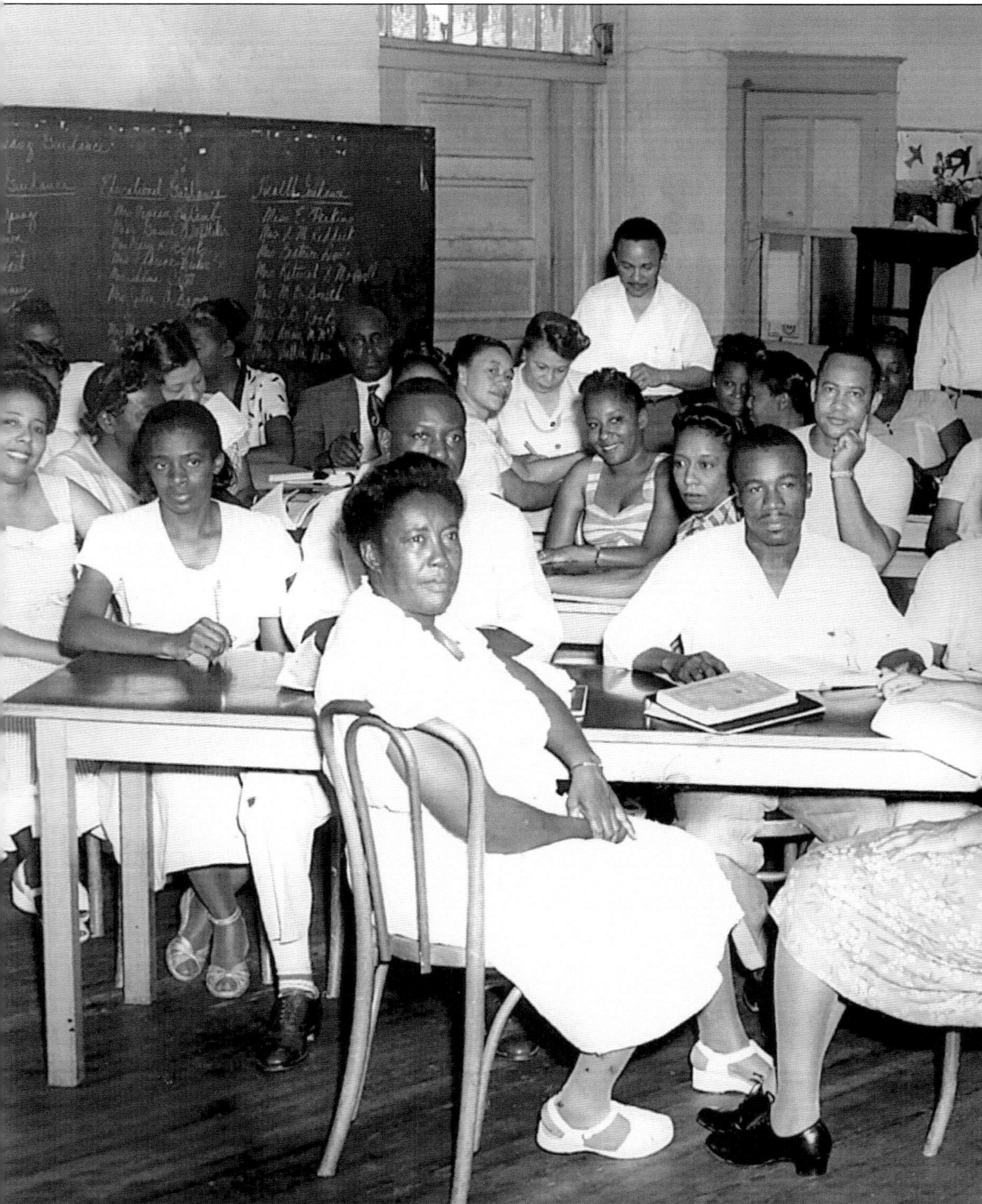

This workshop for Pinellas County African-American teachers includes teachers from Clearwater during the summer of 1949. The workshop was facilitated by Richard Moore, who is standing at

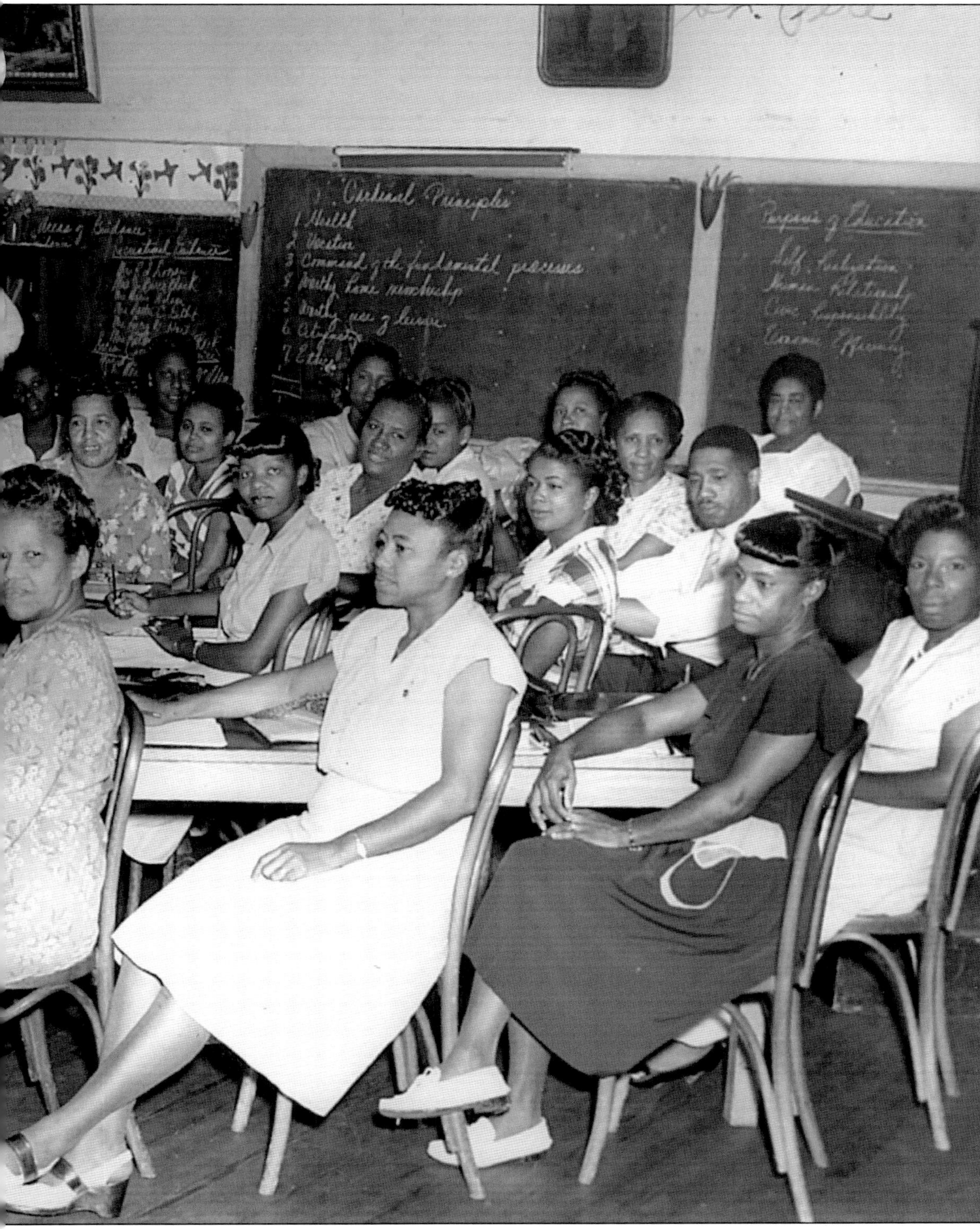

the right in the rear. He later became president of Bethune-Cookman College.

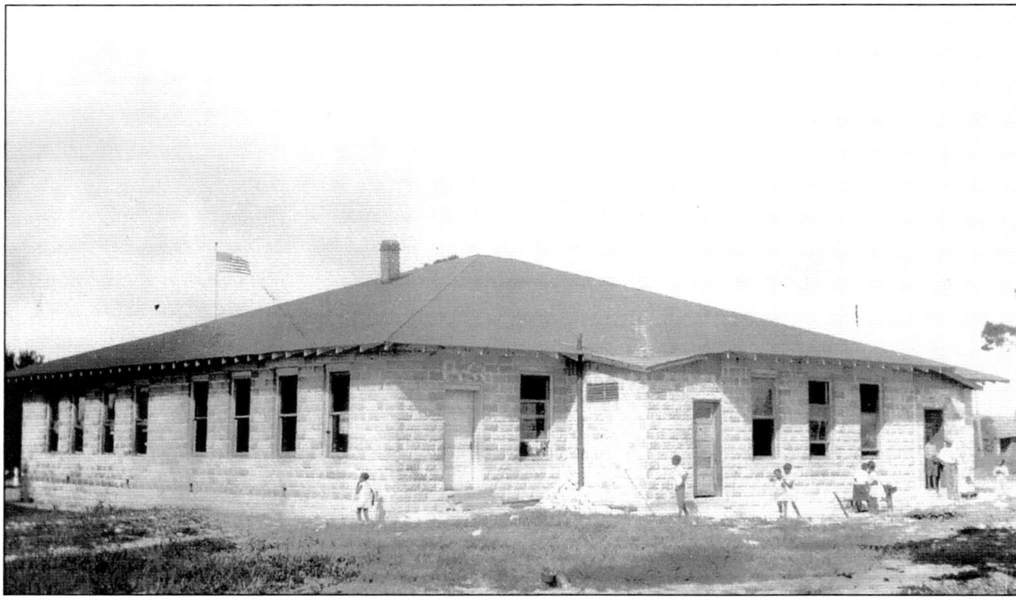

This is Pinellas Junior-Senior High School in 1935.

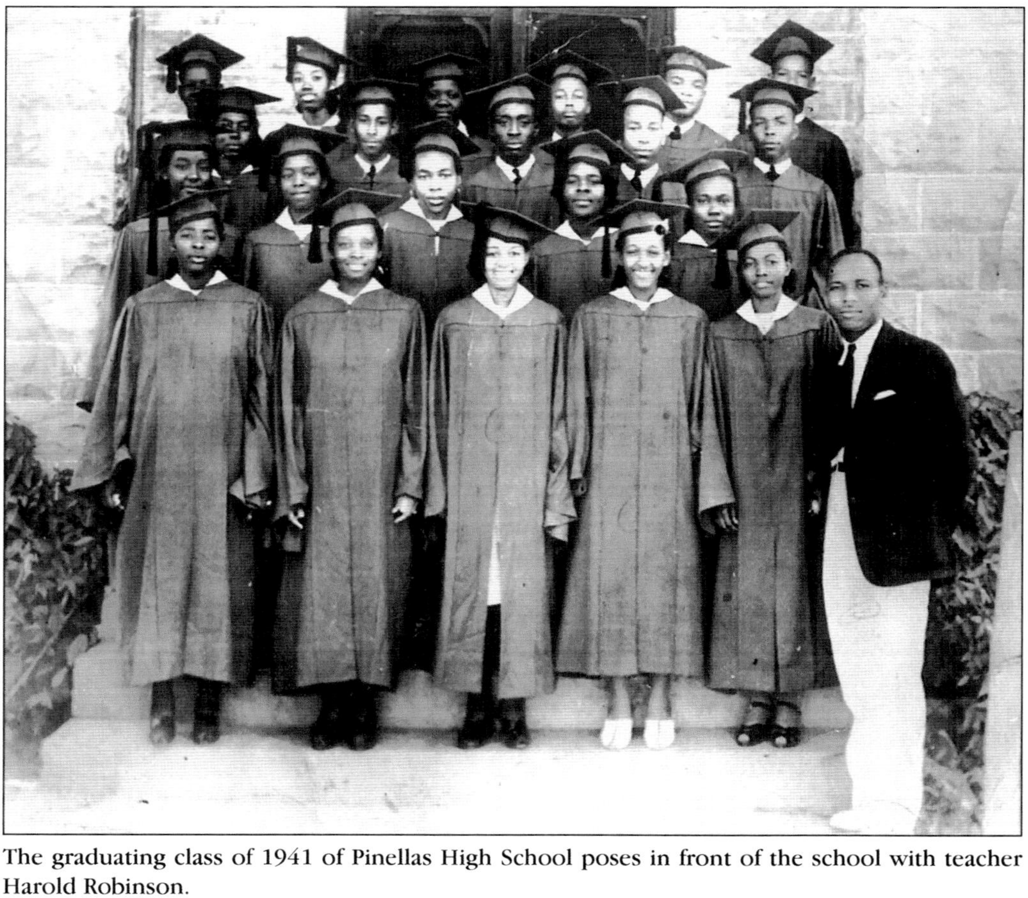

The graduating class of 1941 of Pinellas High School poses in front of the school with teacher Harold Robinson.

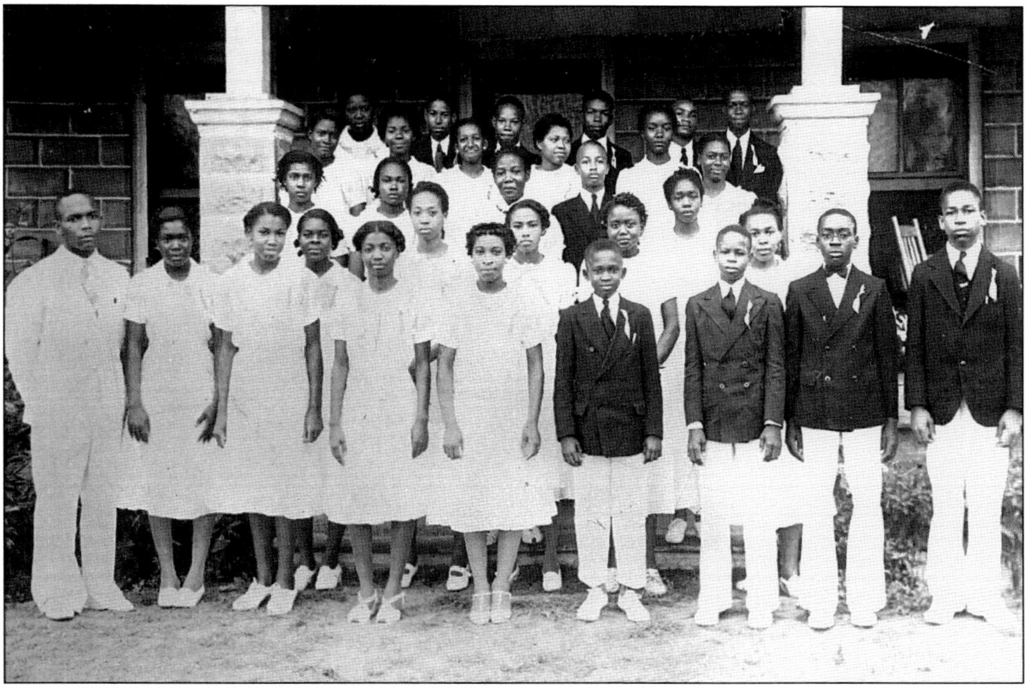

Captured here are the students of Pinellas High School's ninth grade class during the late 1930s.

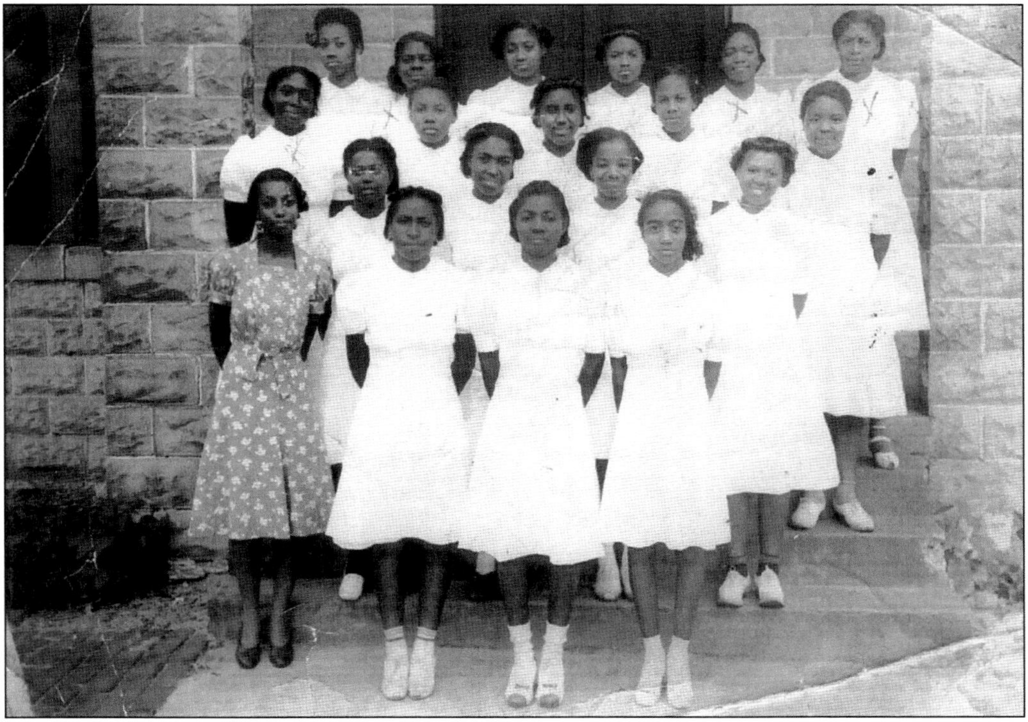

These are the members of the Girls Reserve, an organization very similar to the Girl Scouts of today. It was organized by Vivian Henry, pictured in the flowered dress on the left. The girls did crafts, cooked, and went on field trips.

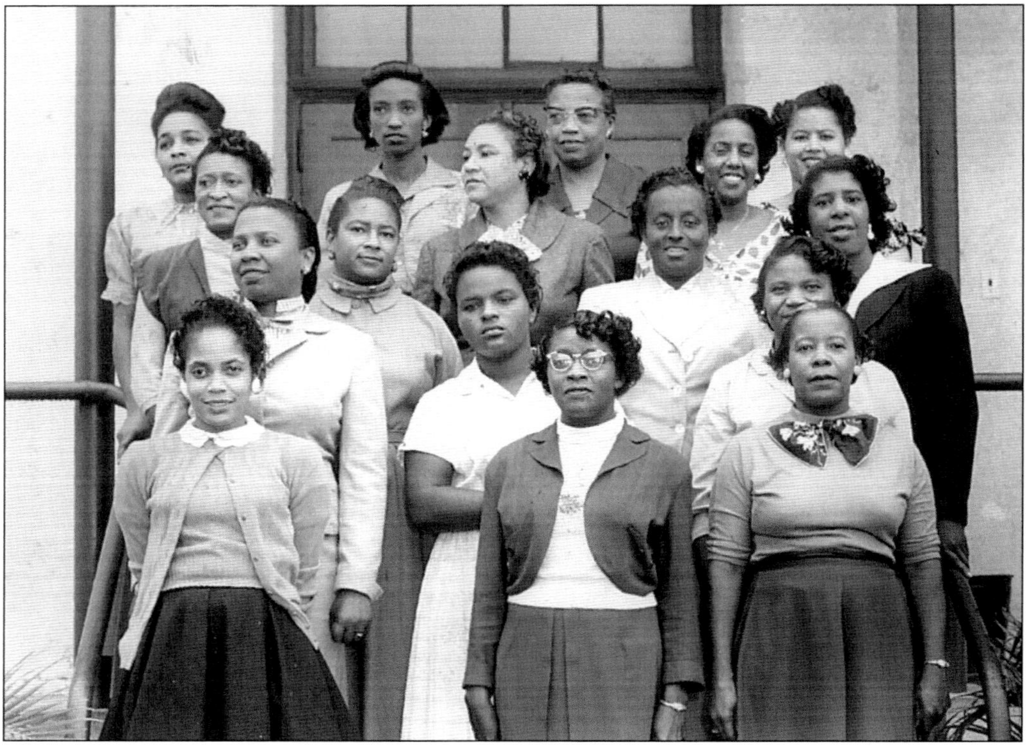

Pictured here is the Curtis Elementary faculty.

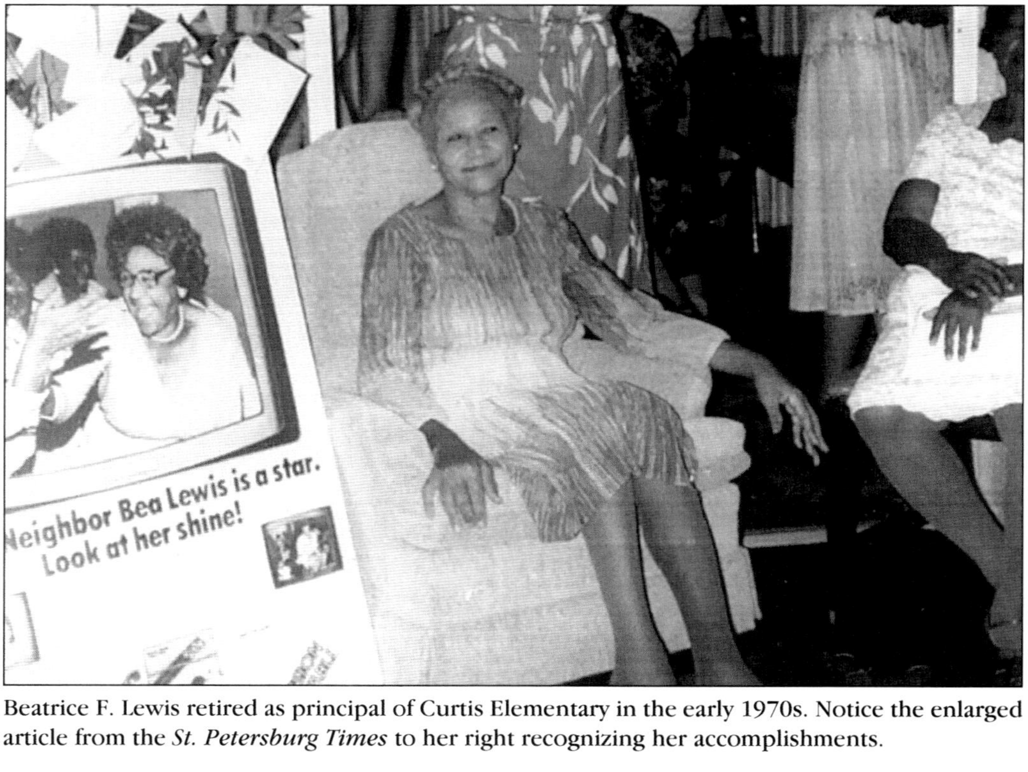

Beatrice F. Lewis retired as principal of Curtis Elementary in the early 1970s. Notice the enlarged article from the *St. Petersburg Times* to her right recognizing her accomplishments.

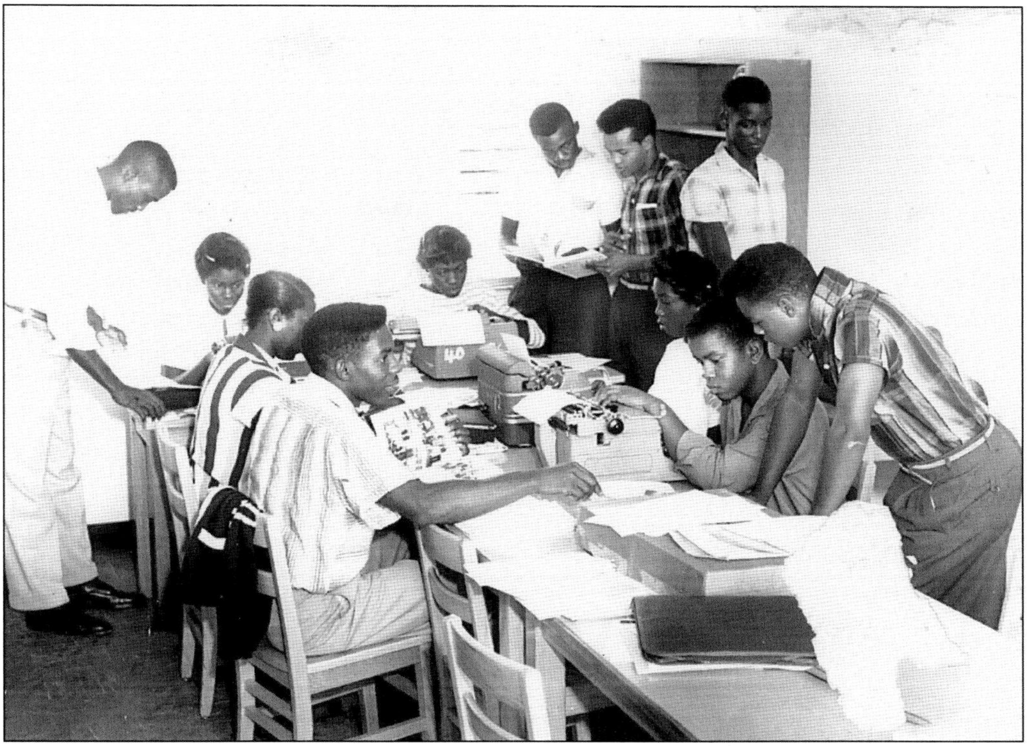

Featured here is the yearbook staff at Pinellas High School in 1957. Standing in the left rear is Paul Hatchett, advisor to the students. He was a 1943 graduate of Pinellas High.

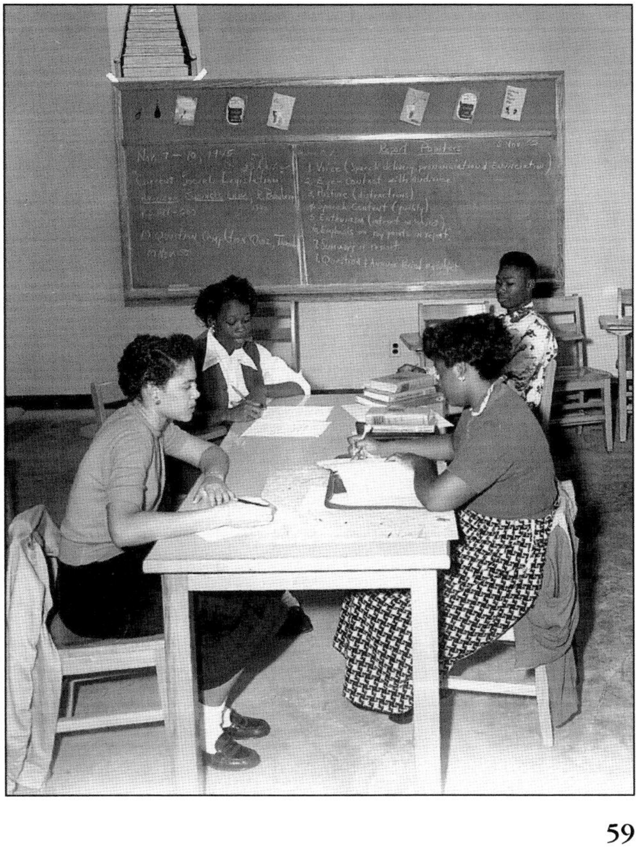

Here is a group of students during a study session in 1955.

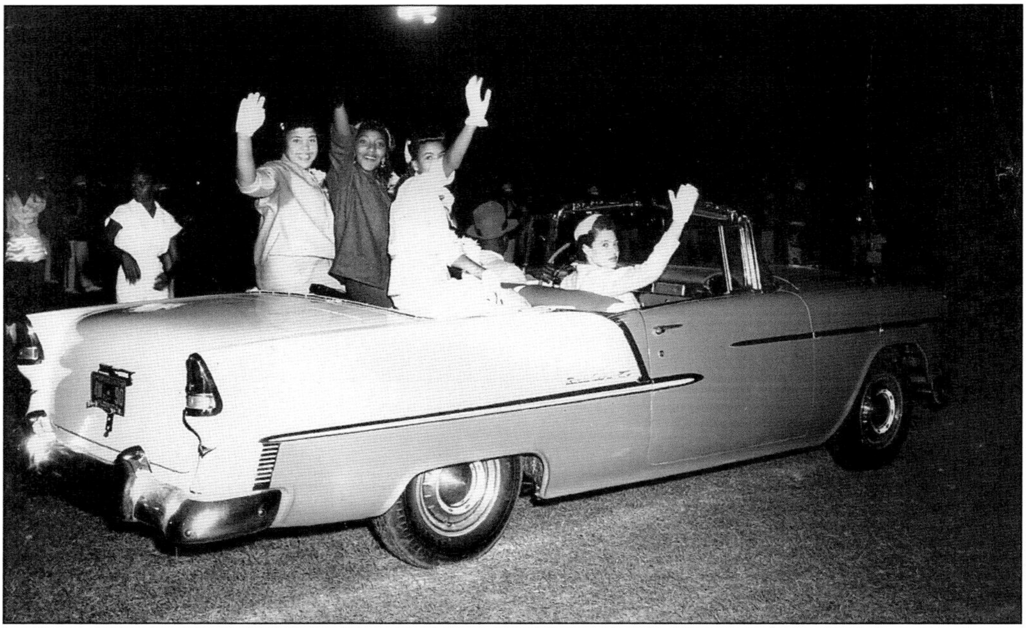

The homecoming queen and attendants wave to the crowd during a homecoming parade in the late 1950s.

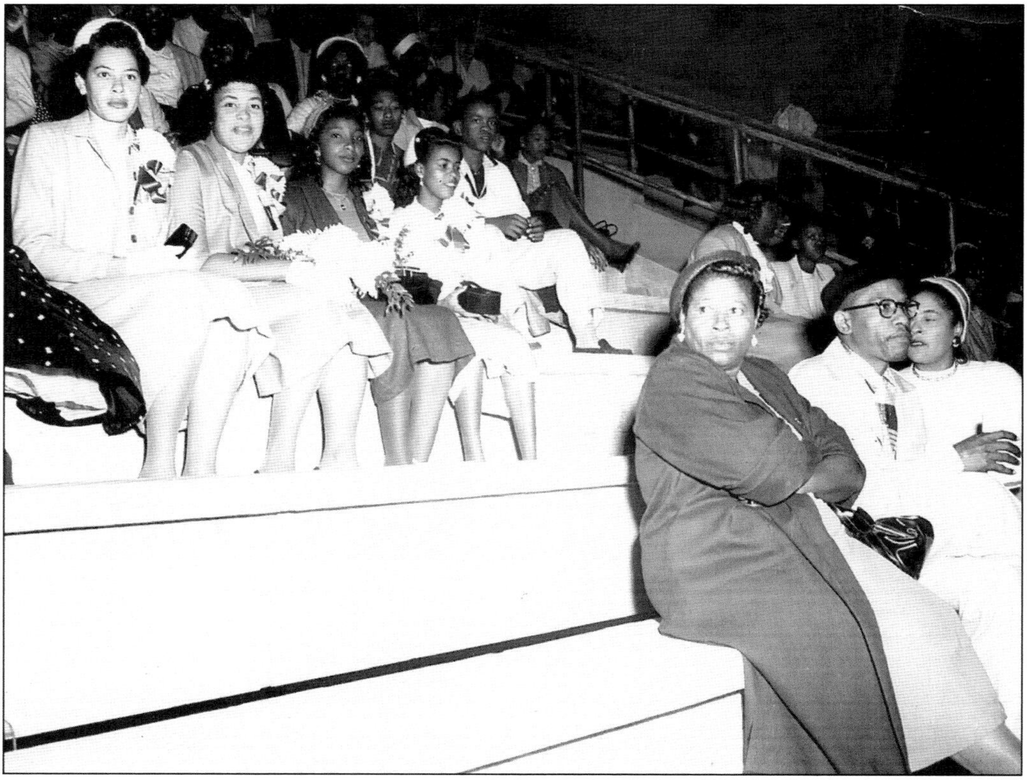

The homecoming queen and attendants enjoy an event in the late 1950s. Emma Larkins is seated in the front to the extreme right.

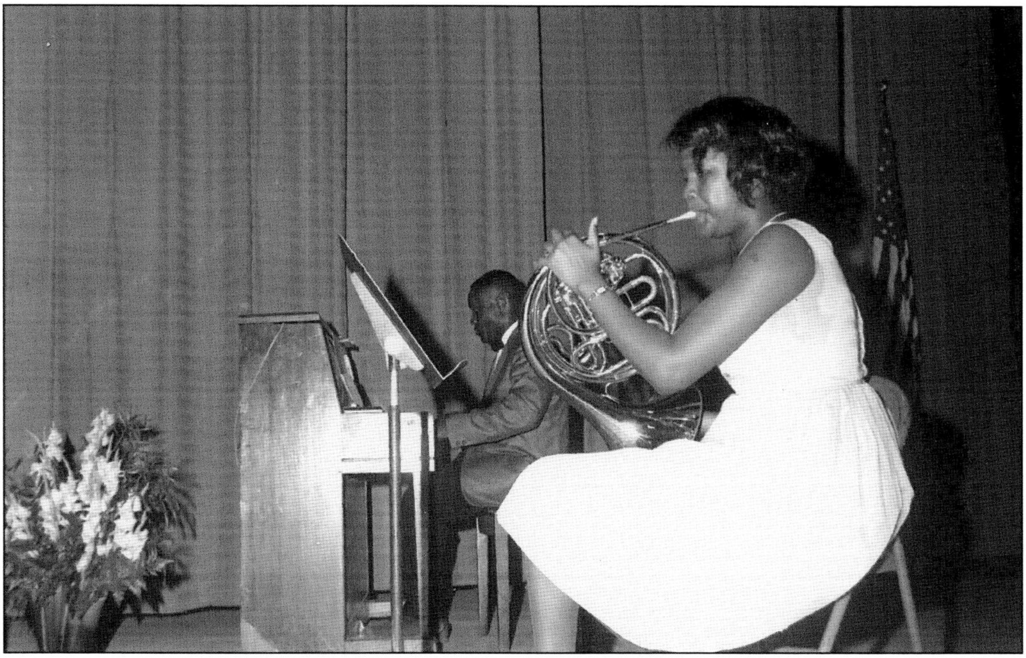

Tommie Ann Hill plays the French horn at Pinellas High and is accompanied by teacher Samuel Hayward in the 1960s.

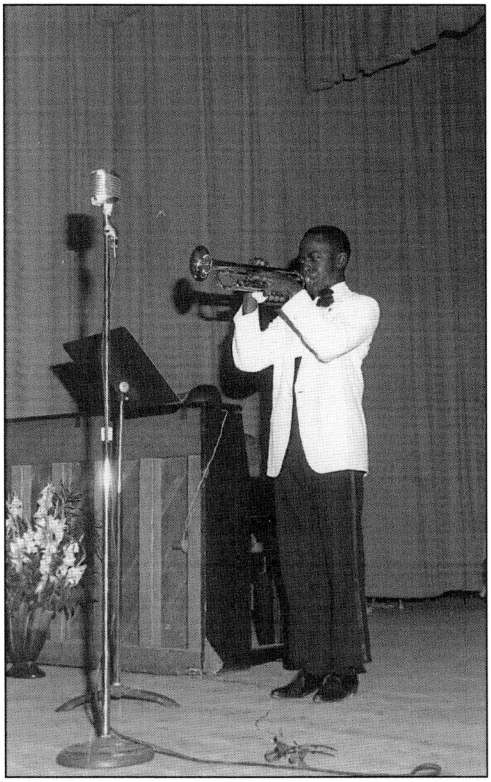

Frankie Neal plays the trumpet.

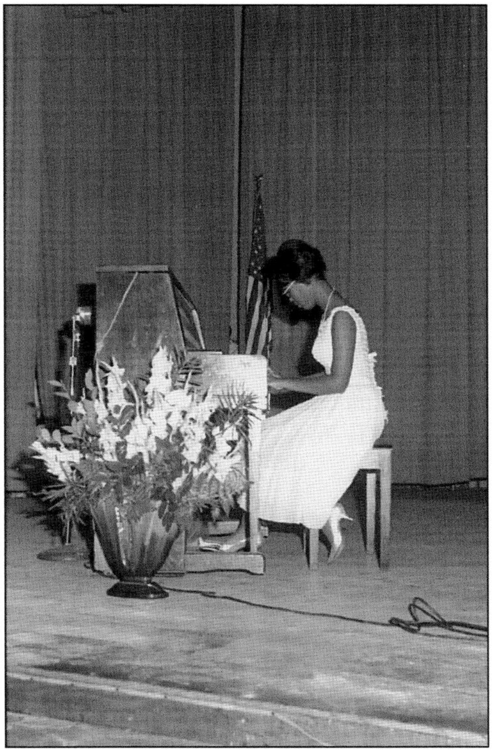

Pinellas High School student Bernice Clark plays the piano.

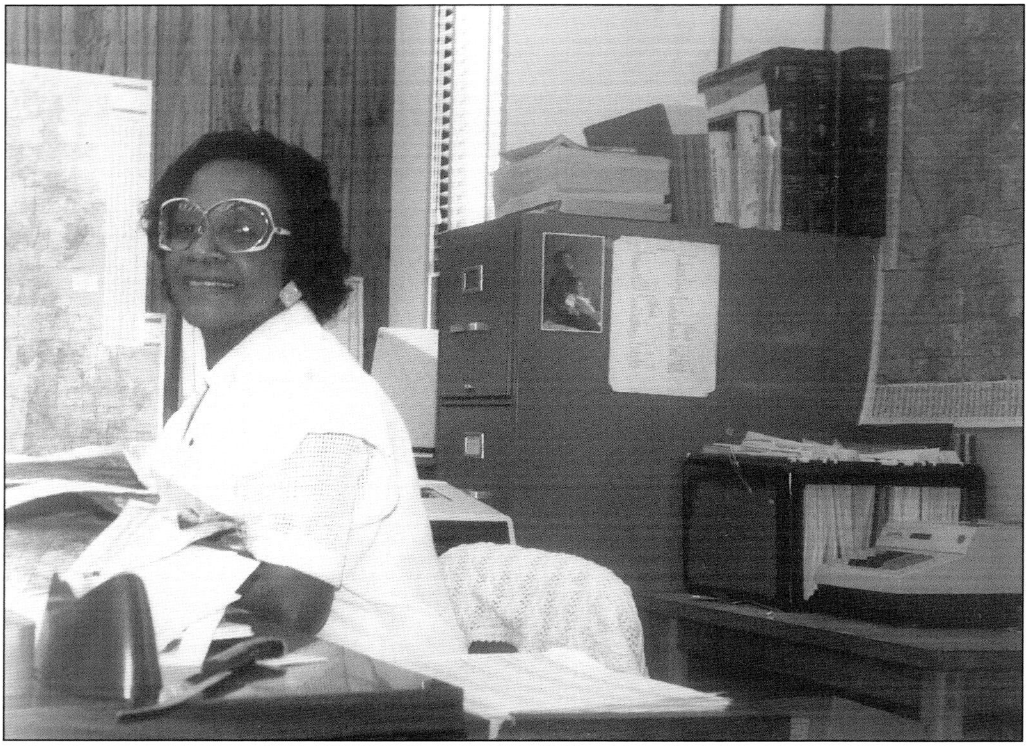

Pictured above is Joyce McCray and below is Ellis M. Montana. Both ladies served as secretaries in Pinellas County schools and later as secretaries at the district office.

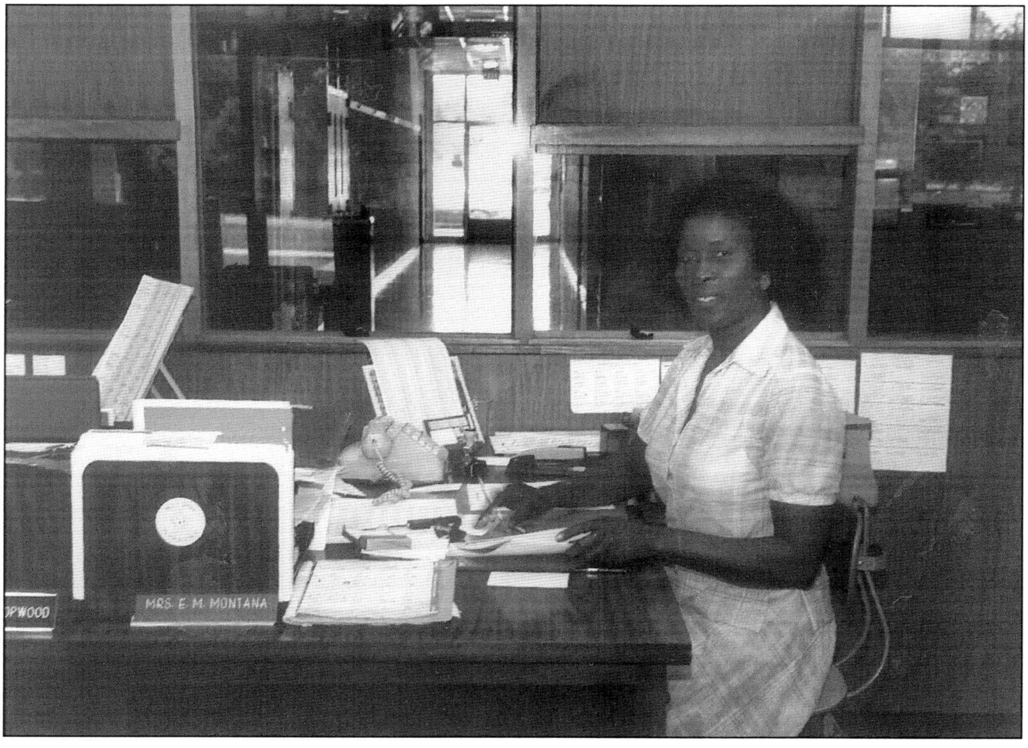

Arlington Nunn, business teacher at Pinellas High, was later named Director of School Operations, Area 3 for the Pinellas County School System.

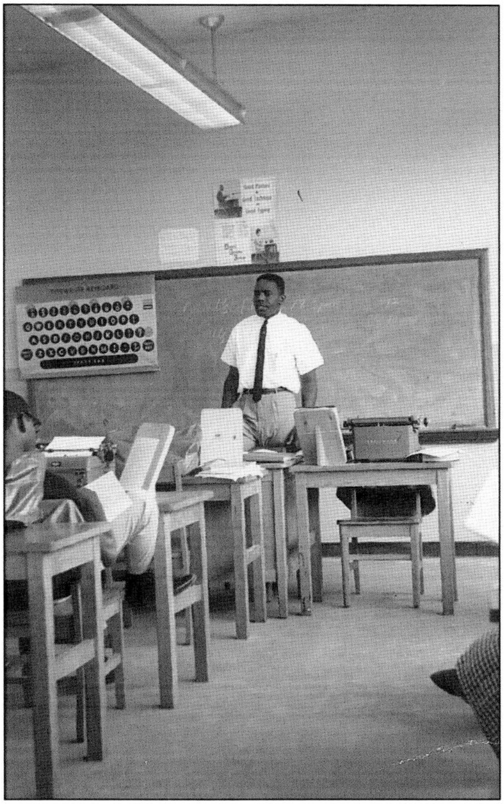

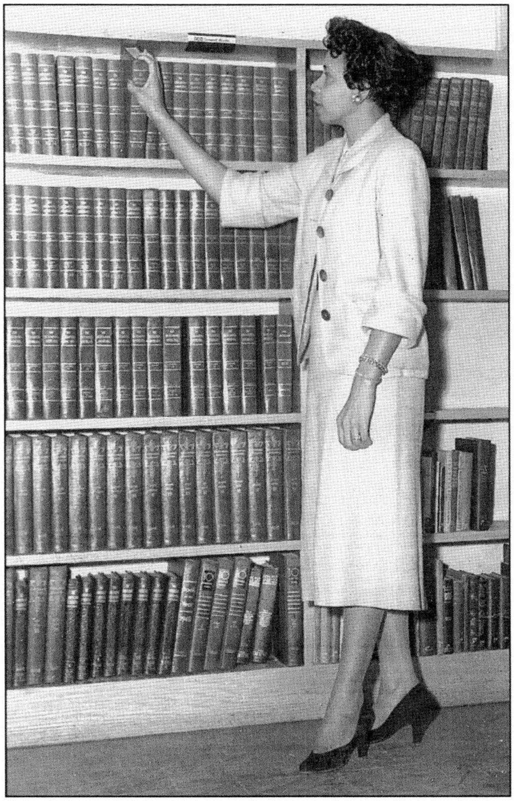

Theresa Goss is pictured here as librarian at Pinellas High School. She later became a librarian at St. Petersburg Junior College.

THE TUSKEGEE
NORMAL AND INDUSTRIAL INSTITUTE
FOR THE TRAINING OF
COLORED YOUNG MEN AND WOMEN
TUSKEGEE INSTITUTE, ALABAMA

June 27, 1914.

Hon. Dixie M. Hollins,
County Sup't of Education,
Clearwater, Fla.

Dear Sir:

I have your letter of June 23rd. We shall be very glad to welcome you at Tuskegee on July 1st, and shall give you every opportunity to see something of the work we are trying to do here.

Our regular session, of course, closed in May, but there is in session now, a summer school for teachers, at which there are in attendance in the neighborhood of four hundred teachers, from all parts of the South, and many from other sections of the country. You will have opportunity of observing something of the work being done for these teachers.

We shall be glad to assist you in any way we can in getting in touch with teachers for the colored schools under your supervision.

I shall be very glad if you will let me know, definitely, the date on which you expect to arrive.

Yours very truly,

Booker T. Washington

MLS

In the letter at left, Booker T. Washington writes the superintendent of Pinellas County Schools, Dixie M. Hollins, inviting him to the Tuskegee Institute for the purpose of recruiting teachers. In the letter below, Superintendent Hollins responds saying that he intends to hire several African-American teachers from Tuskegee.

OFFICE OF
Superintendent Public Instruction
Pinellas County
CLEARWATER · FLORIDA

July, 14, 1914.

Dr. Booker T. Washington,
Tuskegee, Ala.
Dear Sir:

During your recent absence from the Institute I had the pleasure of a days visit there and I must say to you and through you to the people whom I saw there, that it was one of the most pleasant and instructive days that I have every spent. The work that you have done and are doing is certainly an inspiration to any one and the more I reflect on it the more I must admire the spirit and ability that has wrought such results. Your Mr. Scott presented me a copy of your "The Man Lowest Down" which I read entirely on my trip home, and it is needless to say, I enjoyed every page of it. It reflects the spirit of brotherhood that was so much in evidence at Tuskegee.

From your Academic department I expect to employ several teachers to get better results in the negro schools of this county, for which help I am most indebted to you.

Again assuring you of my appreciation of the treatment I received at Turskee, I am, with best wishes,

Very truly,

DMH...B

Shown here is a report card of Pinellas Junior High School graduate Earnell Samuels from the 1943–1944 school year. It was signed by principal Shirley W. Curtis and teacher Portia L. Jackson.

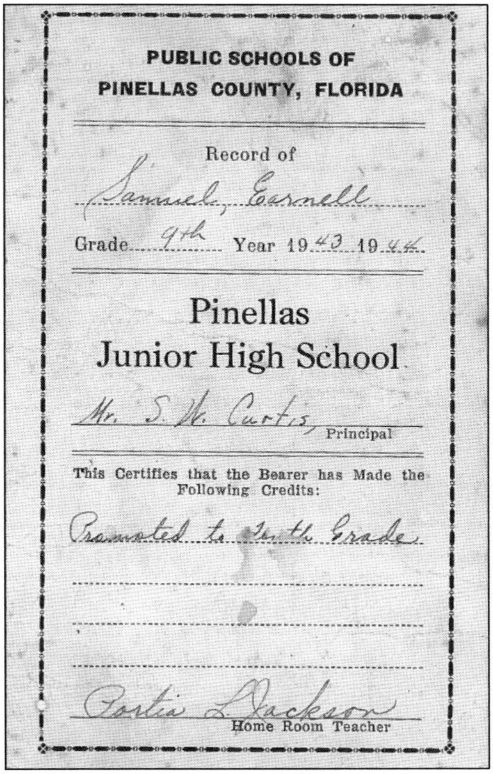

PUBLIC SCHOOLS OF
PINELLAS COUNTY, FLORIDA

Record of
Samuel, Earnell

Grade 9th Year 1943 1944

Pinellas
Junior High School

Mr. S. W. Curtis, Principal

This Certifies that the Bearer has Made the Following Credits:

Promoted to Tenth Grade

Portia L. Jackson
Home Room Teacher

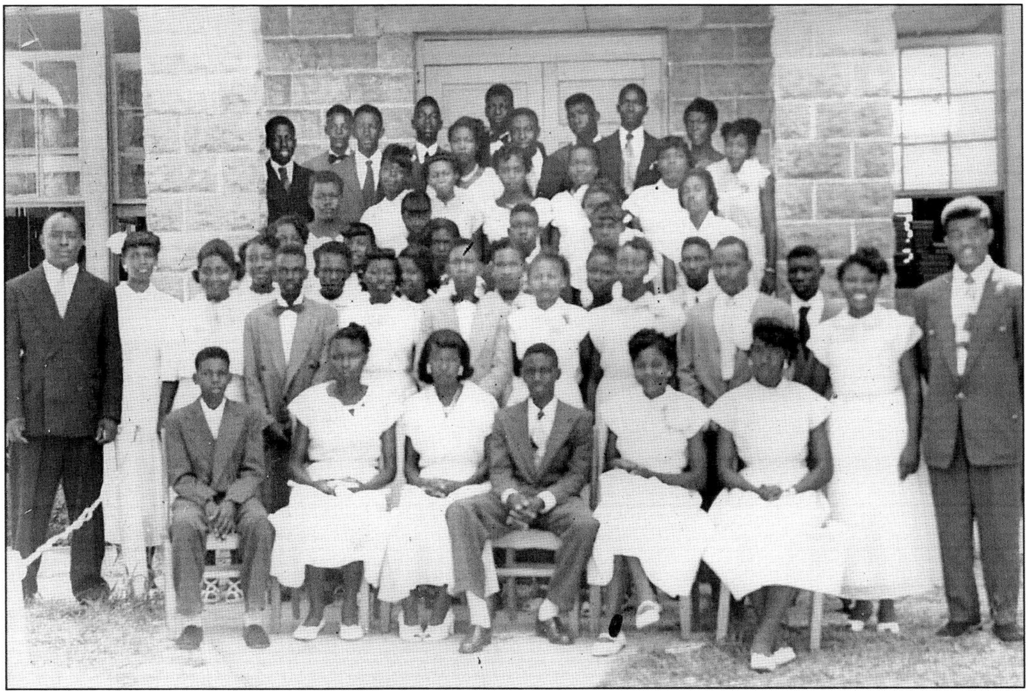

An early 1950s class of Pinellas High School is pictured here. Seated in the front center is Milton Rooks Jr., the son of Milton Rooks Sr., class sponsor.

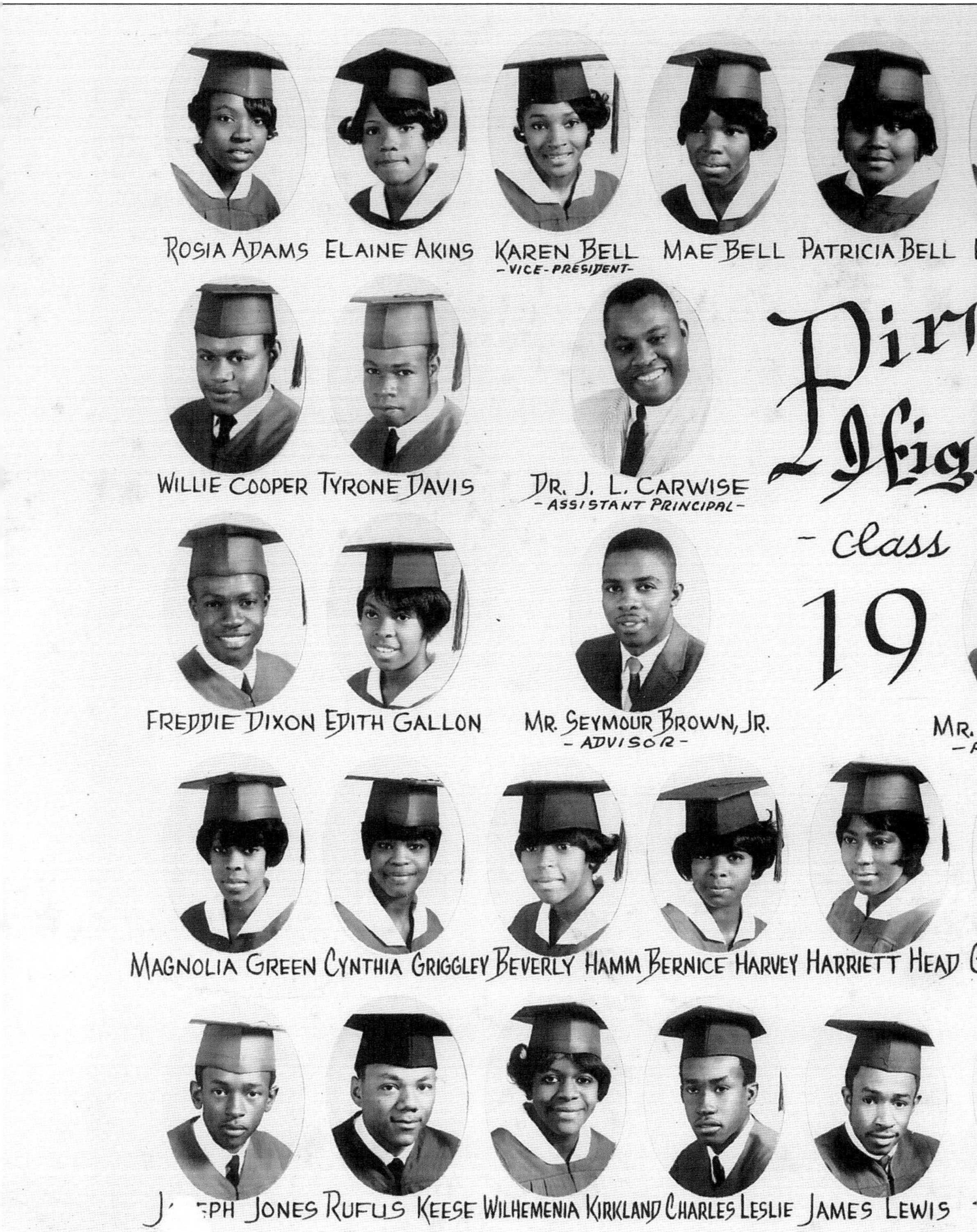

Shown above are Pinellas High School's graduating class of 1968 and faculty members, including

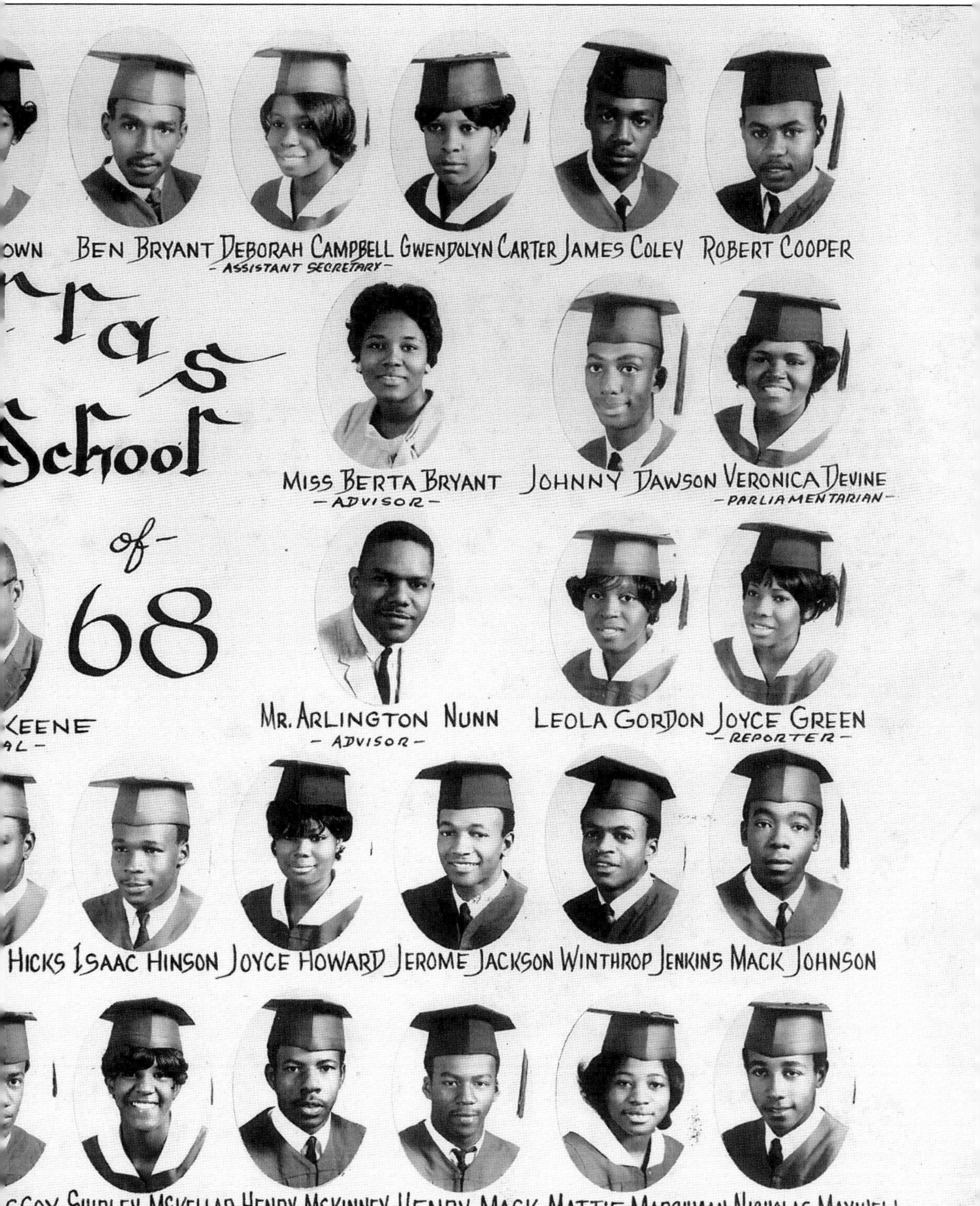

principal Cecil B. Keene and assistant principal Dr. Joseph L. Carwise.

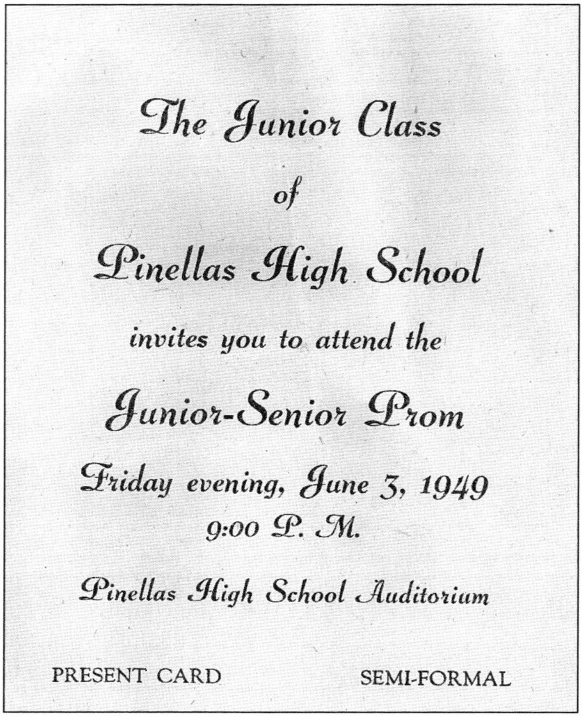

The Junior Class

of

Pinellas High School

invites you to attend the

Junior-Senior Prom

Friday evening, June 3, 1949

9:00 P. M.

Pinellas High School Auditorium

PRESENT CARD SEMI-FORMAL

Shown here is a junior-senior prom invitation held at Pinellas High School on June 3, 1949.

The graduating class of 1945 is photographed with class advisor, Harold Robinson. This picture also appears on the back cover of the book.

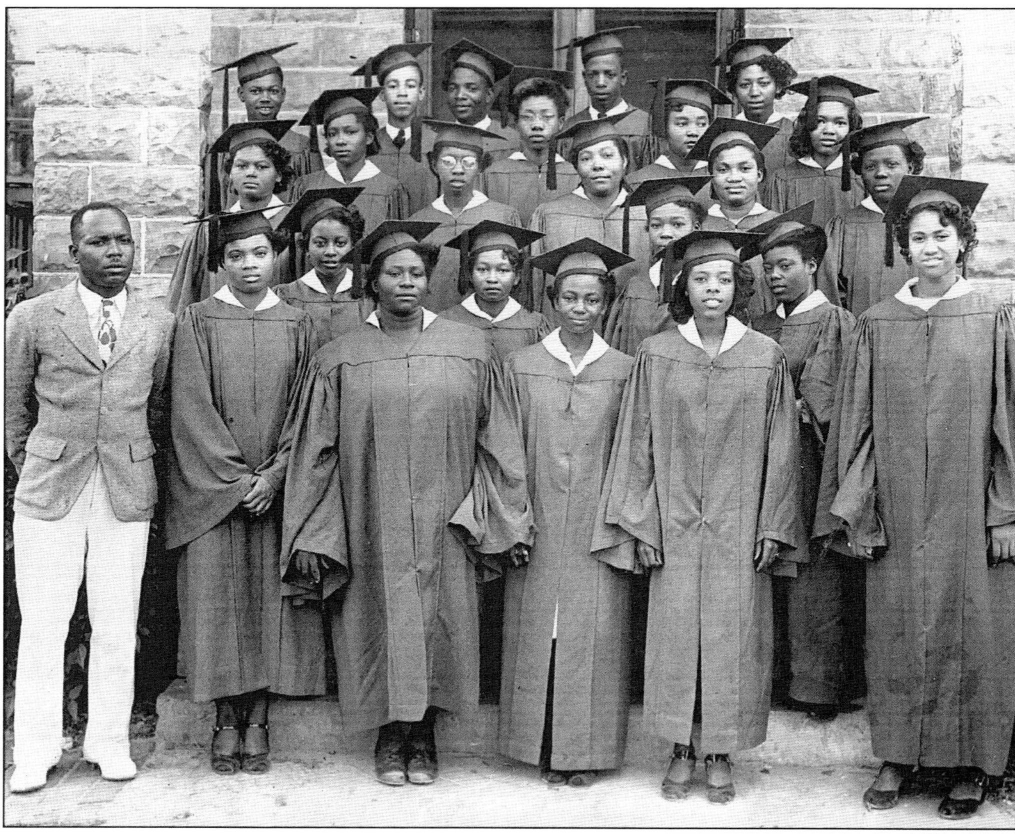

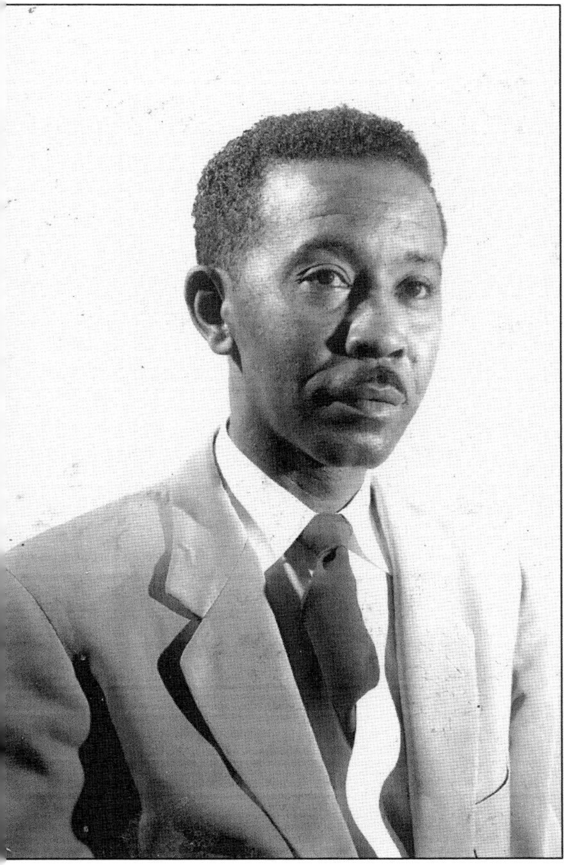 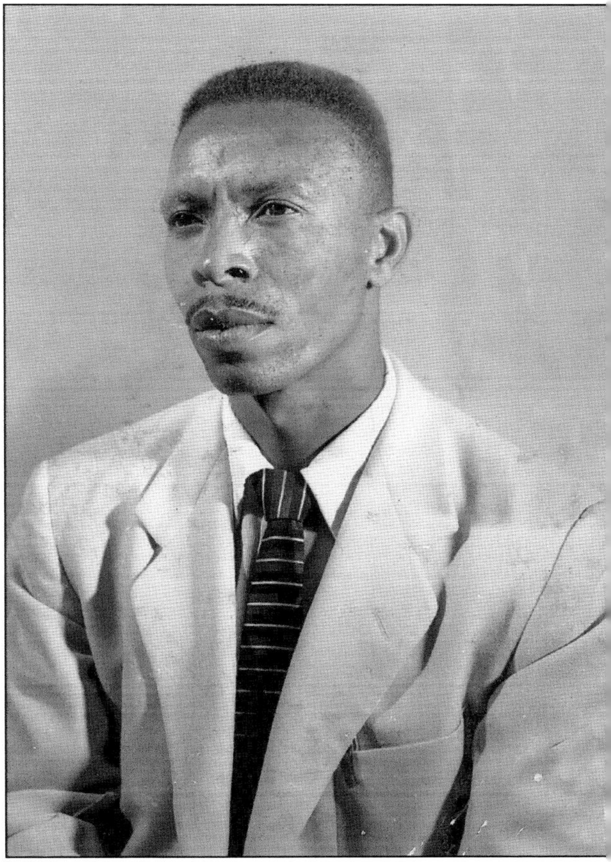

Pictured here are two industrial arts teachers from Pinellas High School during the 1950s. To the left is Reuben J. Triplett and to the right is Nathaniel E. Fitz Jr.

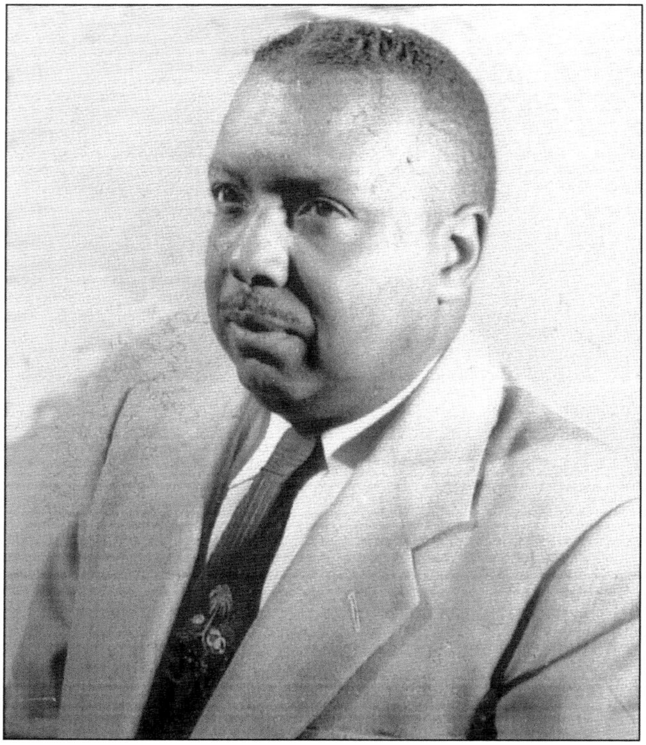

To the left is Edward Henry, who taught tailoring at Pinellas High School.

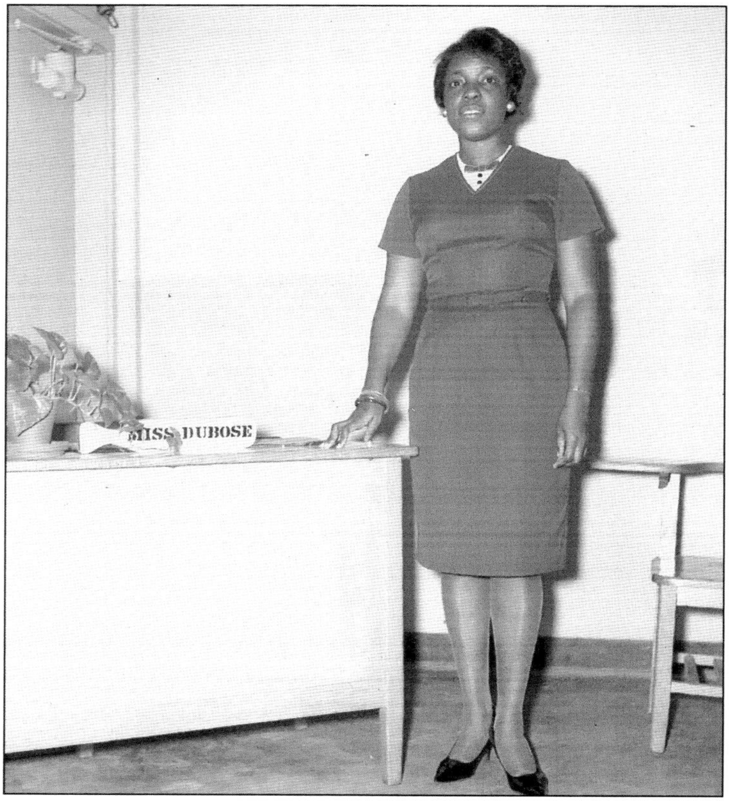

Standing next to her desk is teacher Daisy DuBose Brunson. She taught English at Pinellas High School and Clearwater High.

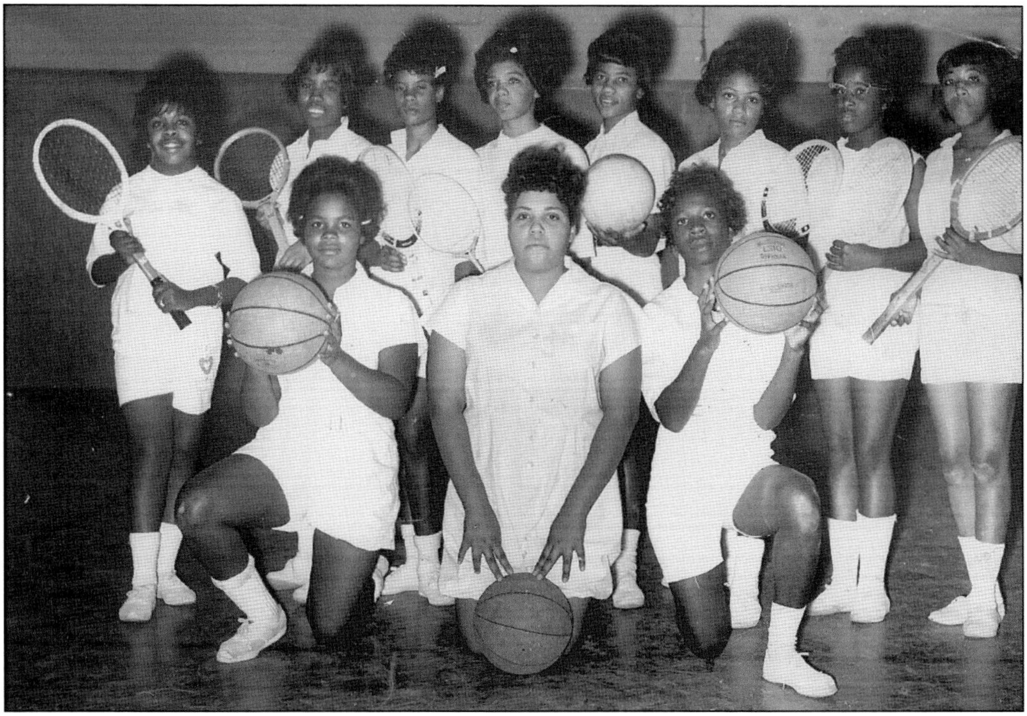

Here is a group photo of female athletes from Pinellas High School. These young ladies participated in tennis, basketball, and volleyball.

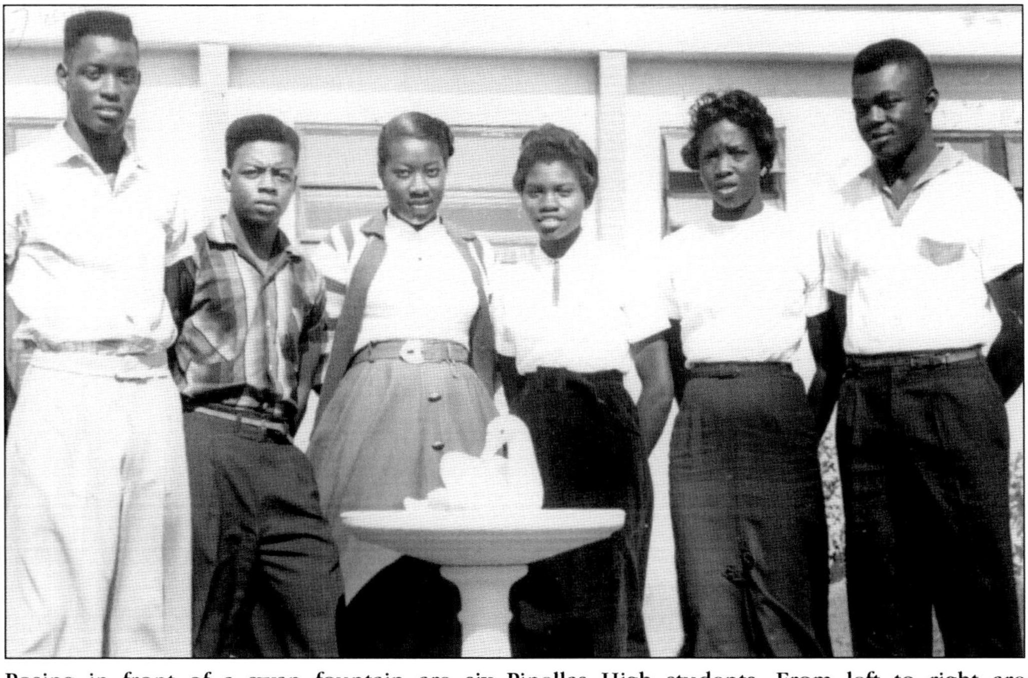

Posing in front of a swan fountain are six Pinellas High students. From left to right are Steve Monroe, Willie James Stewart, Mary Winston, Louise Wallace, Gail Thomas, and William McKinley Harris.

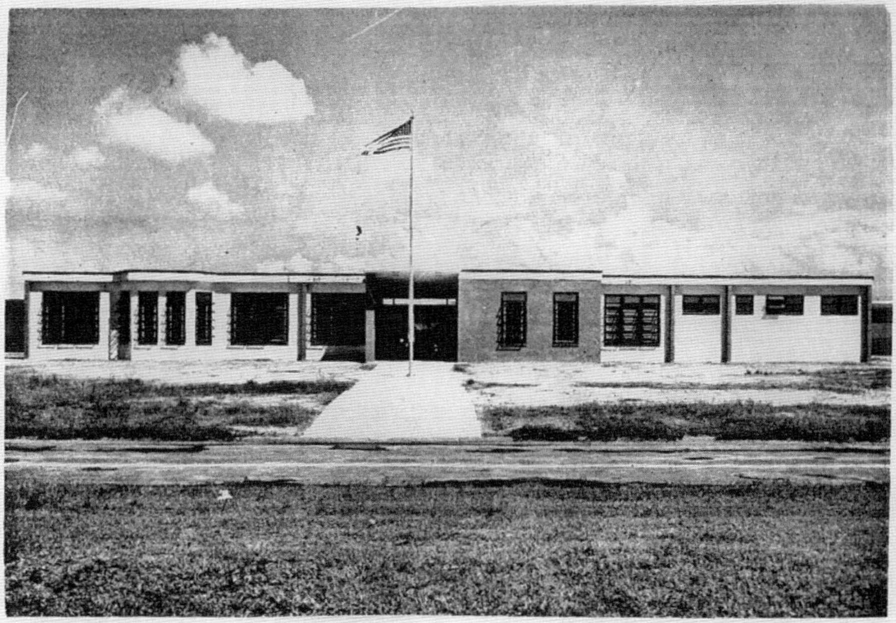

Pinellas Junior-Senior High School

SCHOOL SONG

Dear old Pinellas High School,
You're the world to me.
Dear old Pinellas High School,
You will always be.
For you'll bring us sunshine in the hour of grief.
We will always love our dear school,
When she's up and when she's down,
We will always love our dear school,
When al others turn her down.
Dear old Pinellas High School,
You're the world to me.

This is a photo of Pinellas Junior-Senior High School taken in the mid-1950s. In 1968, Pinellas High was closed and its students transferred to Clearwater High. Featured are the lyrics of Pinellas High's school song from the 1950s. Dorothy Thompson composed the song.

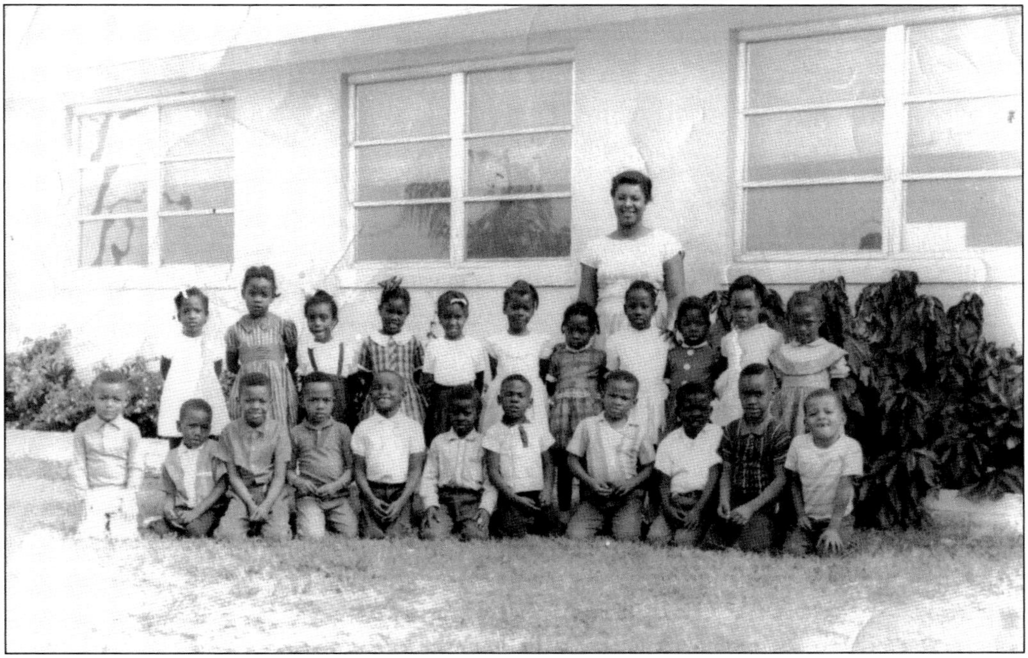

This is an early class of Community Pride Nursery School in the 1960s. The teacher pictured is Verdell Yarn.

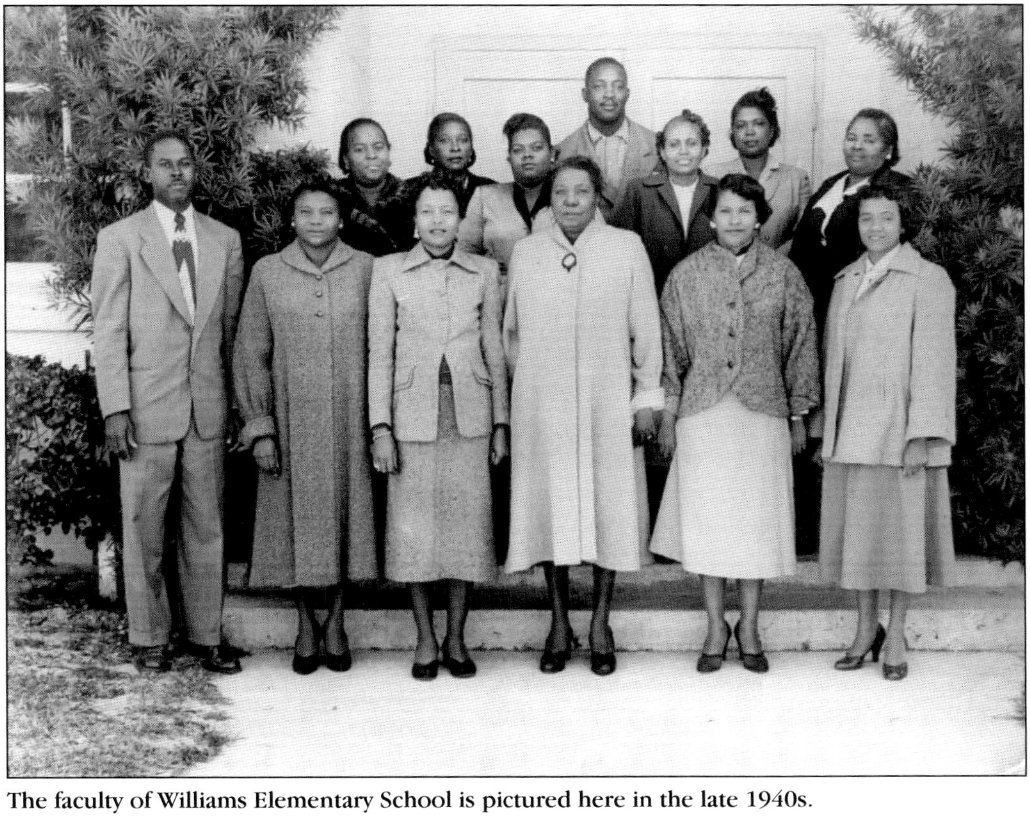

The faculty of Williams Elementary School is pictured here in the late 1940s.

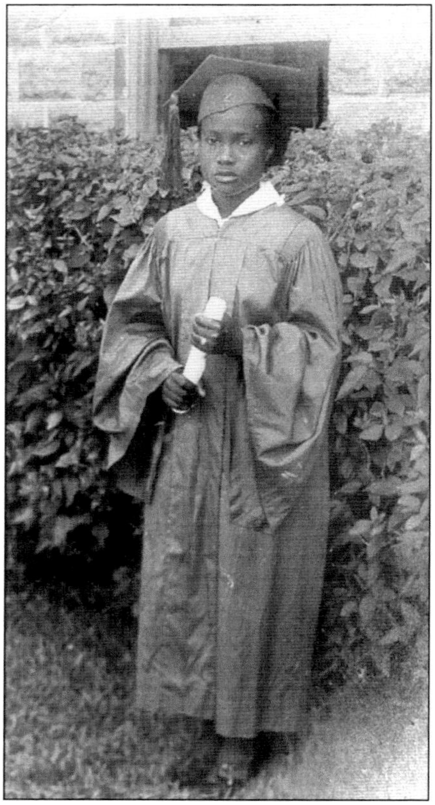

Catherine Jerrido of Pinellas High School is seen here in her graduation attire in 1939.

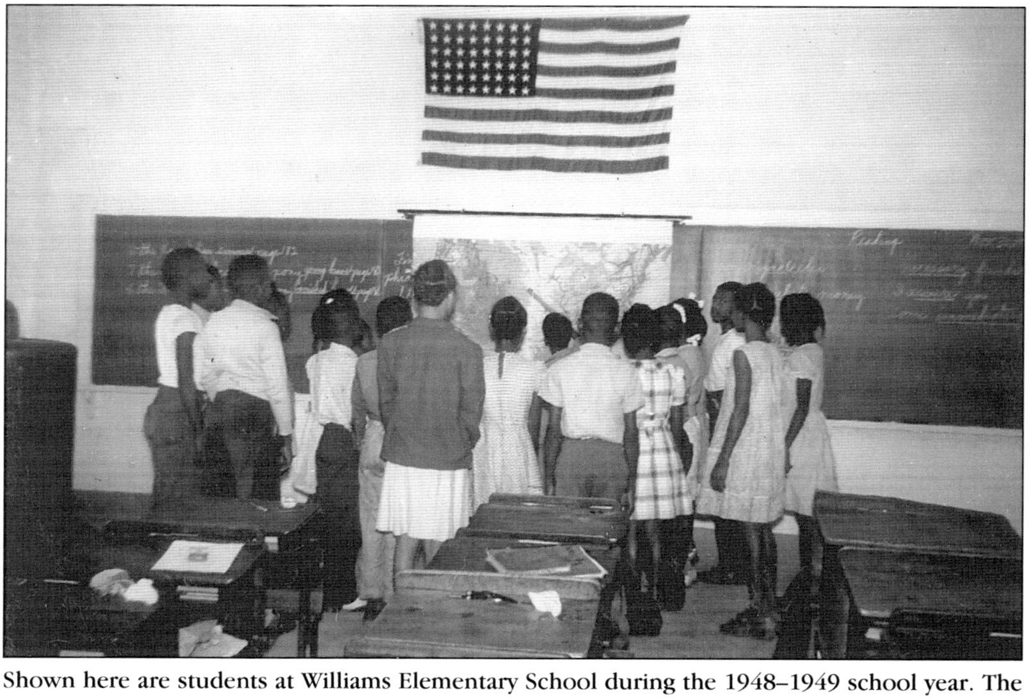

Shown here are students at Williams Elementary School during the 1948–1949 school year. The class was taught by Evelyn Rooks.

Five

Events and Celebrations

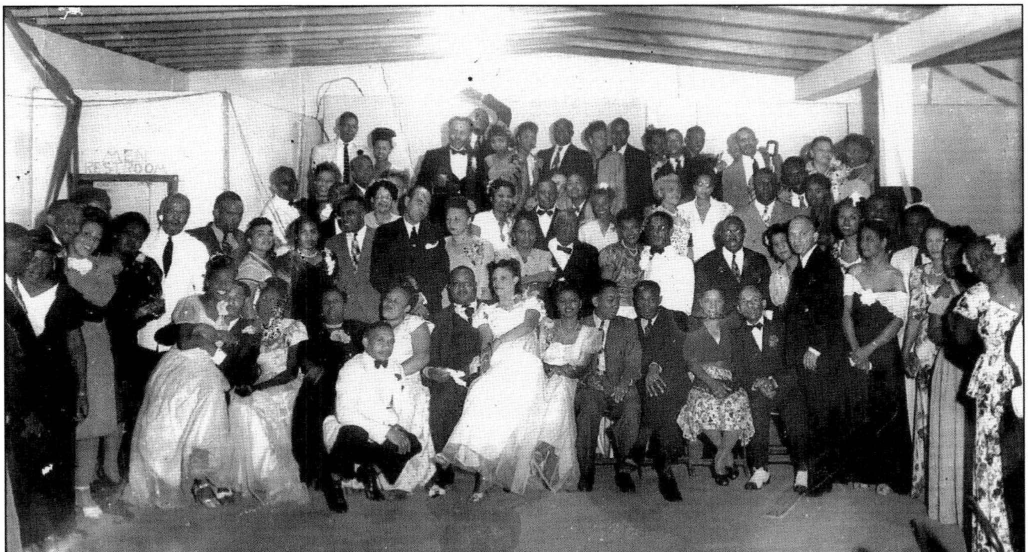

Before integration, African Americans held their formal events at the local school, social club, or fraternal hall. The photo above depicts a formal event hosted by the Women's Progressive Club at the Elks Club on LaSalle Street in the 1950s.

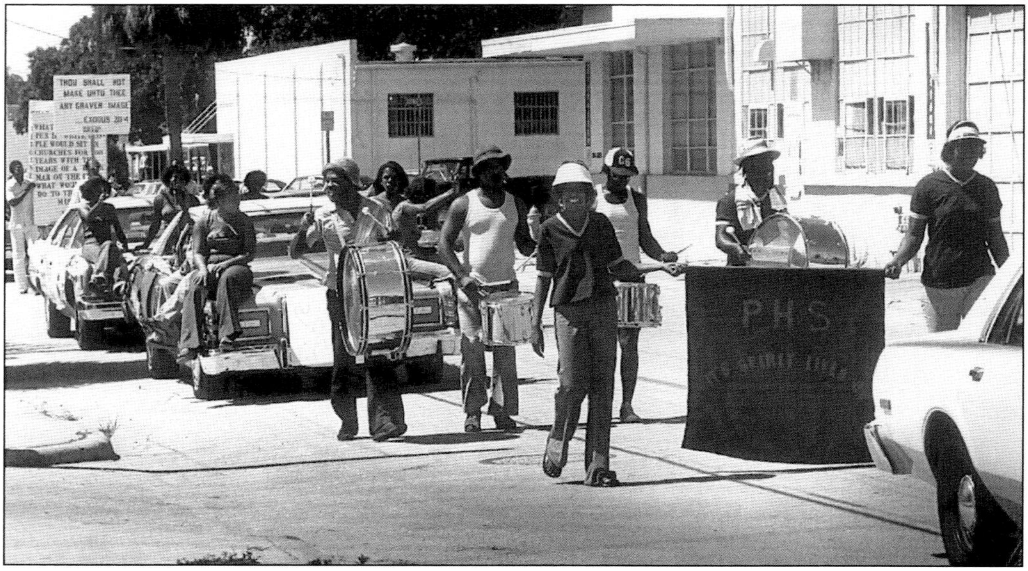

Pinellas High School graduates from classes 1934 to 1968 (integration in 1968 transformed Pinellas from a high school to a middle school) march in a two-mile class reunion parade that started at Mt. Olive A.M.E. Church and ended at the Martin Luther King Center.

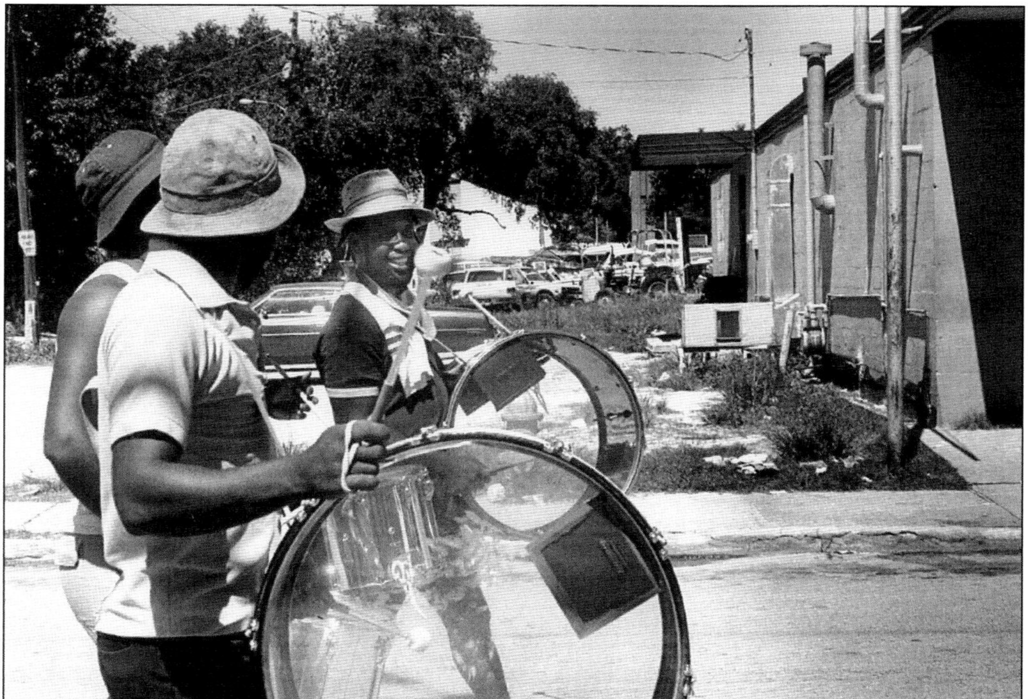

These are former members of the Pinellas High School Drum Corps, leading the reunion parade down Garden Avenue.

A slice of a new life is shared by Earnell Samuel and Lucy Gray Berry.

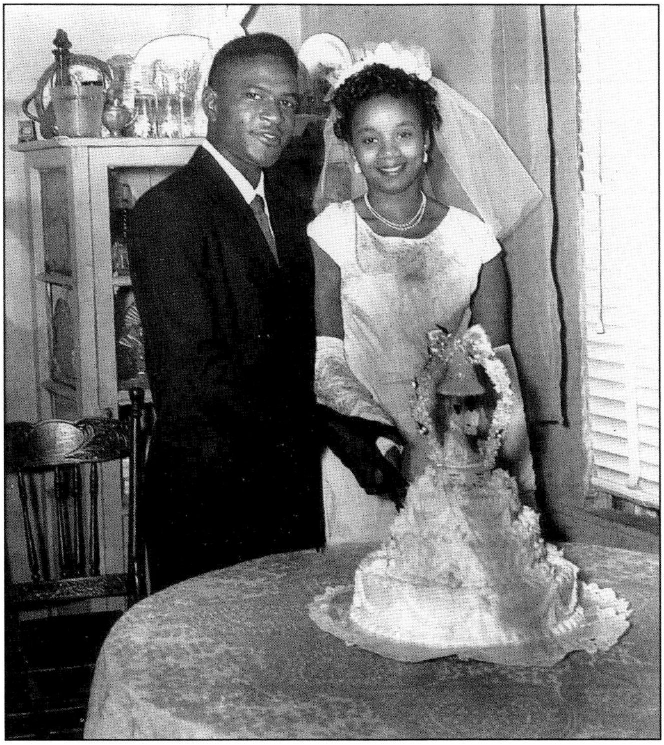

In the photo below, Jack Morris escorts Betty Jo Whitt down the aisle in the 1950s at Mt. Carmel Baptist Church.

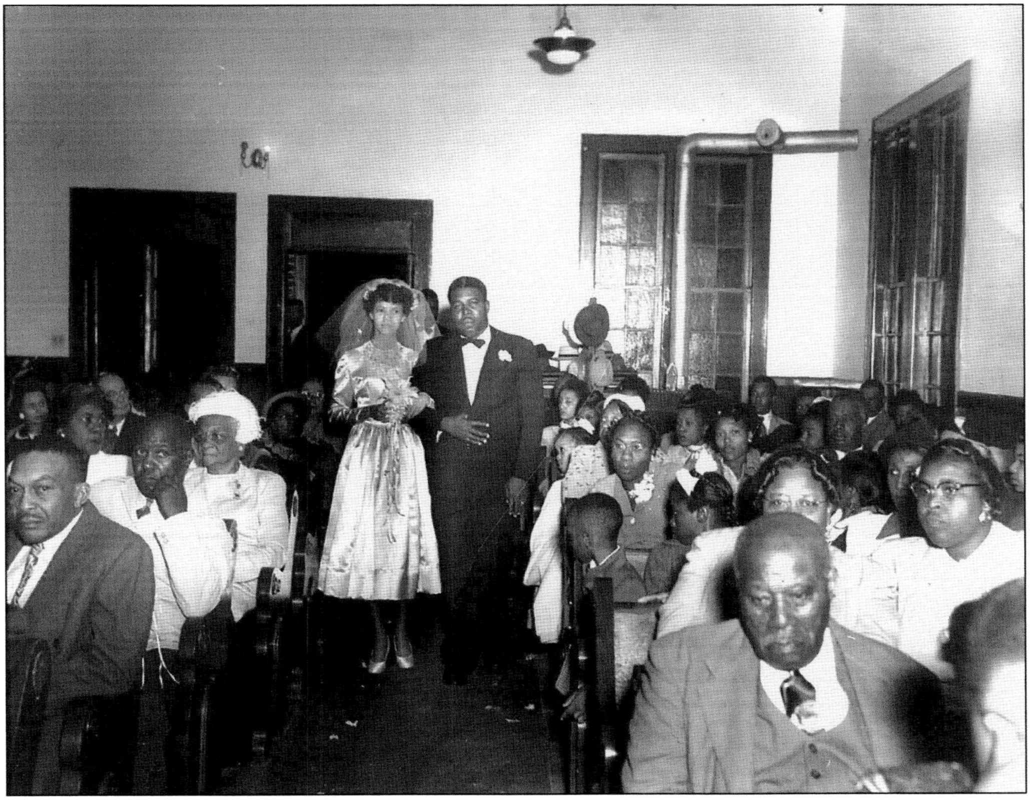

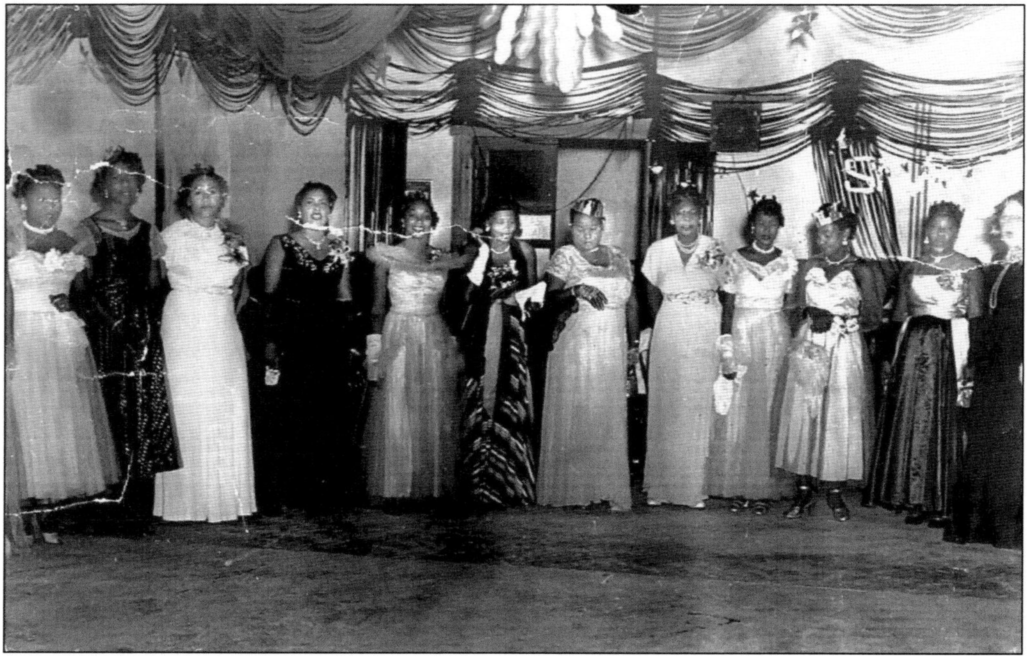

Smart Set Bridge Club was organized in the 1940s for entertainment. They met at different members' homes to play weekly bridge games. Scores were kept and the club hosted an annual dance to present trophies to the members with the highest scores obtained during the year.

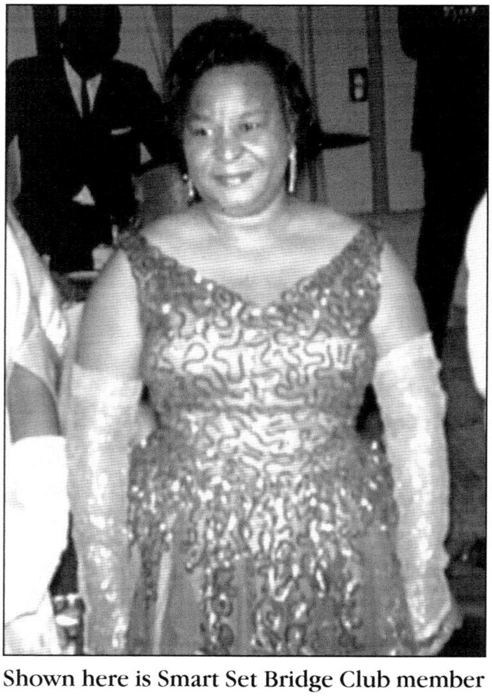

Shown here is Smart Set Bridge Club member Bessie Gibson. Alice Harold was contracted by the club to produce the formal wear for the event and made many of the gowns.

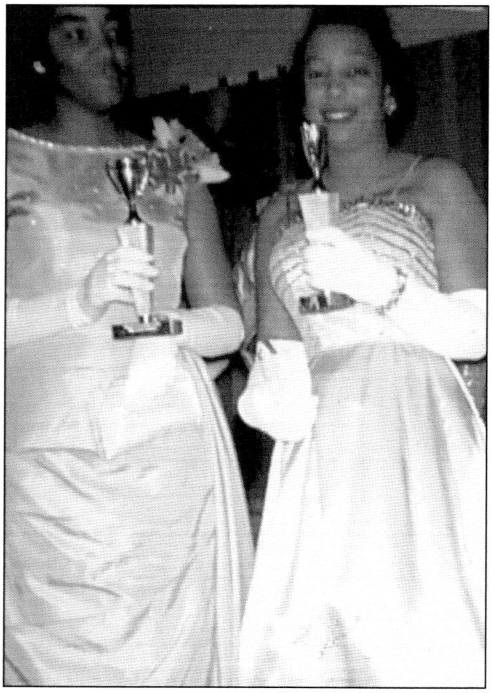

Smart Set Bridge Club members Victoria Pompey and Vivian Henry each hold a trophy awarded for their bridge skills.

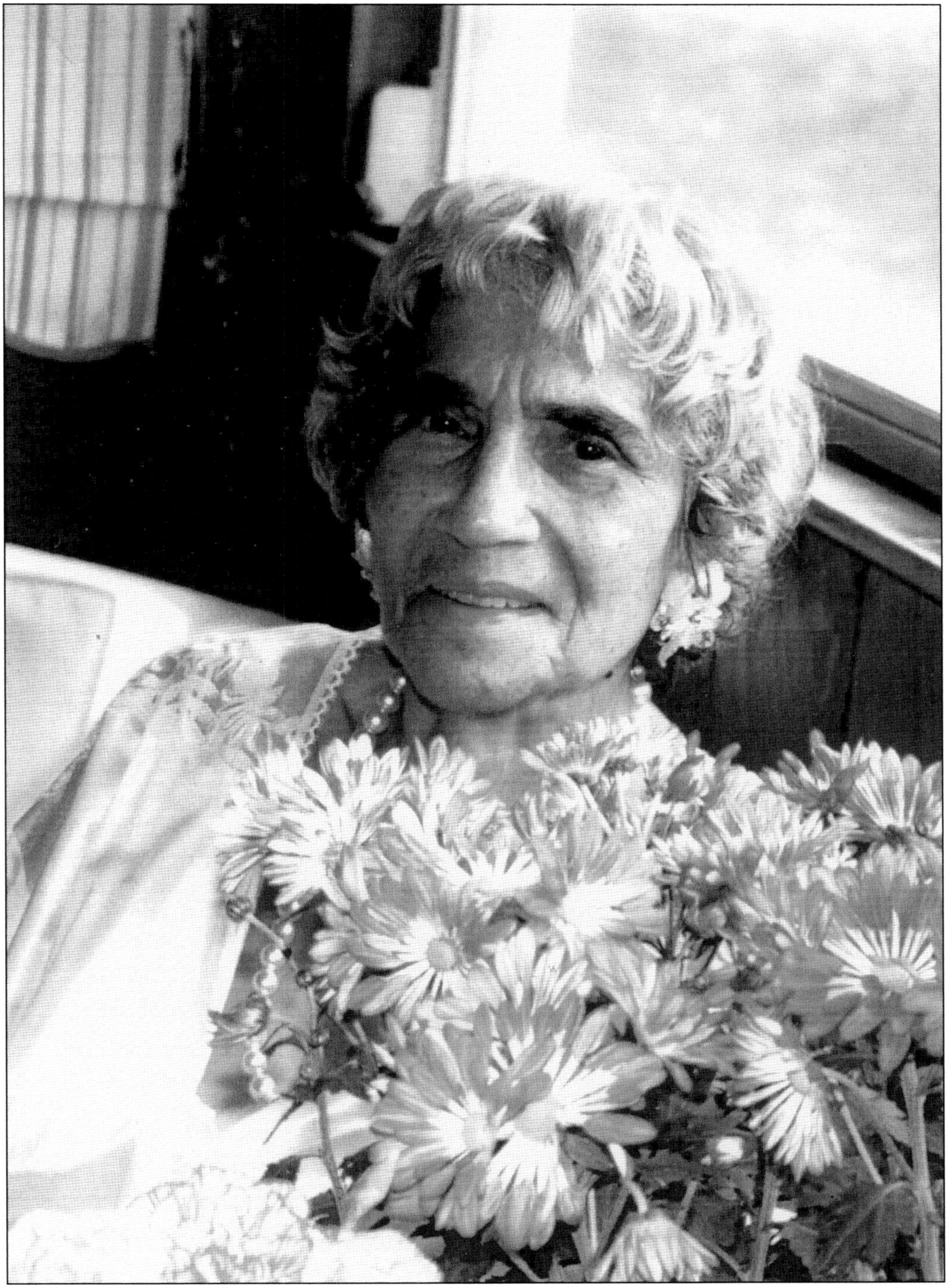

Cherry Harris is portrayed in this photo. Mrs. Harris was a dedicated lifelong member of the NAACP and fought to make Clearwater a better place to live for all of its citizens. Cherry Harris Park is named in her honor.

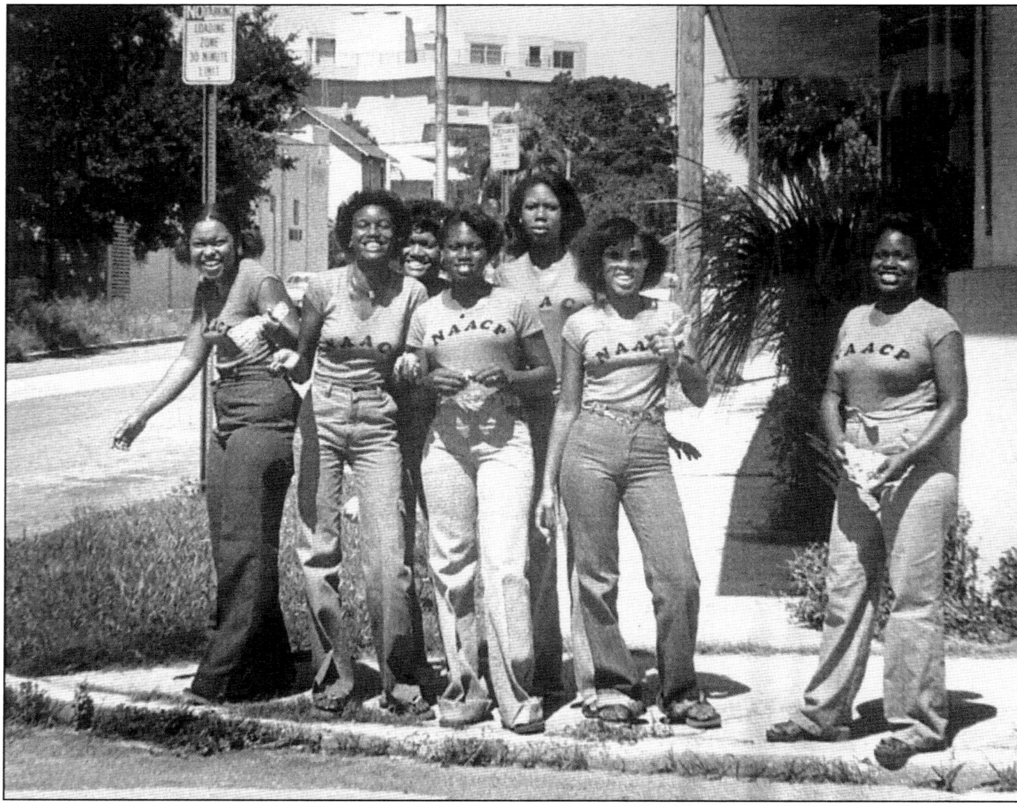

Members of the Clearwater NAACP Youth Council prepare to join the Pinellas High reunion parade for all classes (1934–1968) at the corner of Jones Street and Garden Avenue.

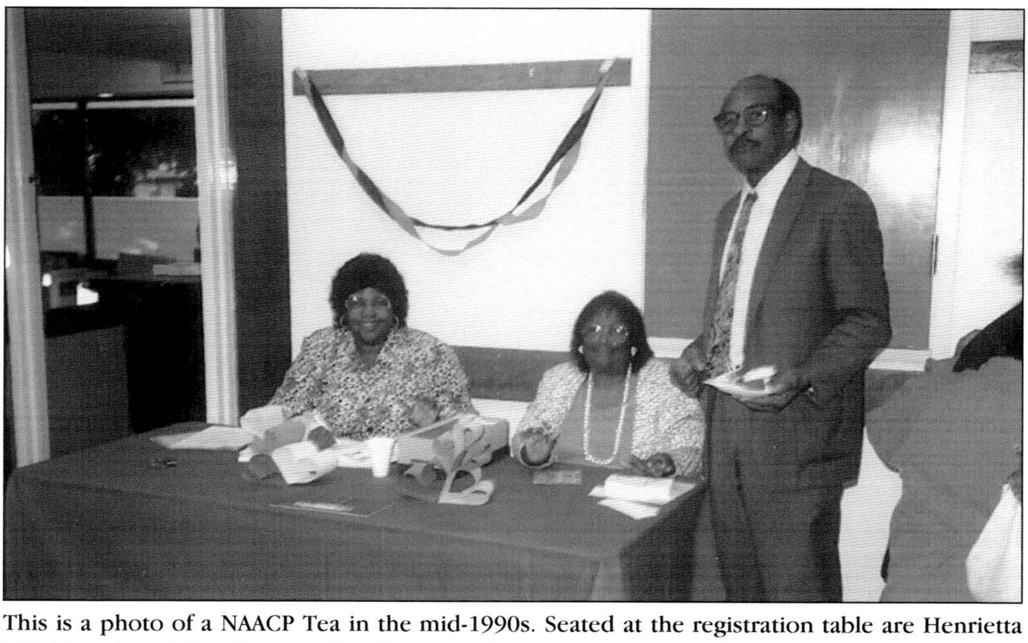

This is a photo of a NAACP Tea in the mid-1990s. Seated at the registration table are Henrietta Wright and Leola Washington. Standing is Tal Rutledge.

This is the cover of the souvenir program of Le Cercle des Jeunes Femmes social club. The club was hosting its first annual dance at the National Guard Armory in March 1965.

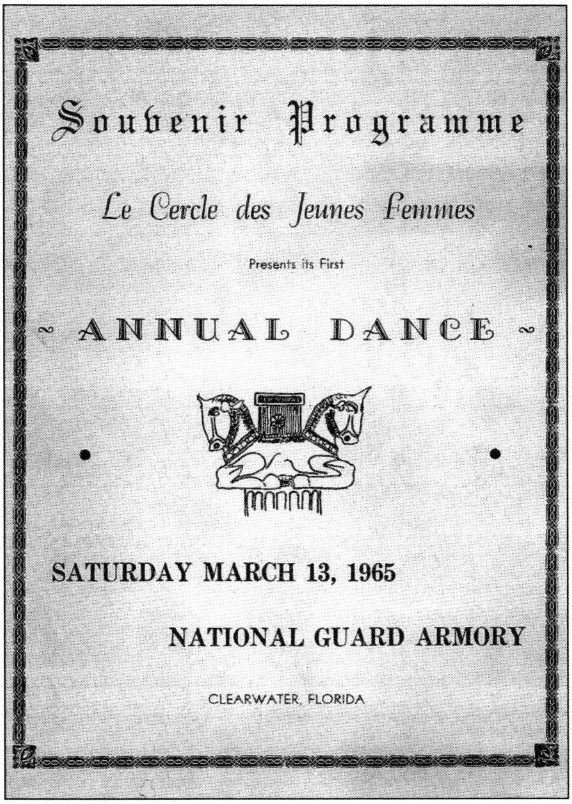

Souvenir Programme

Le Cercle des Jeunes Femmes

Presents its First

~ ANNUAL DANCE ~

SATURDAY MARCH 13, 1965

NATIONAL GUARD ARMORY

CLEARWATER, FLORIDA

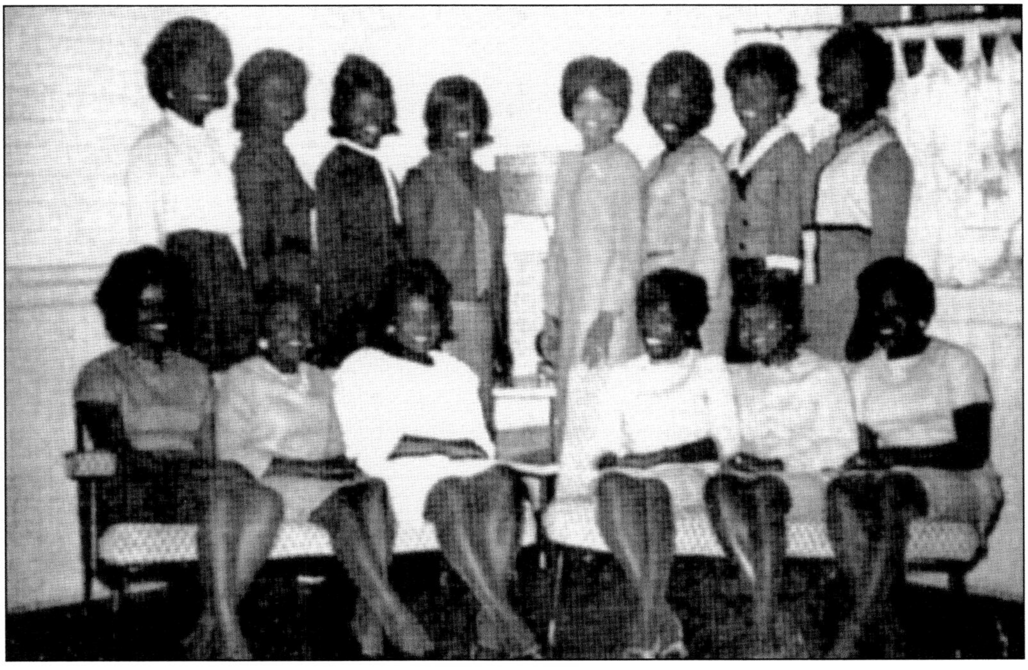

Pictured are the officers of the Le Cercle des Jeunes Femmes social club. The president of the organization was Twynette McIver.

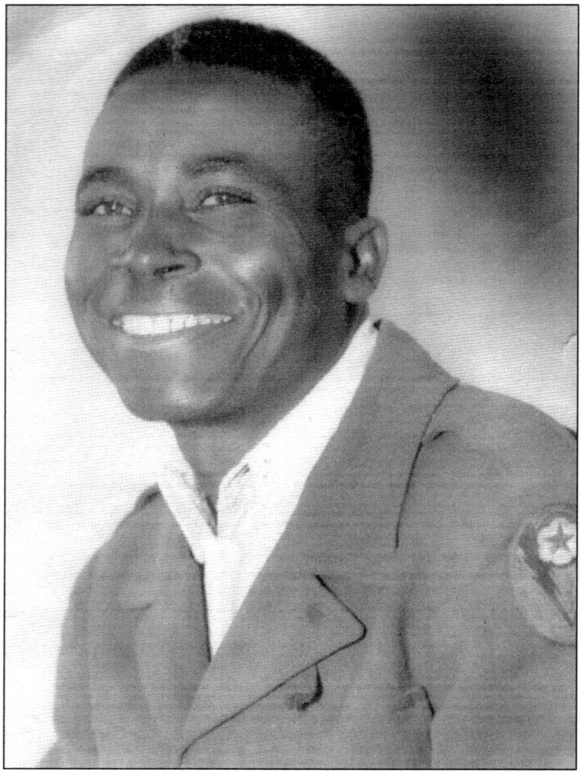

Caleb Jones is pictured in the 1950s in his Boy Scout uniform. He was the first African-American Boy Scout leader in Clearwater.

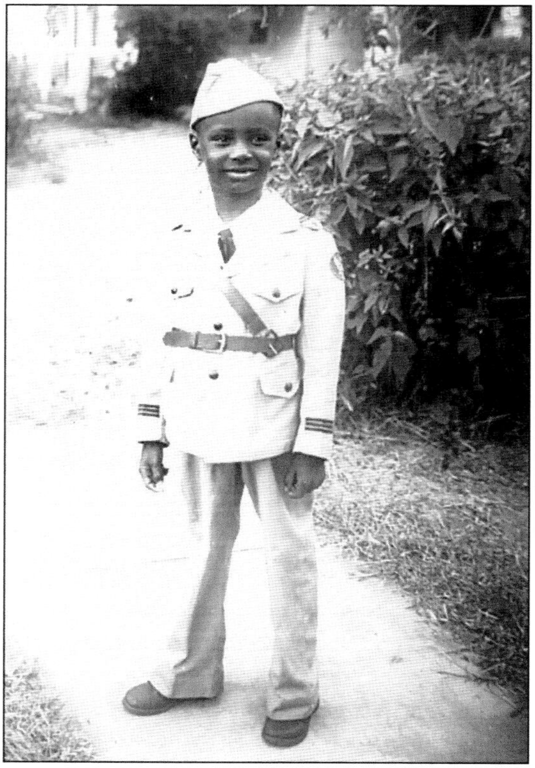

Milton Rooks Jr. poses outfitted in his army uniform in the mid-1940s.

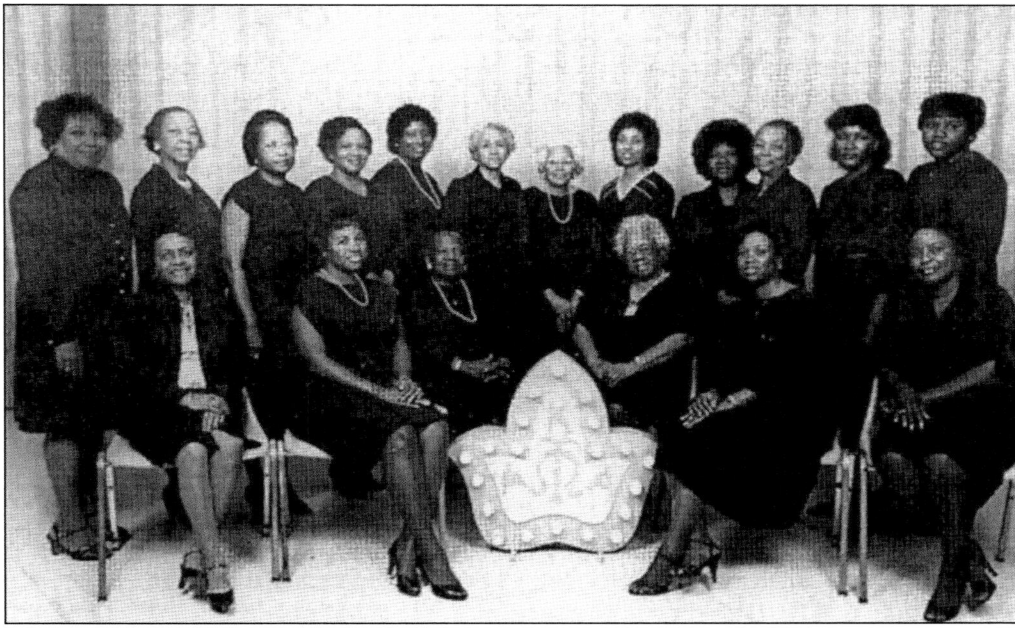

This is the Nu Beta Omega Chapter of Alpha Kappa Alpha Sorority, Inc. in a 1984 photo. From left to right are (seated) Alyce Bennett, Gwendolyn Jackson, Annie McLin, Dorothy Thompson, Dorothy Bailey, and Erma Johnson; (standing) Joyce Nelson, Portia L. Jackson, Mamye Hodges, Carrie Hayward, Marva Lane, Beatrice Lewis, Evelyn Rooks, Clayvonne McElrath, Jean Rivers, Vivian Henry, Karen Jones, and Eleanor Breland.

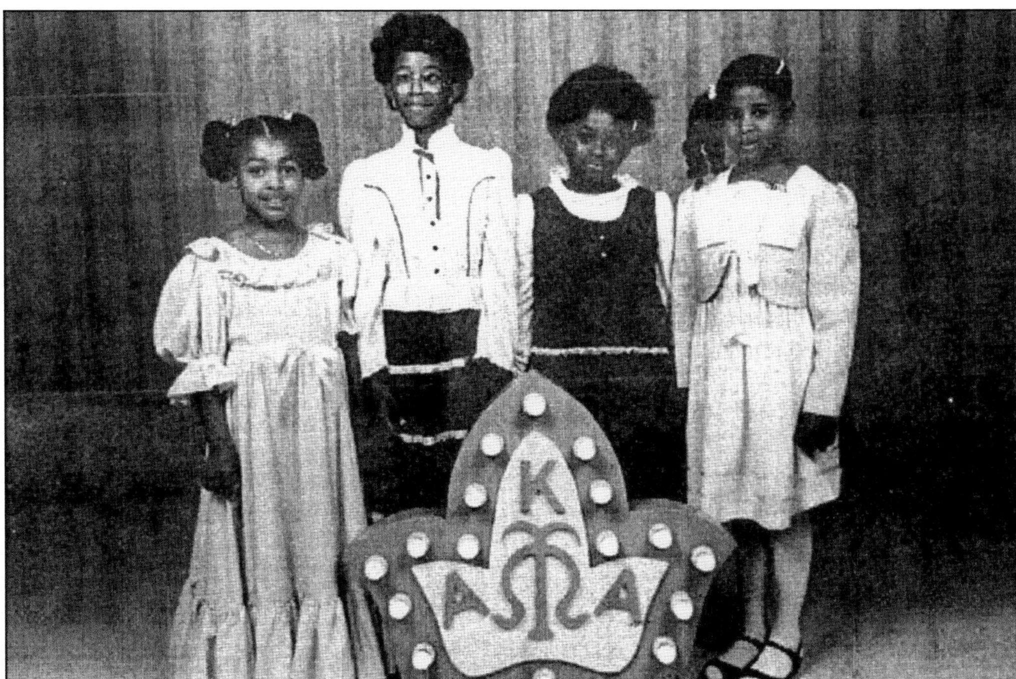

"Miss Fashionetta" contestants are pictured in 1984, sponsored by Nu Beta Omega. Pictured from left to right are Antoinette Winthrop, Portia Gibbs, Virginia Walker, and Gerlanna McElrath.

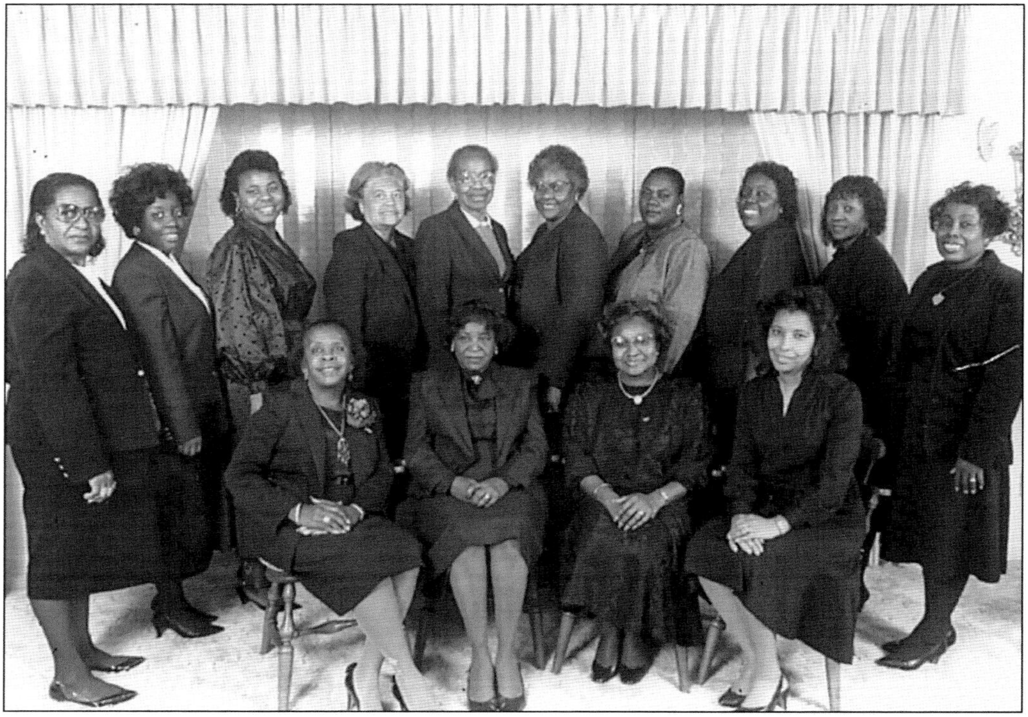

Members of Delta Sigma Theta Sorority, Inc. are photographed in the 1980s. From left to right, they are Panchitta Carwise (chapter president), Sarayl L. Detreville, Brenda Hunter, Louise Coleman, Lois Martin, Louise Rutledge, Rosa Tarver, Daisy Brunson, Kellis Glenn, and Louetta Williams; (seated) Willie M. Merthie, Willa Carson, Annette Faison, and Ruth Nunn.

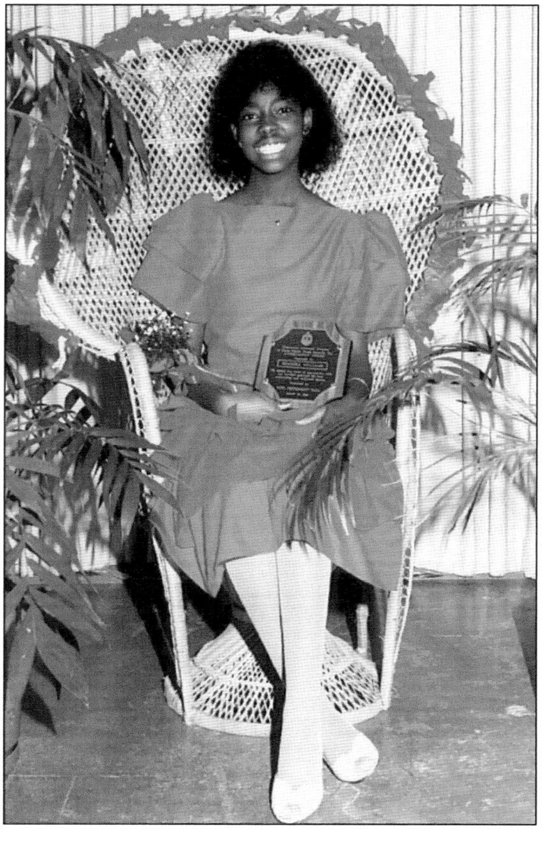

Shamika Williams is crowned Little Miss Peppermint in the 1980s.

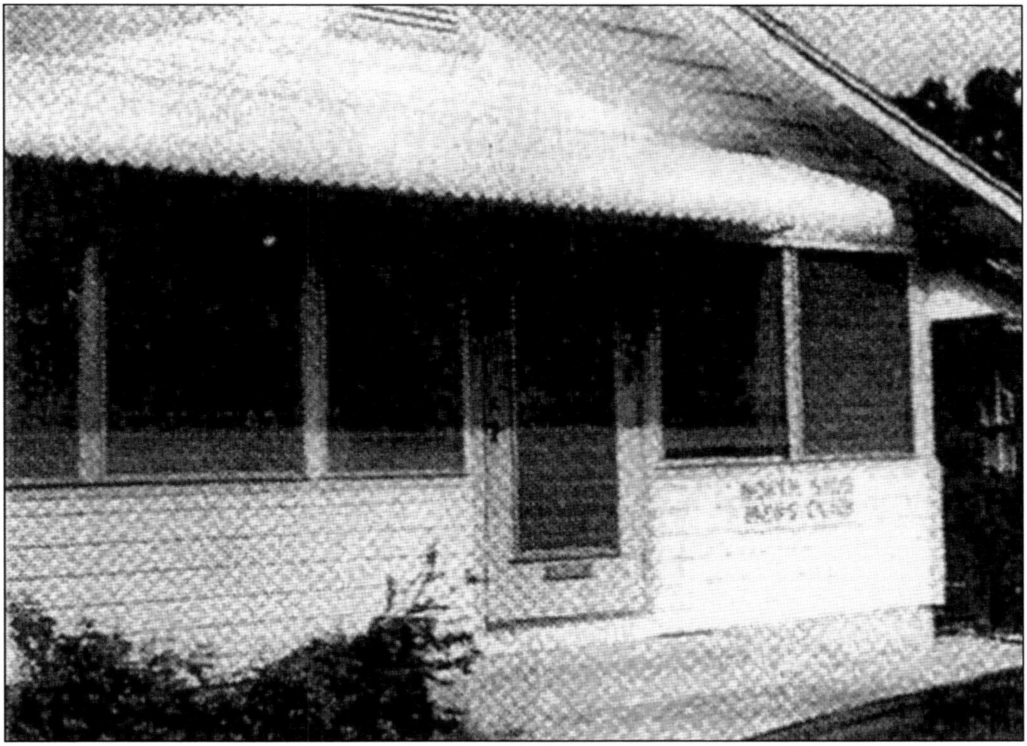

Depicted here is the North Side Men's Club headquarters on Carlton Street. The North Side Men's Club was one of the oldest chartered civic and benevolent organizations in Clearwater. It was organized in the early 1950s and chartered in 1968.

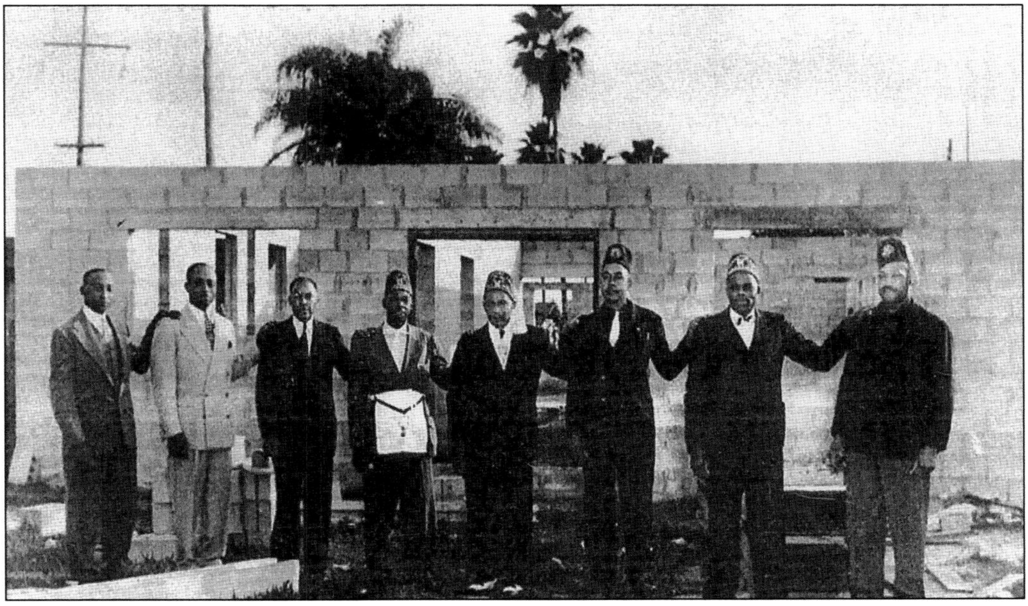

Members of Springtime Lodge #592 are pictured in front of an addition to the lodge still under construction in the mid-1950s. Pictured here, from left to right, are George Mack, Tenia Pettis, Jake Richardson, Willie Williams, Dewey Davis, Mack Tidwell, Arnold Jackson, and Mack Dixon Jr.

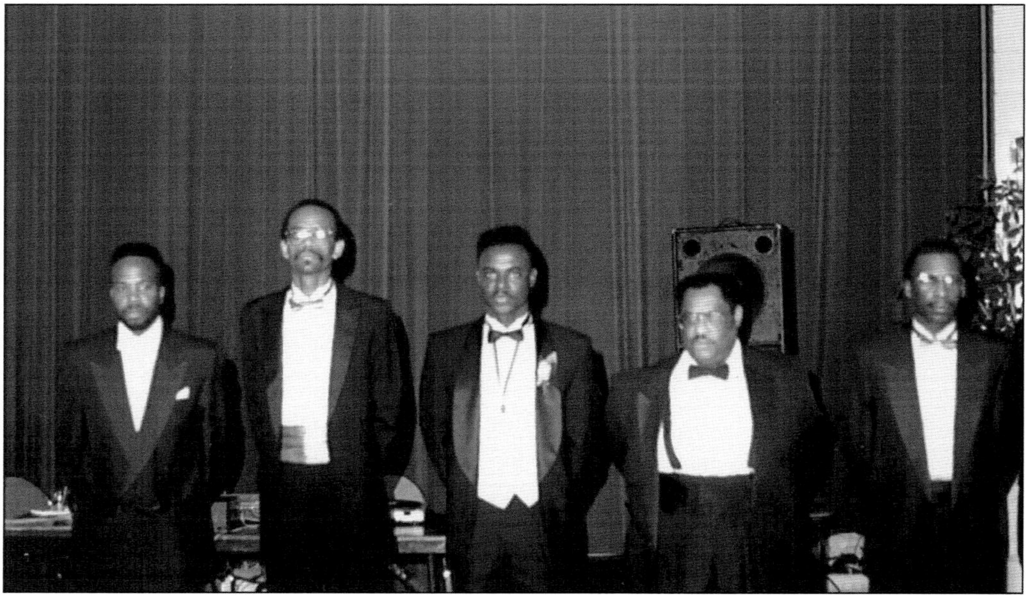

Members of Omicron Beta Lambda Chapter of Alpha Phi Alpha Fraternity, Inc. are shown at the 1988 Miss Black and Gold Ball. Pictured from left to right are Philip Boone, Joseph Smiley, James Waters, Joseph Carwise, and Louis Ladson.

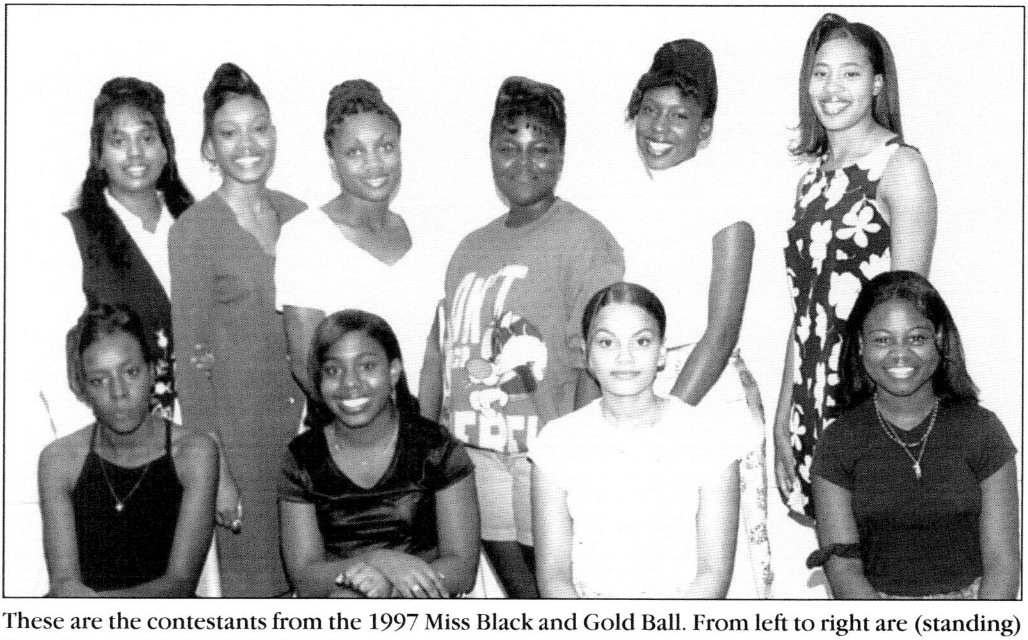

These are the contestants from the 1997 Miss Black and Gold Ball. From left to right are (standing) Kerri Kaizer, Sabrina Brinkley, Anquanita Hearns, Regina McKinnes, Tierra Tisdale, and LaWanda Hunter; (seated) Elaine Pittman, Artia Davis, Angela Hunsinger, and Kelli Bailey.

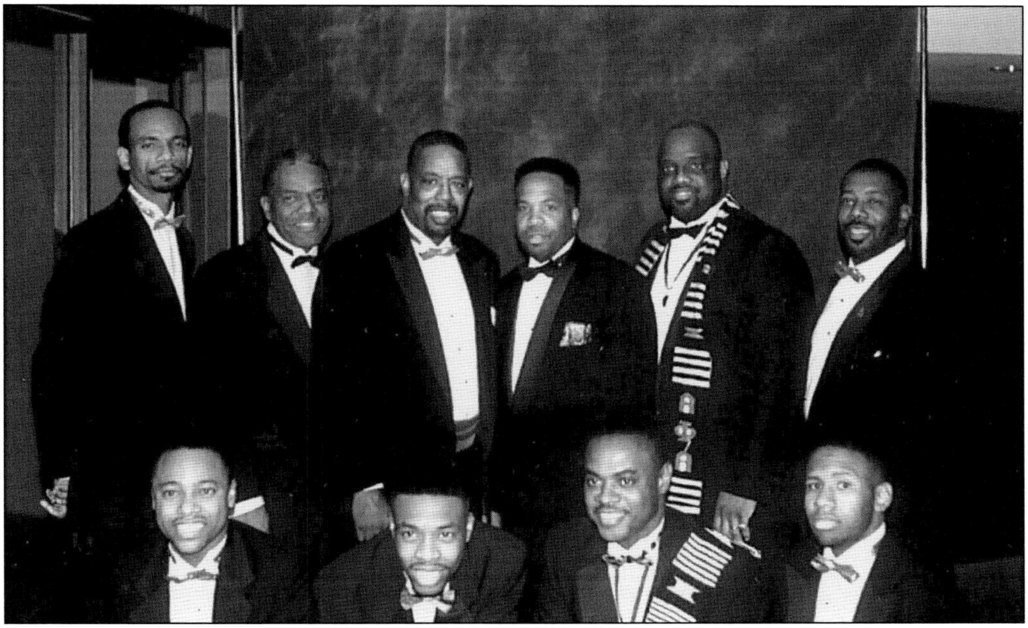

Members of Omicron Beta Lambda Chapter of Alpha Phi Alpha Fraternity, Inc. pictured, from left to right, are (front row) LaVaughn McNary, Scott Marshall, James Waters, and Jon Marina; (back row) Joseph Smiley, Arlington Nunn, Charles McCray, Philip Boone, Edward McKahand, and Randolph Lightfoot.

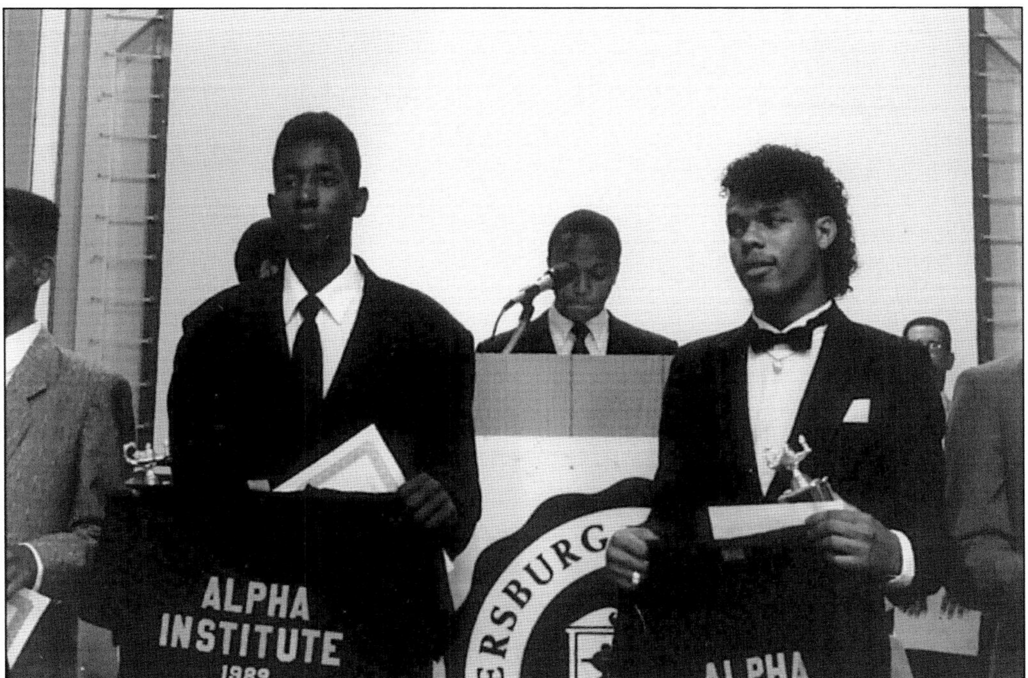

Omicron Beta Lambda sponsors the Alpha Institute—a mentoring program that meets with young men ages 12 to 18 and emphasizes academics, entrepreneurial skills, and leadership development. Pictured are some of the graduates of the class of 1989.

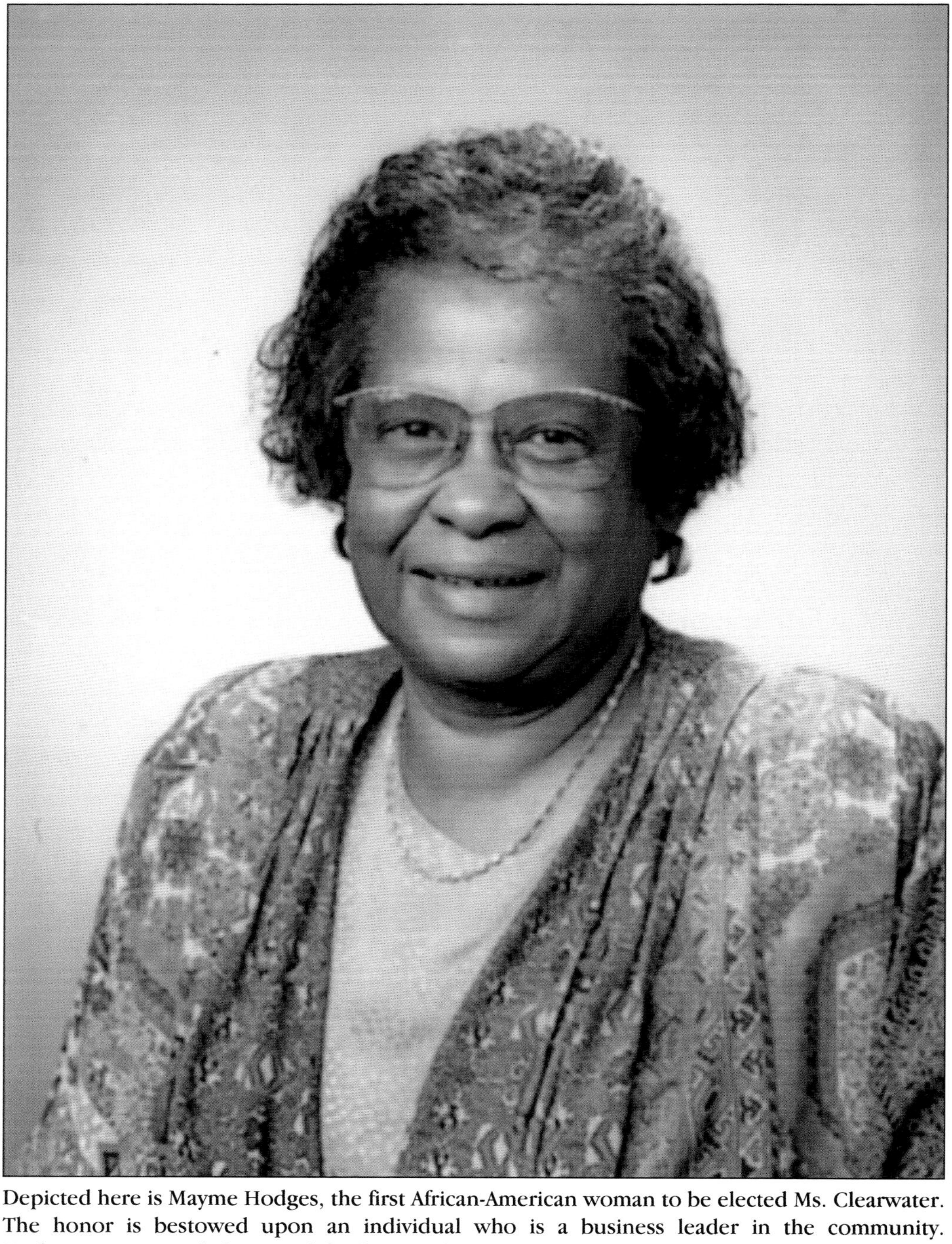

Depicted here is Mayme Hodges, the first African-American woman to be elected Ms. Clearwater. The honor is bestowed upon an individual who is a business leader in the community. Hodges was granted the award for her involvement with more than 22 civic and professional organizations over the years. She also served as interim city commissioner in 1993.

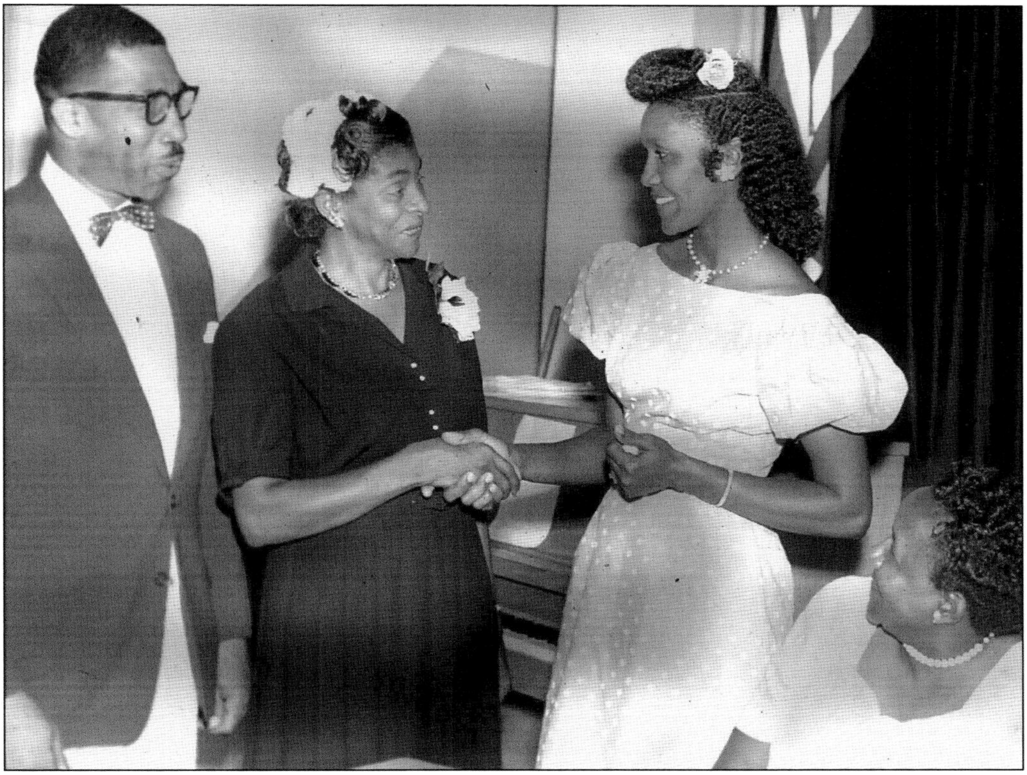

Shown in this photo is Rose Brewton, scout leader of the first African-American Girl Scout troop. She is being congratulated for her election as president of the Williams Elementary P.T.A. Also pictured, from left to right, are Fred Burney, Johnnye Black, and Carolyn Green.

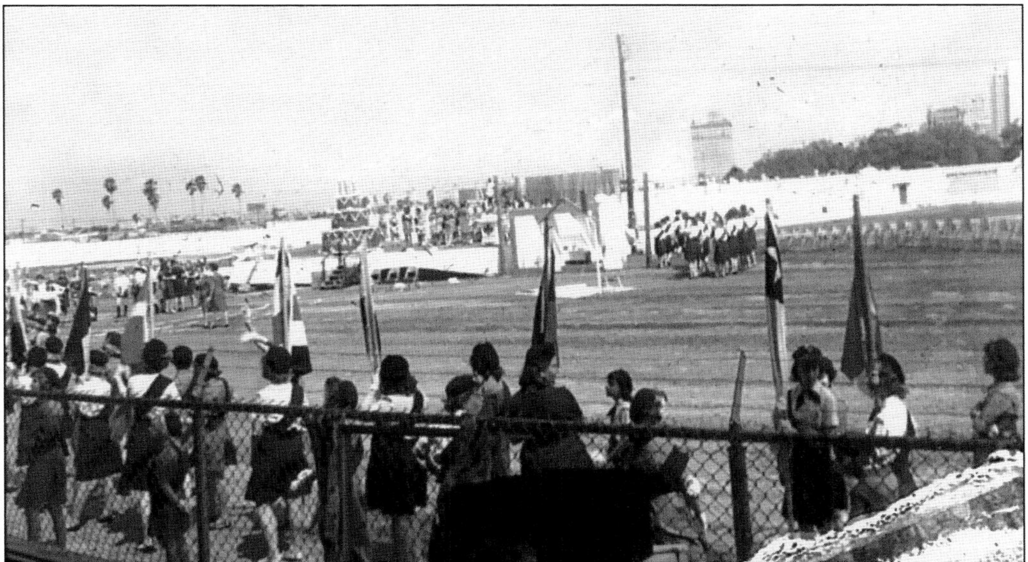

Here is a picture of the Girl Scout troop that Mrs. Brewton led in 1966. The occasion is a celebration in Tampa of the birthday of Juliet Law, founder of the Girl Scouts of America.

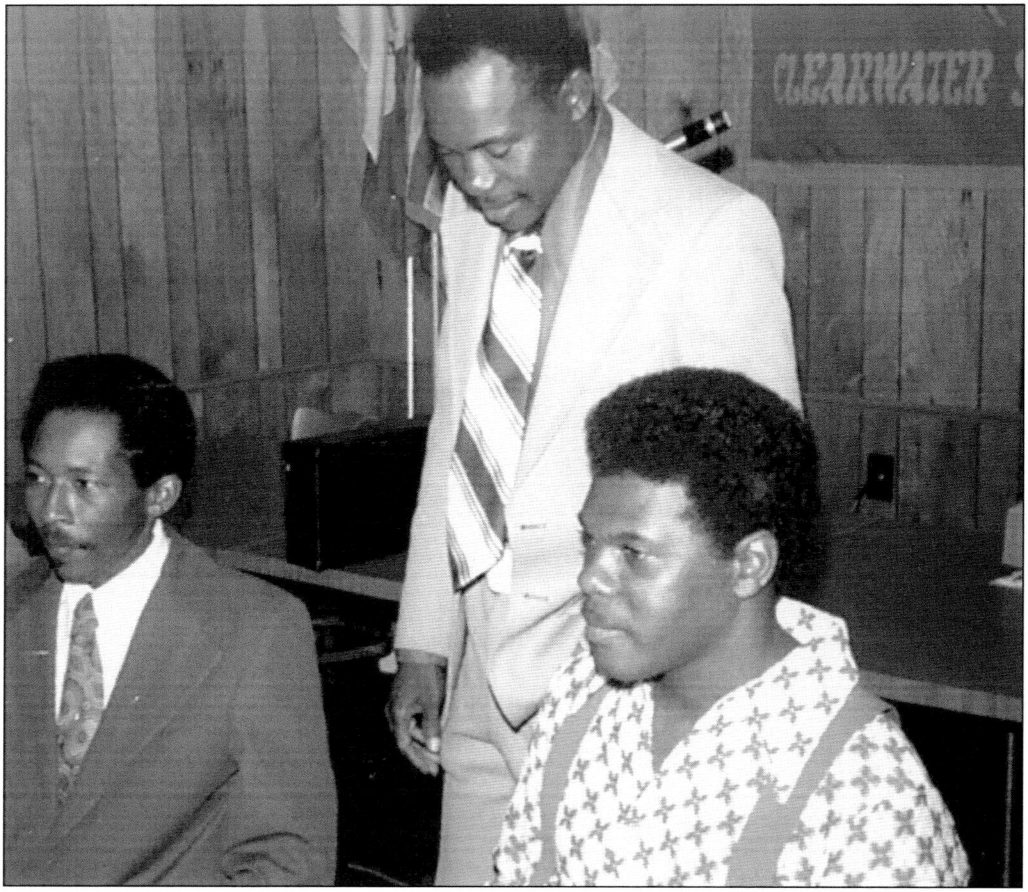

Pinellas High class of 1955 holds a 20-year reunion in 1975. Pictured from left to right are Henry Jones, Carlton McCray, and Robert Williams.

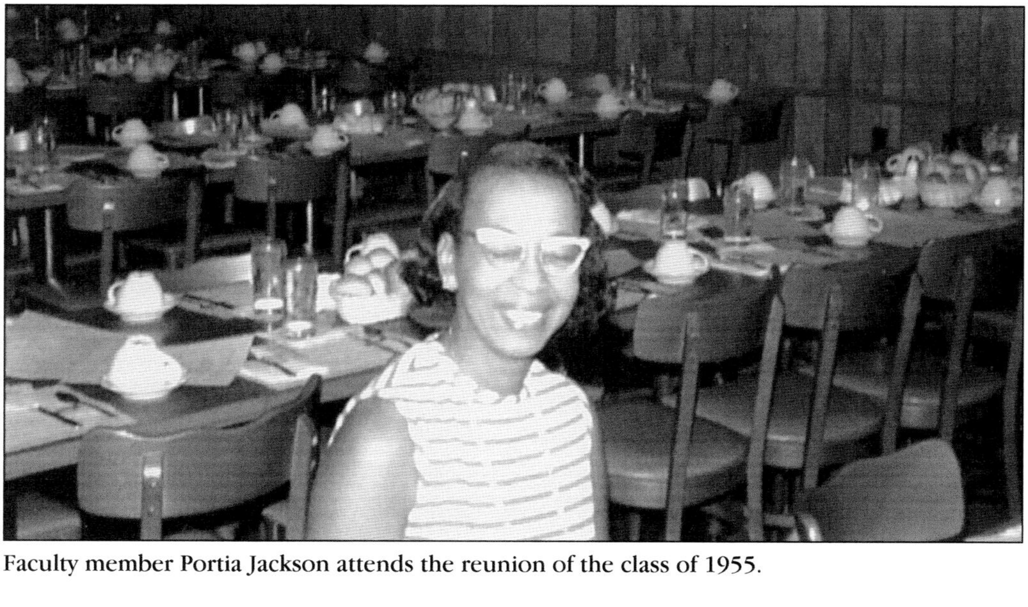

Faculty member Portia Jackson attends the reunion of the class of 1955.

Six

Government

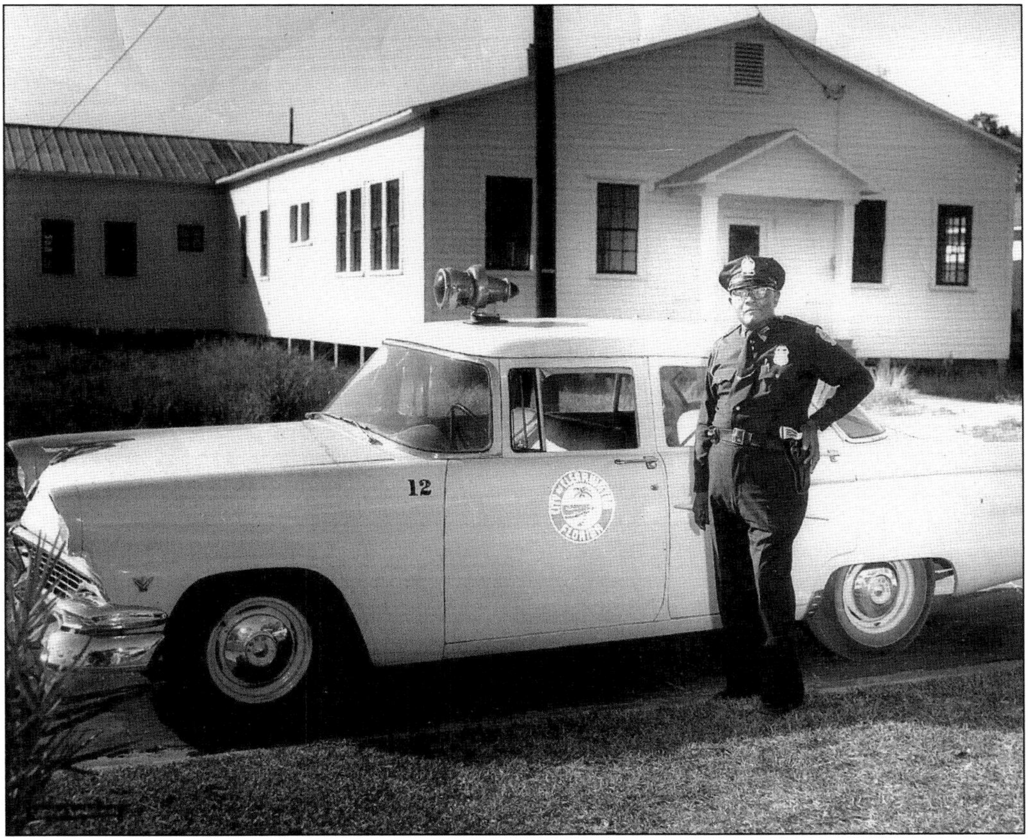

Featured here is Oscar "Sport" McCullom standing in front of his squad car in the late 1950s. McCullom was one of the first African-American police officers in Clearwater.

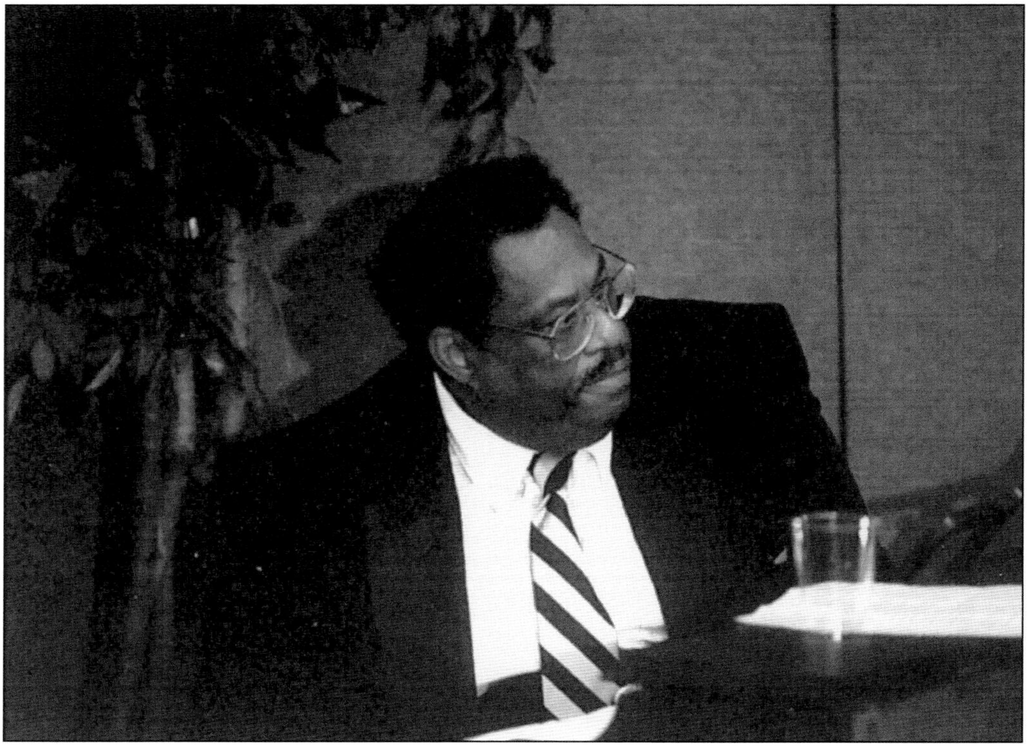

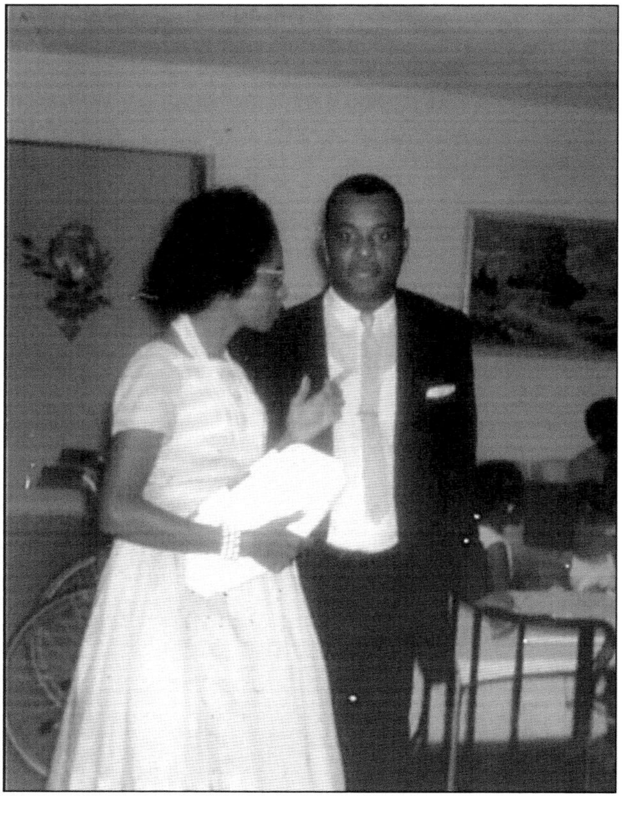

Joseph Carwise Sr. waged a successful election campaign in 1971 to become Clearwater's first African-American city commissioner.

Shown here is Joseph Carwise Sr. accompanied by his wife, Panchitta Carwise.

Mayme Hodges was appointed interim city commissioner in 1992 to fill the term vacated by Lee Regulski.

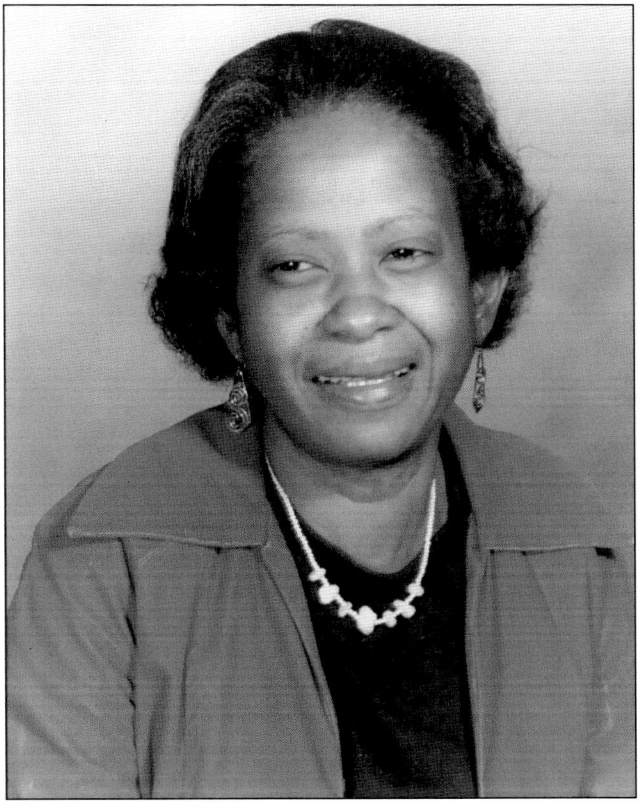

Below, Mayme Hodges poses in front of her campaign trailer, which she used when she ran for school board in 1994.

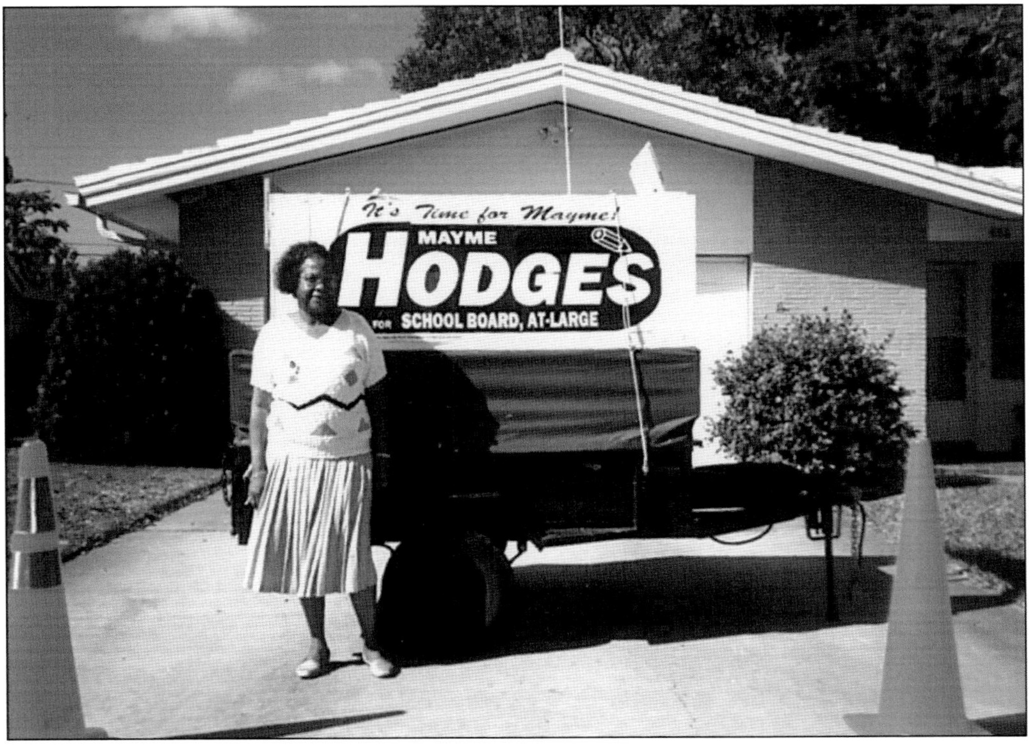

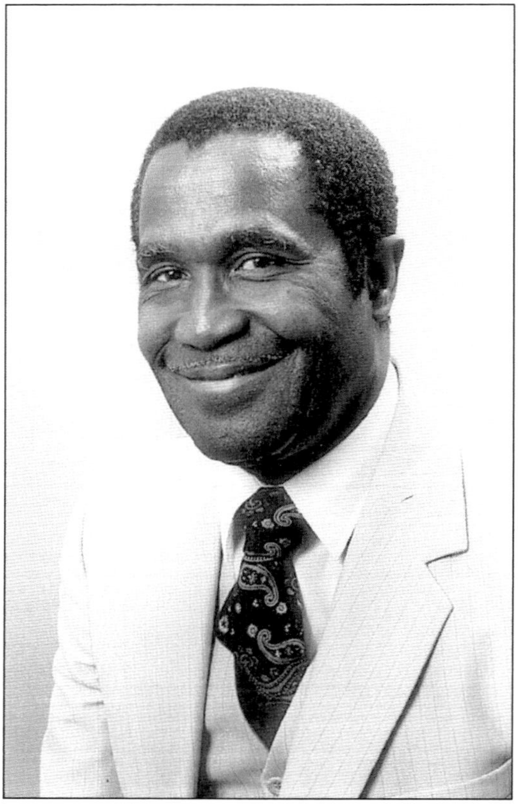

Paul Hatchett served on the Clearwater City Commission from 1978 until 1982. He was the second African American in the city's history to serve on the commission.

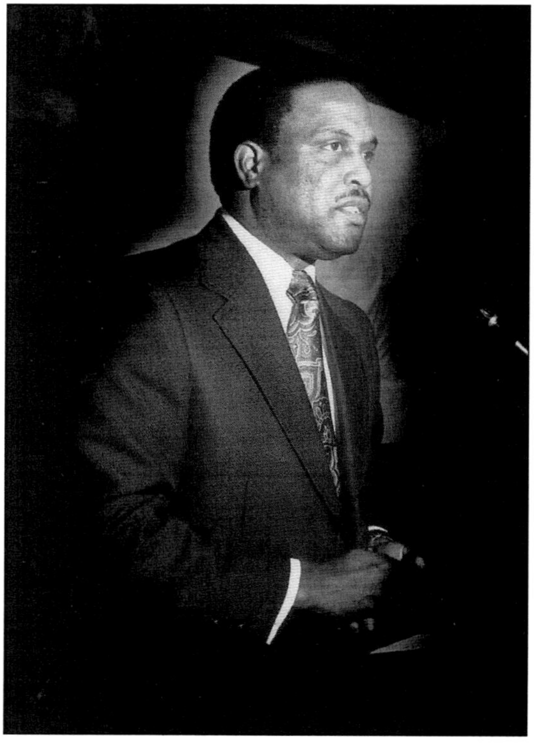

Judge Joseph W. Hatchett, brother of Commissioner Paul Hatchett, became the first African American to serve on the Florida State Supreme Court and later became the first African American to serve on the federal bench in the South.

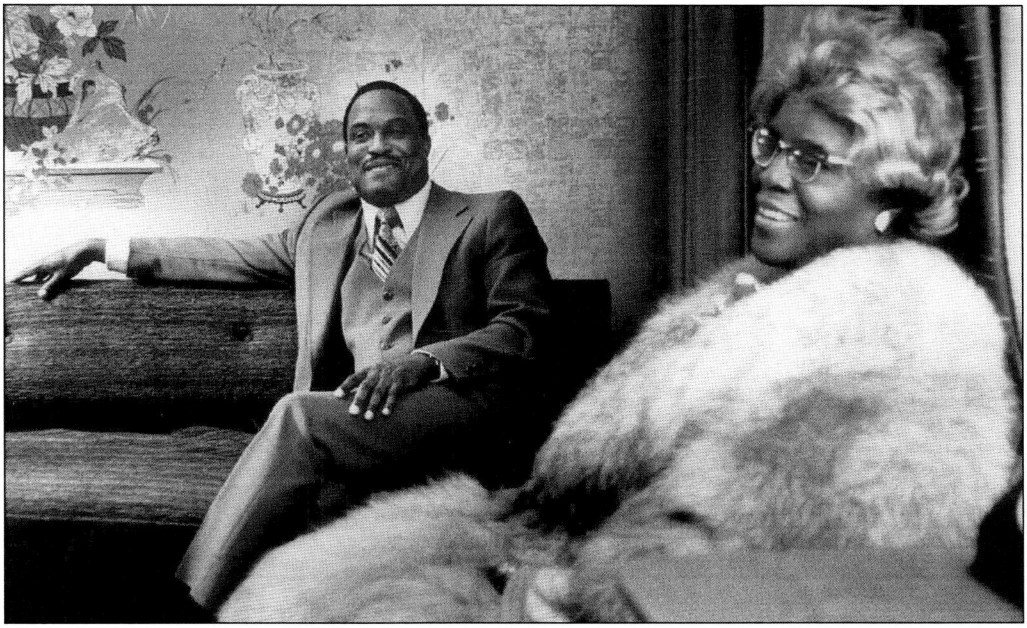

Judge Hatchett shares a peaceful moment with his mother, Lula Hatchett.

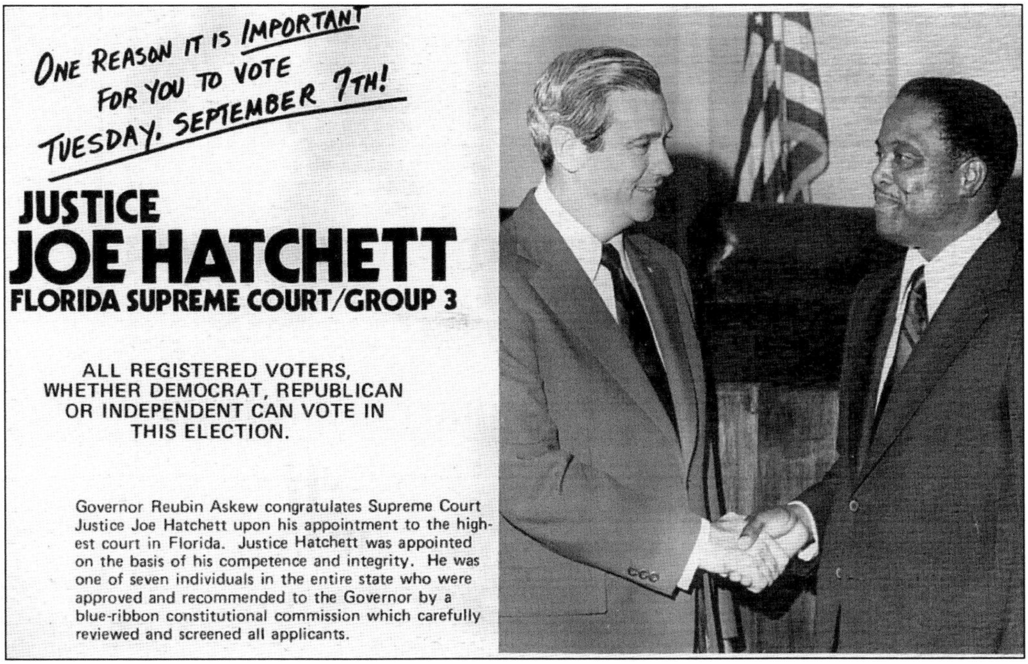

This is a campaign brochure for Judge Joe Hatchett. Pictured with the judge is Florida governor Reubin Askew, who appointed him to the Florida Supreme Court in July 1975.

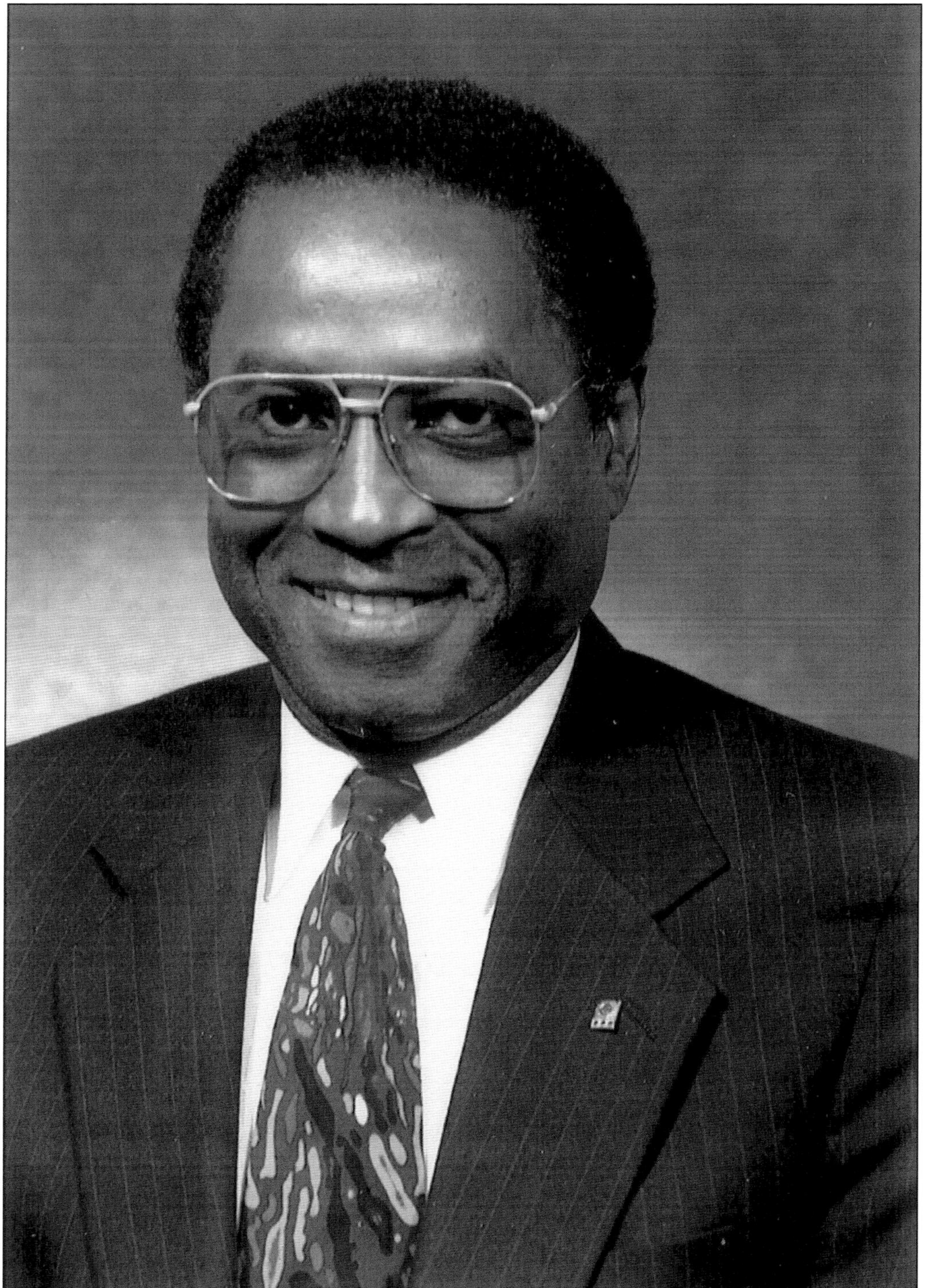

Pictured is Calvin Harris, a former administrator at St. Petersburg Junior College. On November 3, 1998, Pinellas County voters elected him to the county commission. He became the first African American elected to the commission in the history of the county.

Seven

Fashion and Style

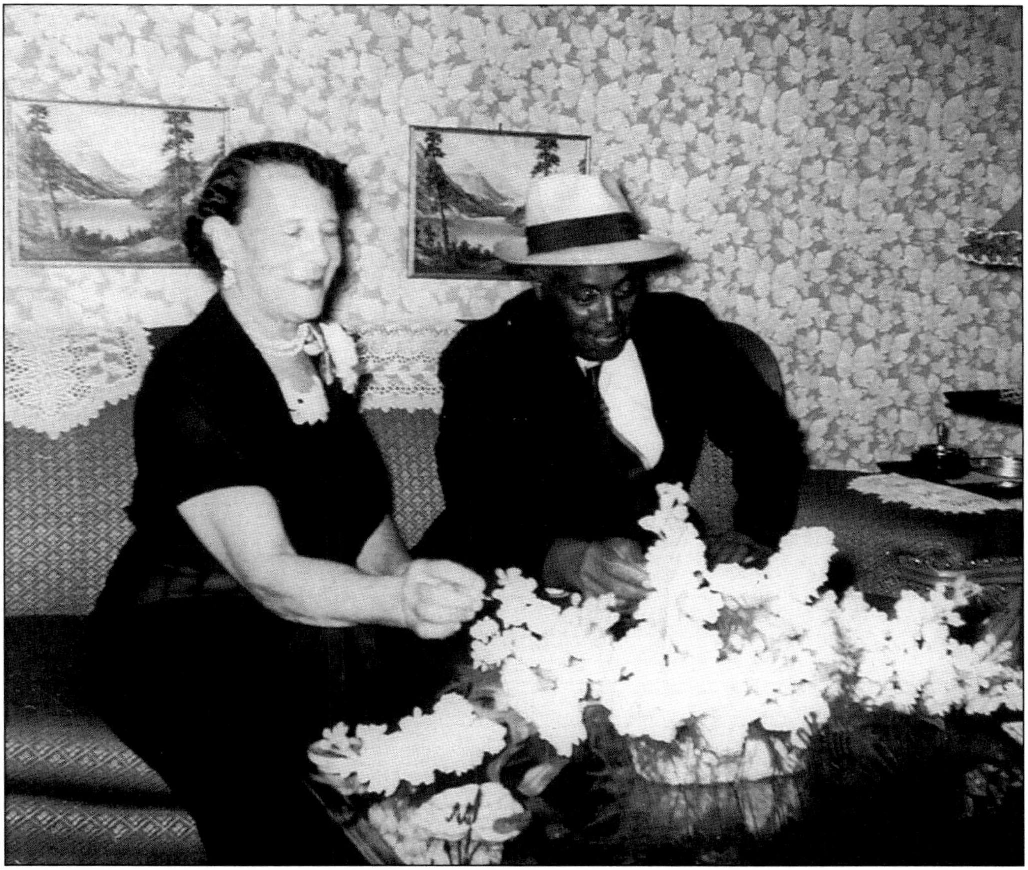

Mr. and Mrs. Calvert Charles Rutledge Sr. are elegantly dressed in their home. The couple is arranging flowers for an evening of entertainment.

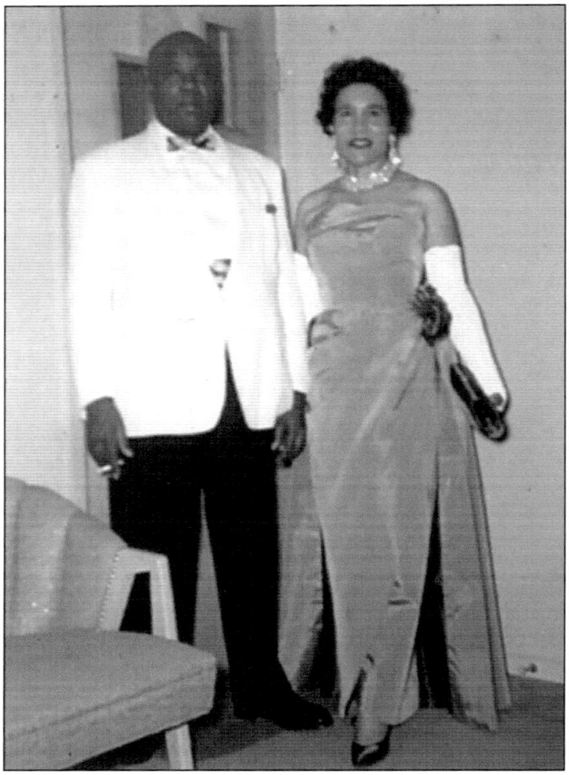

Cherry Harris and her brother-in-law, Jack Bryant, are pictured here. Mrs. Harris is dressed in a formal taffeta gown and long white gloves. The two are on their way to a club dance.

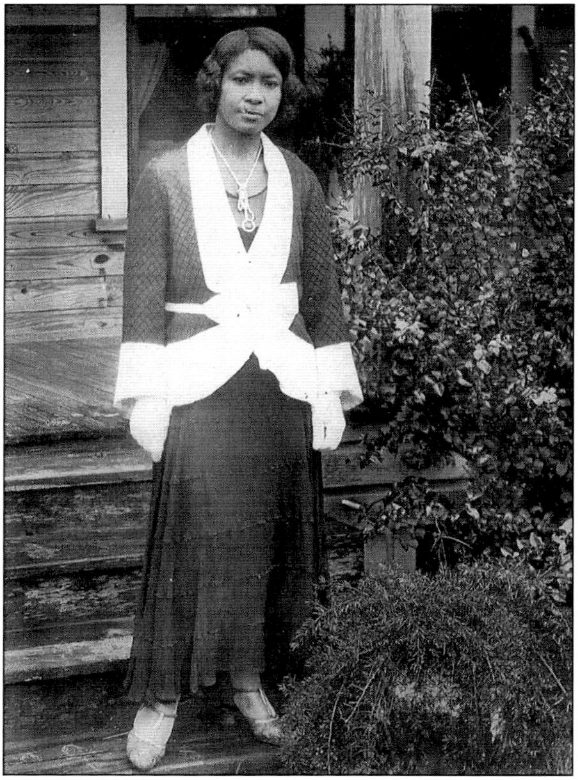

Rosa Jones is photographed in an elegant chiffon dress in the 1920s.

Dorothy Pearson, a former Curtis Elementary School teacher, is dressed in brocade satin as she pours coffee at a social function.

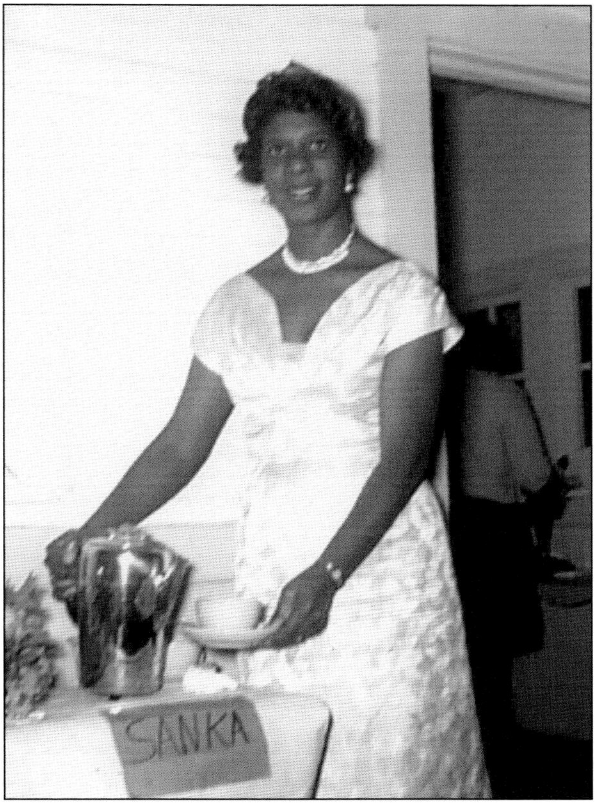

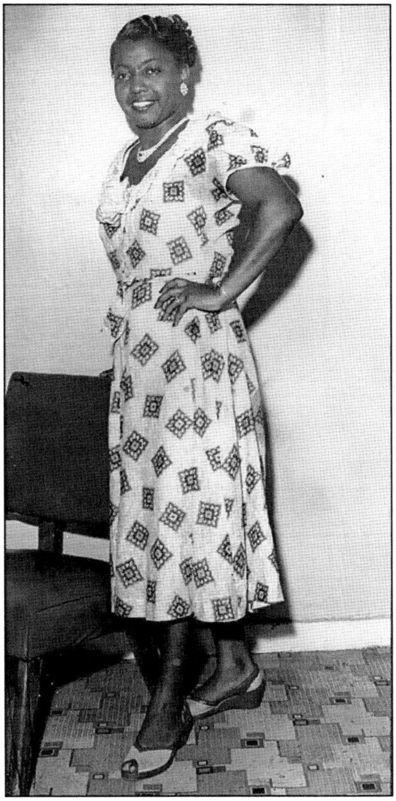

Christine Morris was photographed in 1959 while in Philadelphia. She is exemplifying class and style.

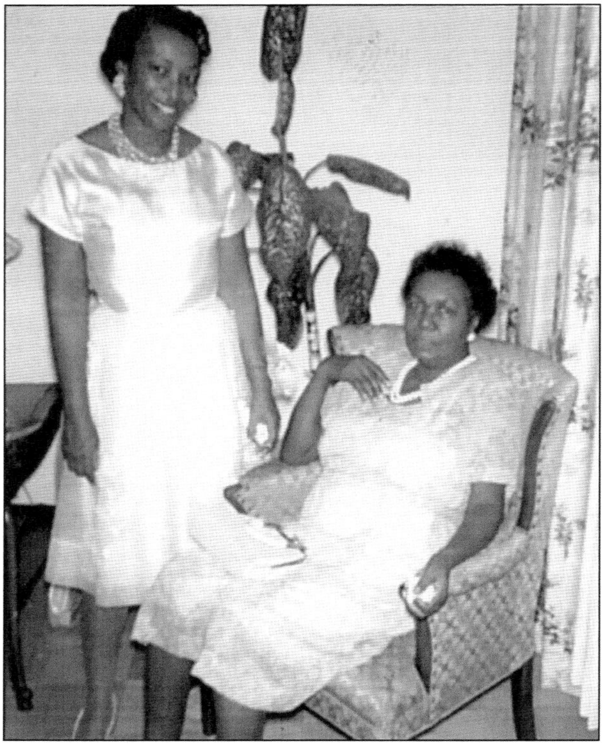

Pinellas High School teacher Vivian Henry stands dressed in a satin top and chiffon bottom dress. She is alongside Arabella Faust, principal of Williams Elementary, who is dressed in a print with lace trim.

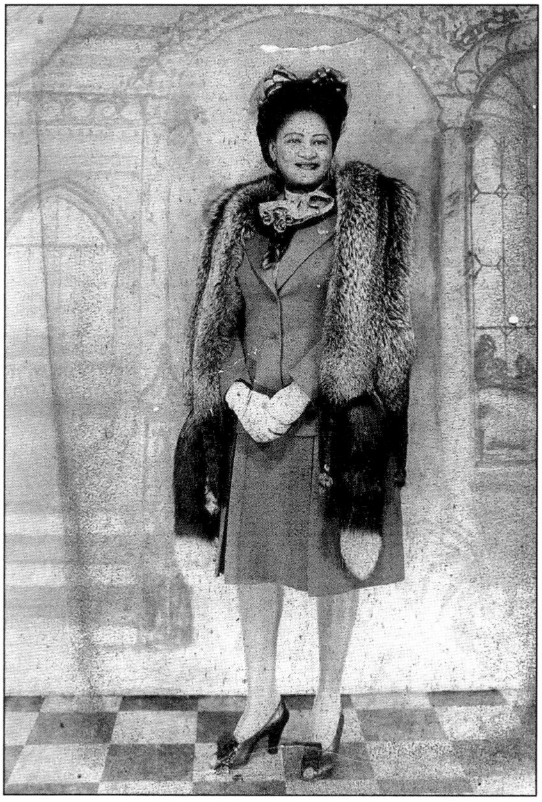

Clealia Jackson elegantly poses in the late 1940s, wearing a two-piece suit and furs.

Family gathers for a birthday celebration for Della Jackson. Seated on the sofa is Emma Sanchez (on left) in a print dress, Della Jackson (center) also in a print dress, and Clealia Jackson (on right) dressed in a print dress of silk. Seated on the floor is Eliza Sims in a lovely lace dress.

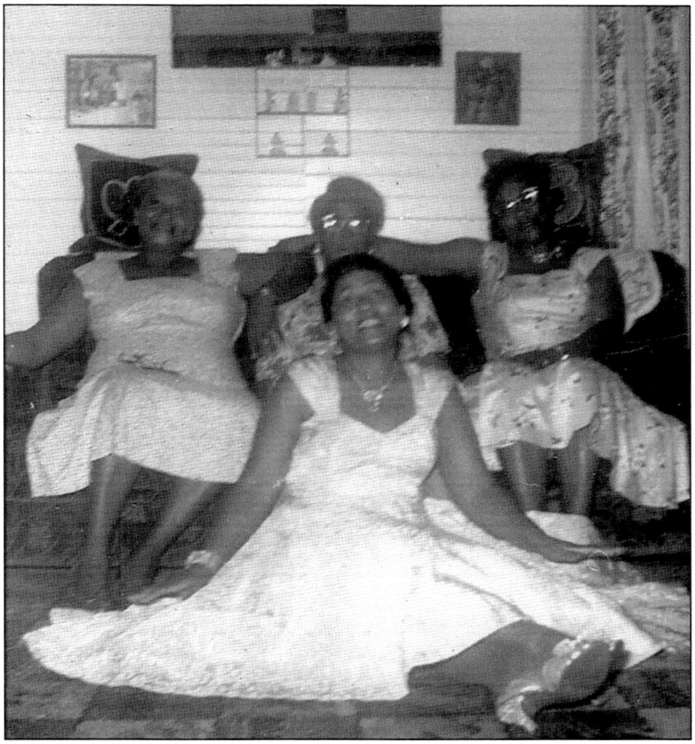

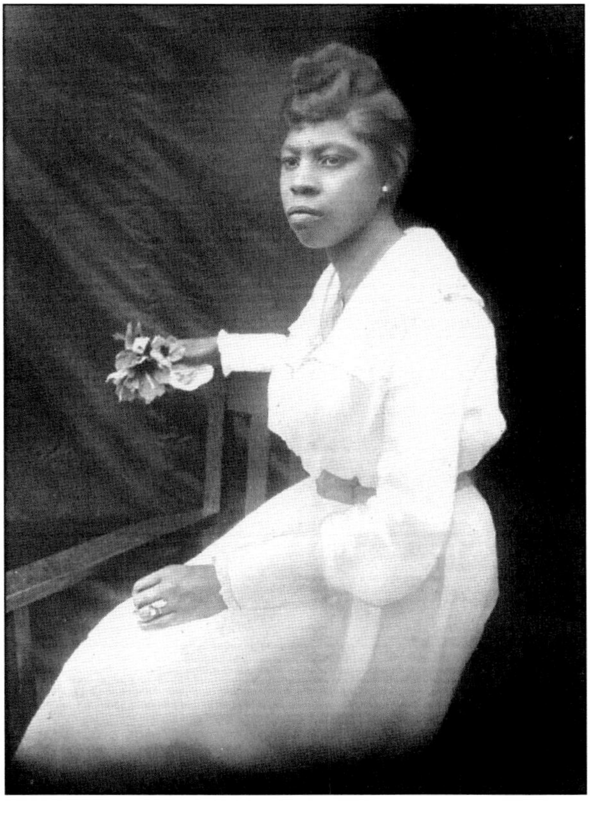

Pictured here is Gertrude Johnson Cobbs, principal of Curtis Elementary School. She is wearing an elegant white dress and holding a small bouquet of flowers.

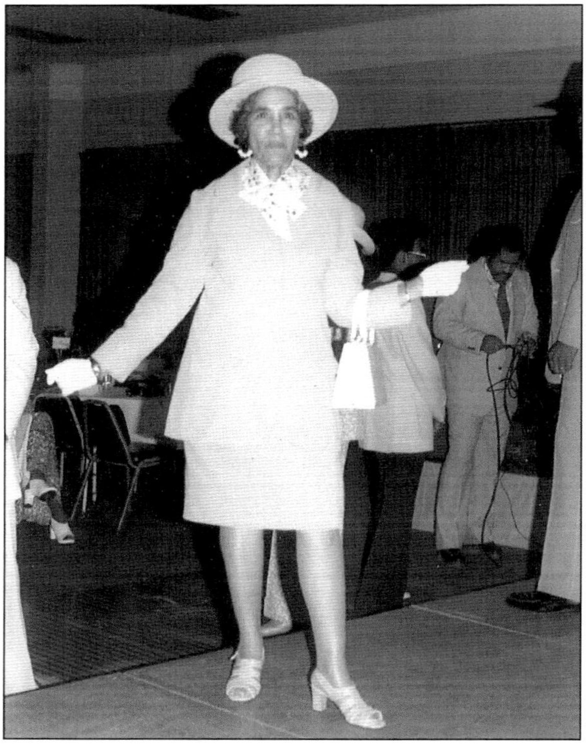

This photo was taken of Cherry Harris modeling a yellow two-piece suit with a matching hat and shoes with white gloves and a white purse.

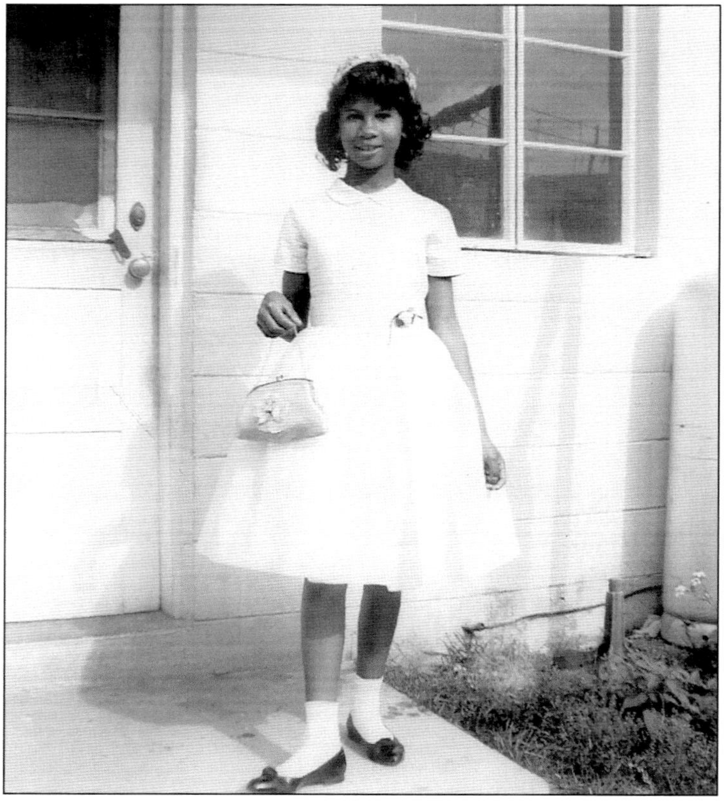

A young Zanith Lofton Toomes sports an organza dress with a trim and flower at the waist and wears patent leather shoes. She carries a stylish purse also featuring a flower.

Shown here is Willie Brewton Sr. in a 1949 photo looking suave and debonair.

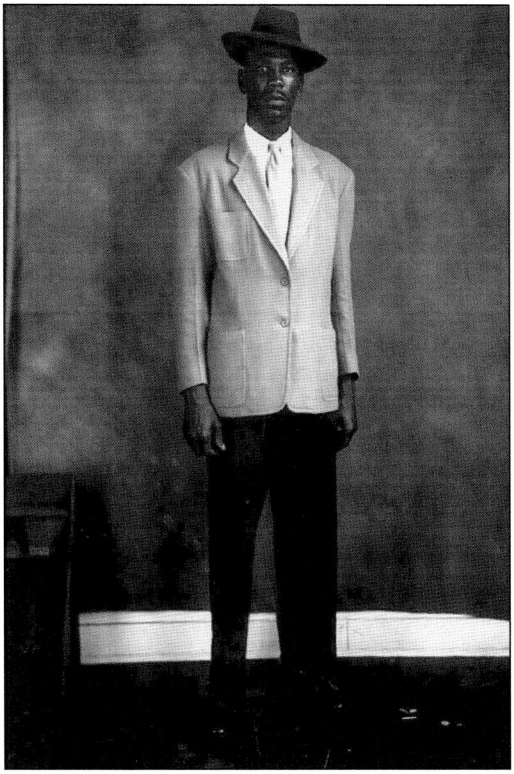

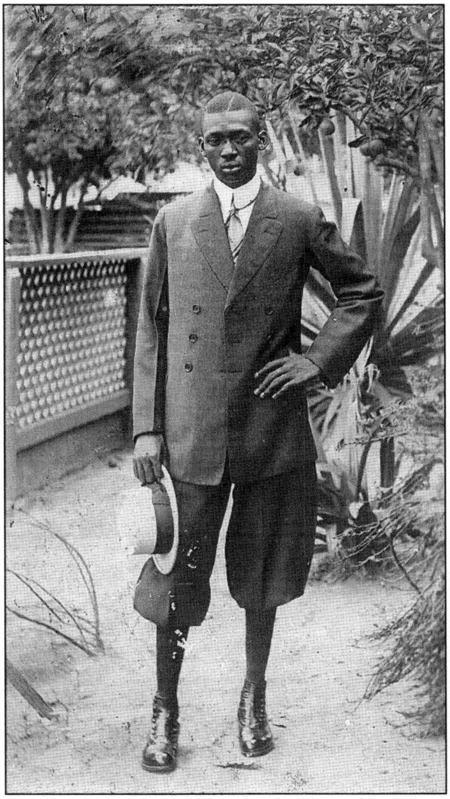

An unidentified man was photographed in the late 1800s or early 1900s sporting a double-breasted knickerbocker suit. Striking a unique pose, he also wears boots buttoned up on the sides.

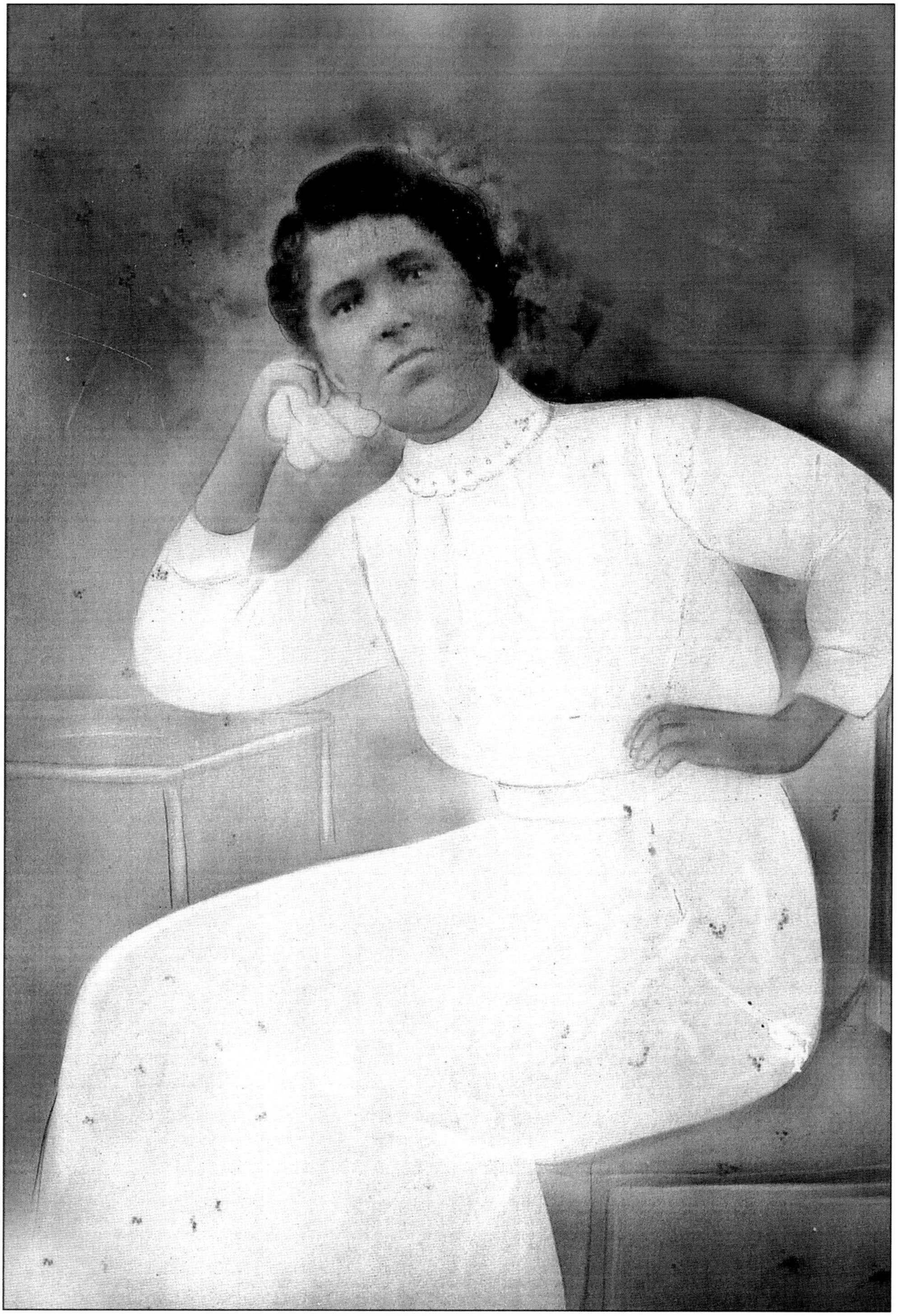

This is an early photograph of Julia Samuels, paternal grandmother of Rosalie Robinson. She is outfitted in a light-colored dress with an embroidered collar, which she created and sewed herself.

Seen here is Bessie Gibson, former teacher of Williams Elementary, standing behind a car in a light-colored dress with matching shoes and hat. This photo was taken in 1966.

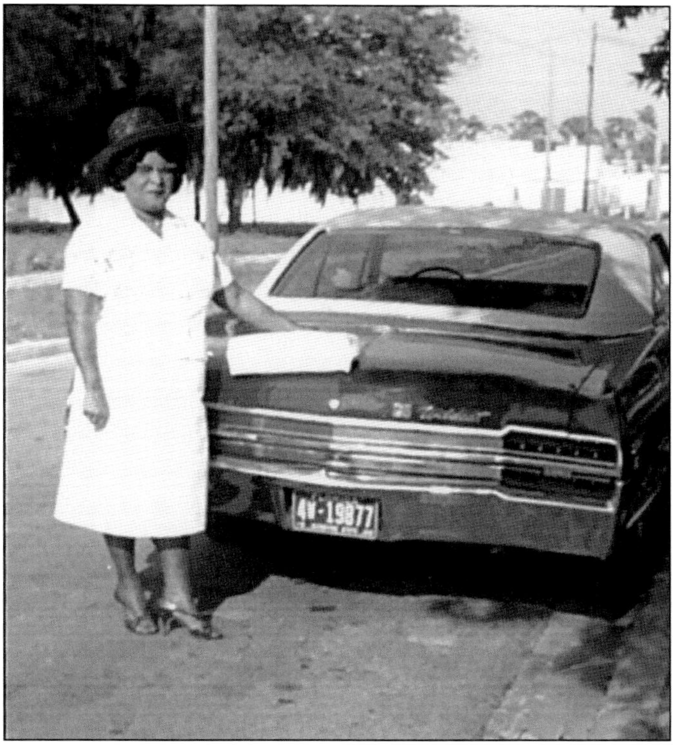

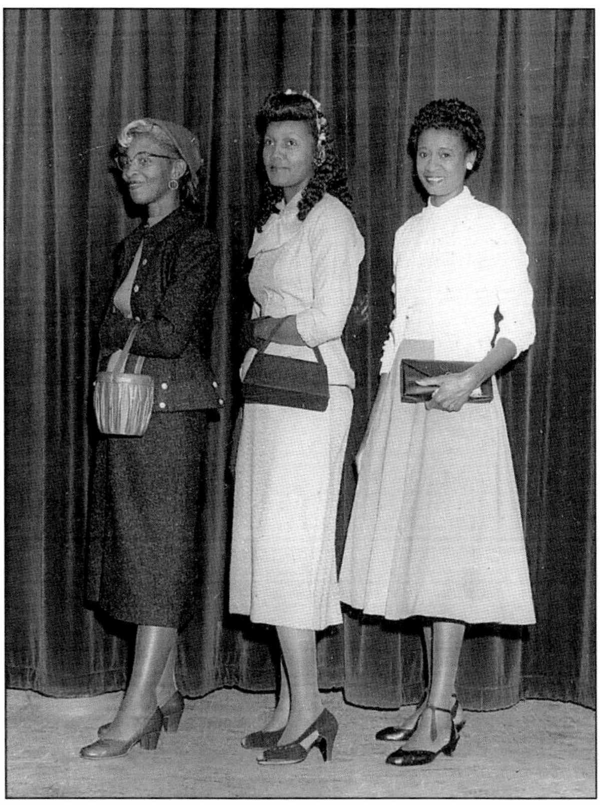

Three stylish women, each carrying a purse, pose for this 1959 photo.

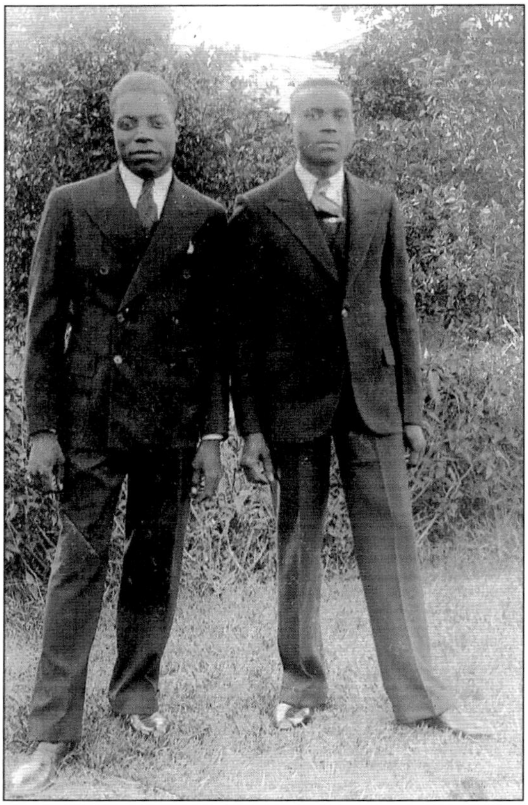

Robert Kitchen and Caleb Jones sport their sleek suits and neatly buffed shoes.

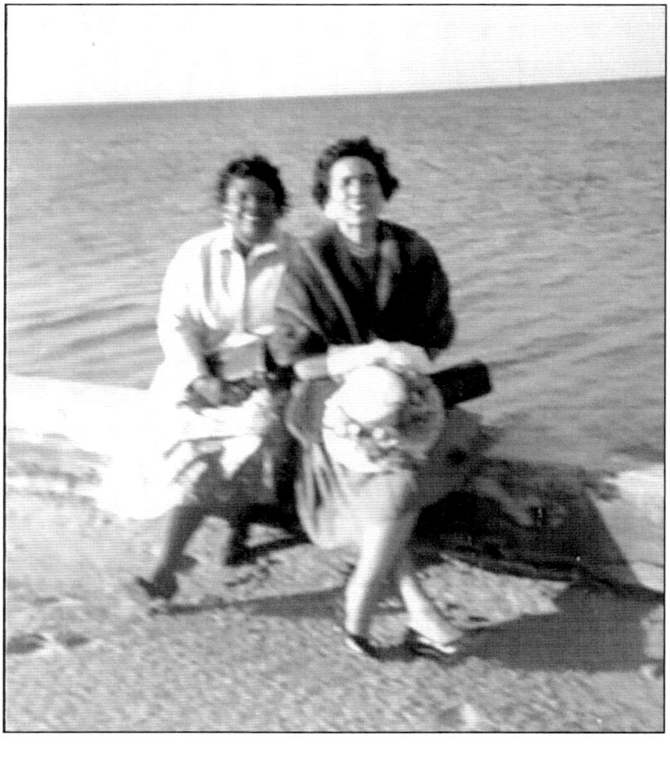

Stylish, even at the beach, are Cherry Harris and her niece, Leola Washington. Mrs. Harris is draped in fur on a breezy February day in 1960.

Eight

Faces and Places

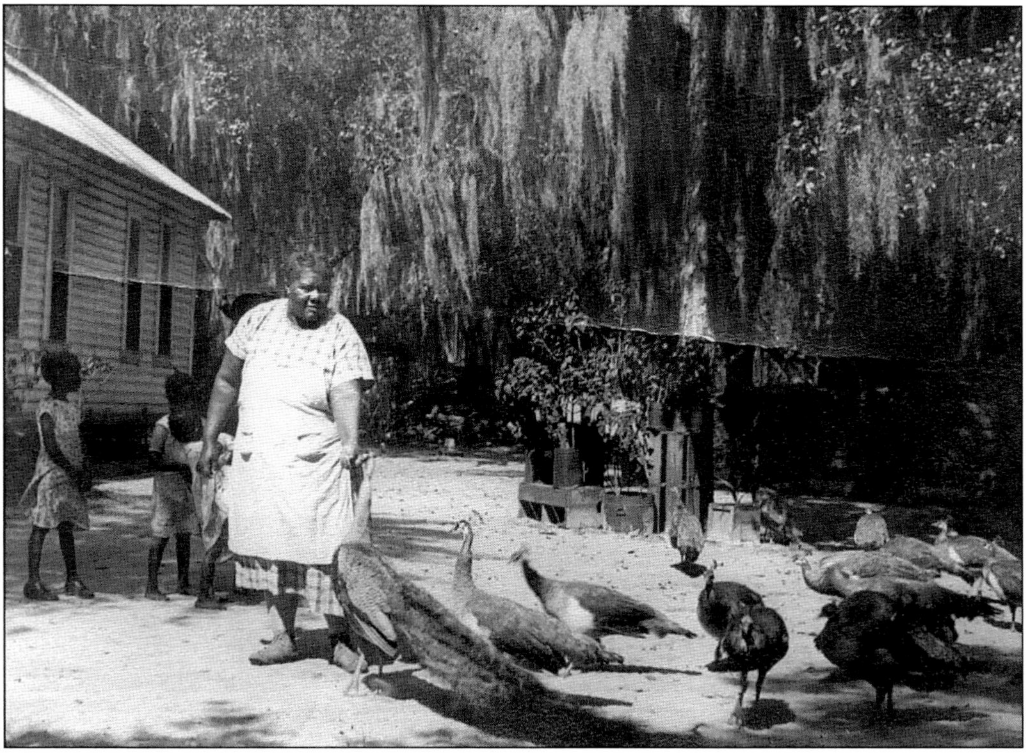

A popular Clearwater tourist attraction in the 1920s was a peacock farm owned by Ethel Williams. The farm was located where the Clearwater Mall later stood. The mall no longer exists.

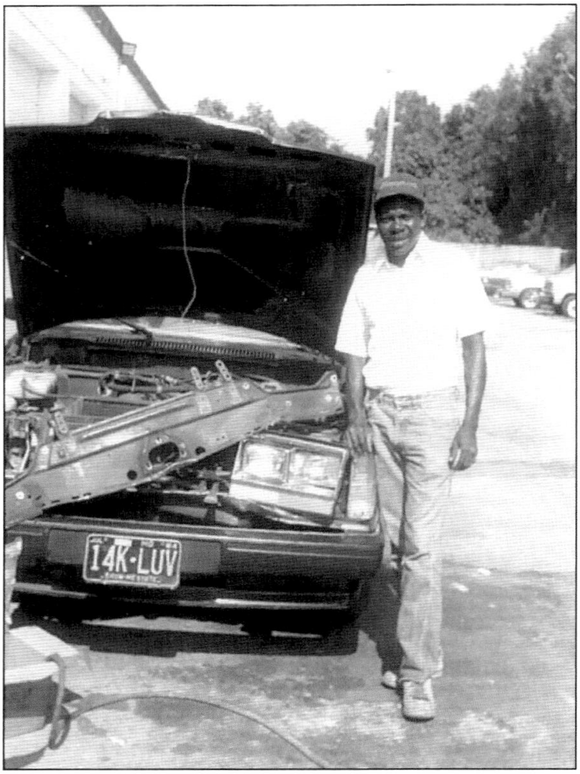

Carlton McCray poses beside an automobile that is in desperate need of repair.

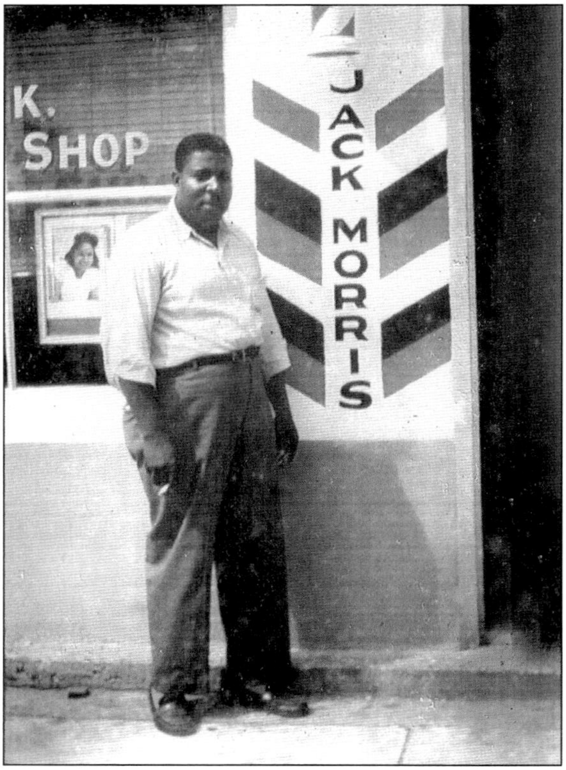

Jack Morris stands in front of his barbershop, which was relocated from Garden Avenue to Greenwood Avenue.

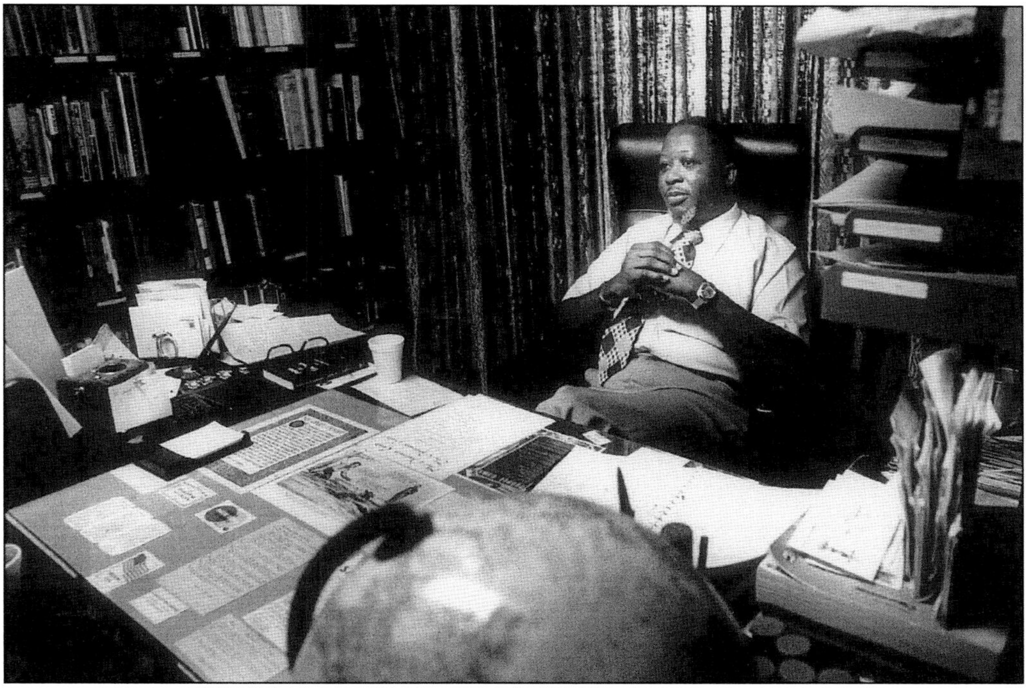

Rev. Mac Williams, pastor of Mt. Carmel Baptist Church and former president of the Clearwater Upper Pinellas NAACP, takes a breather inside his office. His surroundings indicate the breadth of his work and responsibilities.

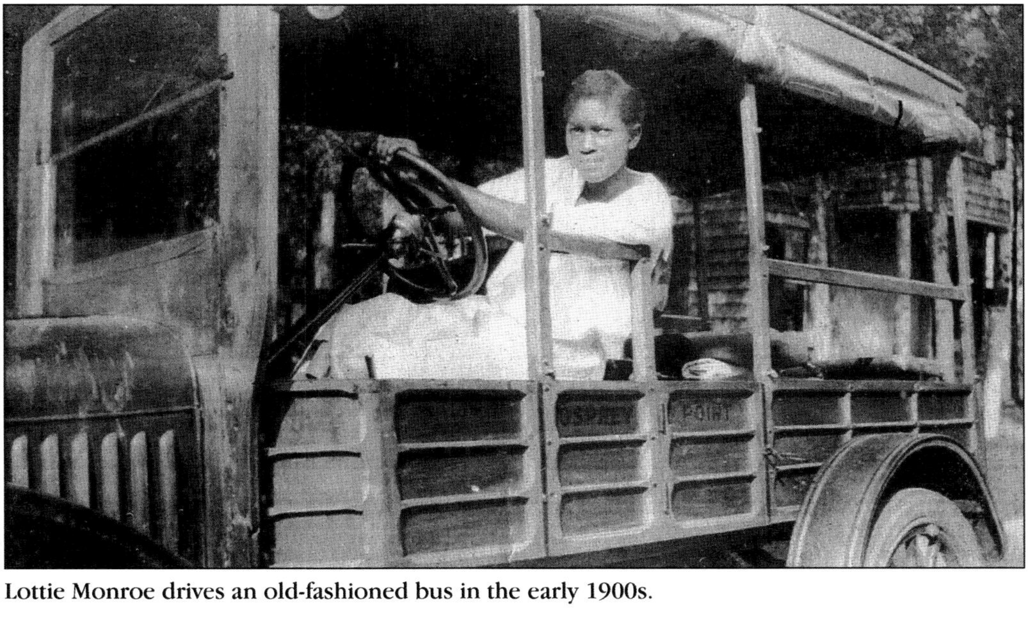

Lottie Monroe drives an old-fashioned bus in the early 1900s.

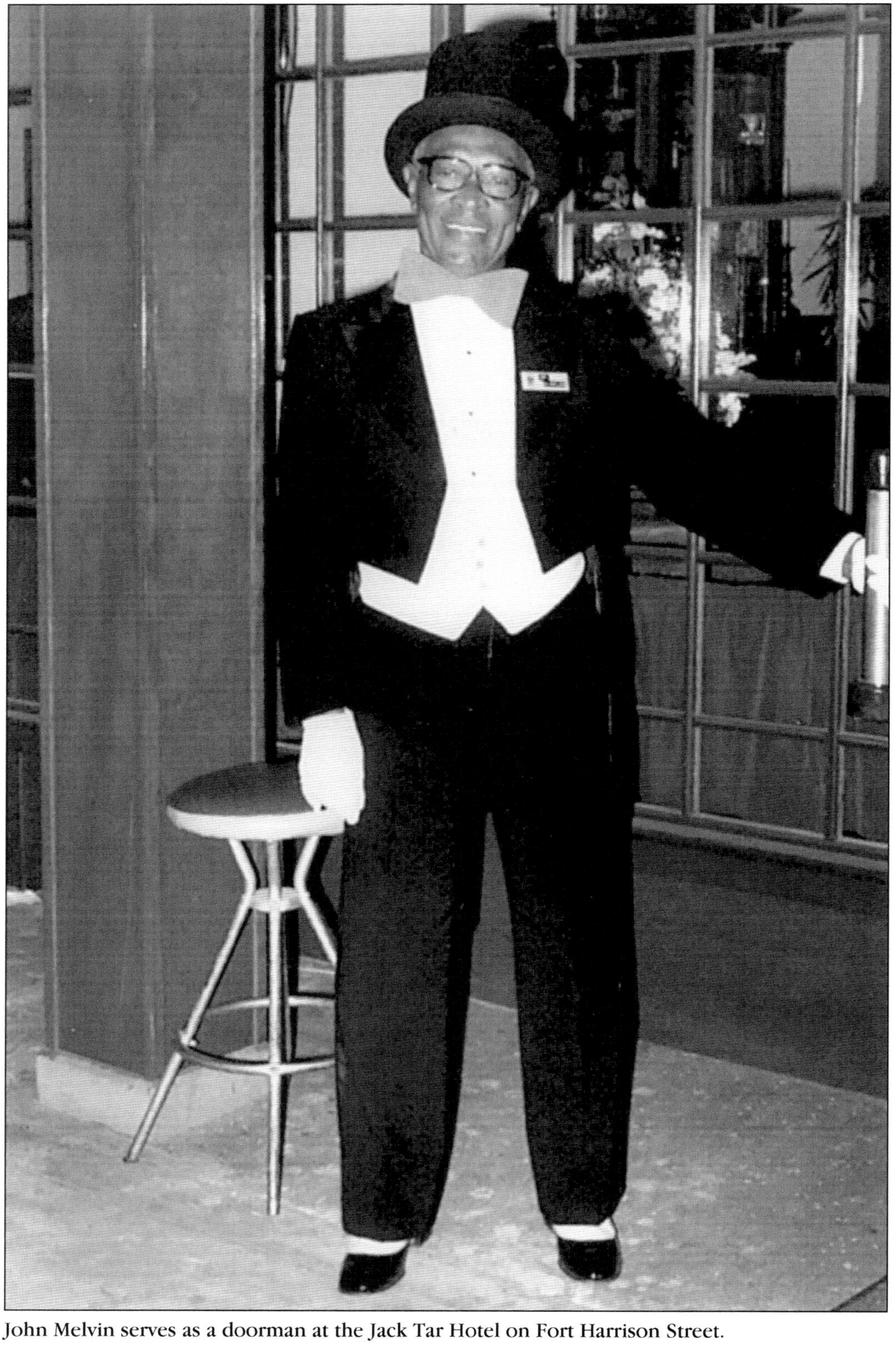

John Melvin serves as a doorman at the Jack Tar Hotel on Fort Harrison Street.

Eleanor Breland, a class of 1965 Pinellas High graduate, poses in front of a classic mid-1950s Chevrolet.

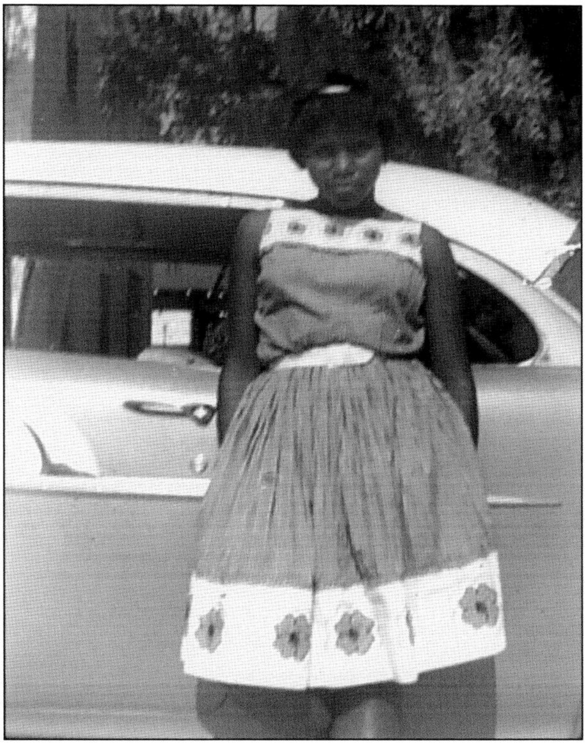

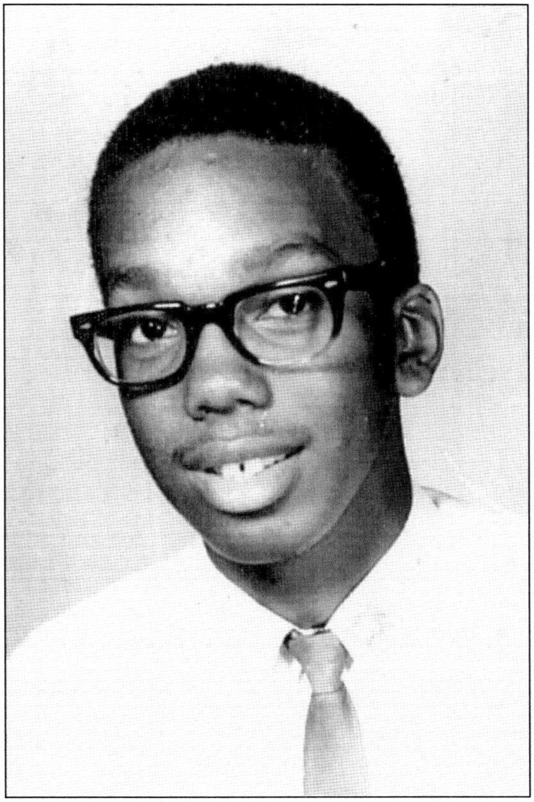

At left is a photo of Edward Henry Jr., who was also a class of 1965 graduate.

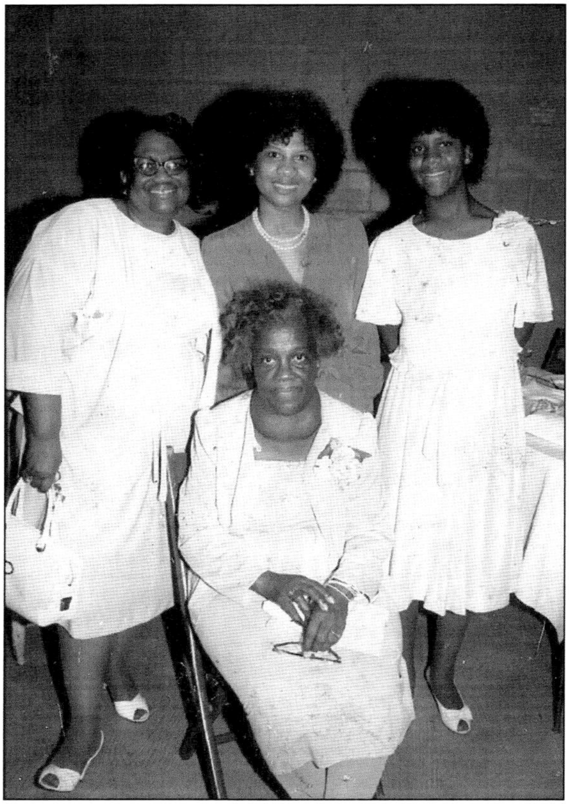

Pictured here are four generations of Bryant ladies. Seated is Ethel Bryant. From left to right in back are Leola Bryant Washington, Zanith Copes Toomes, and Zanetta K. Robinson.

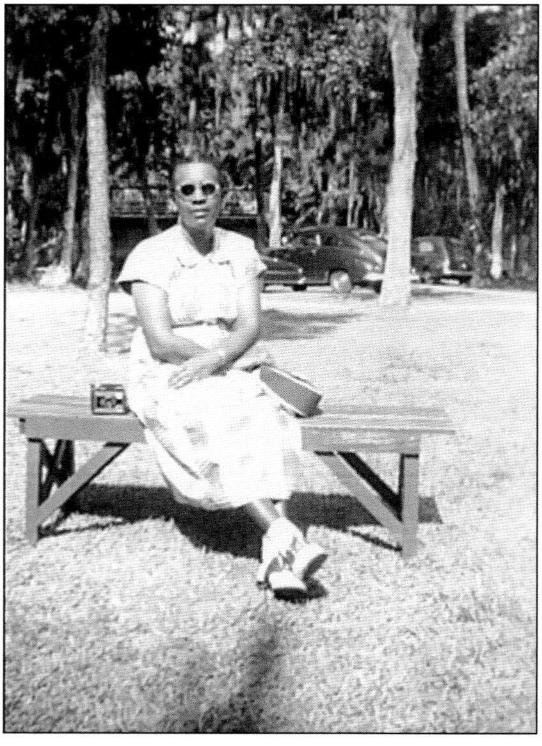

Mary Edwards, sister of Evelyn Rooks, takes a break on a park bench.

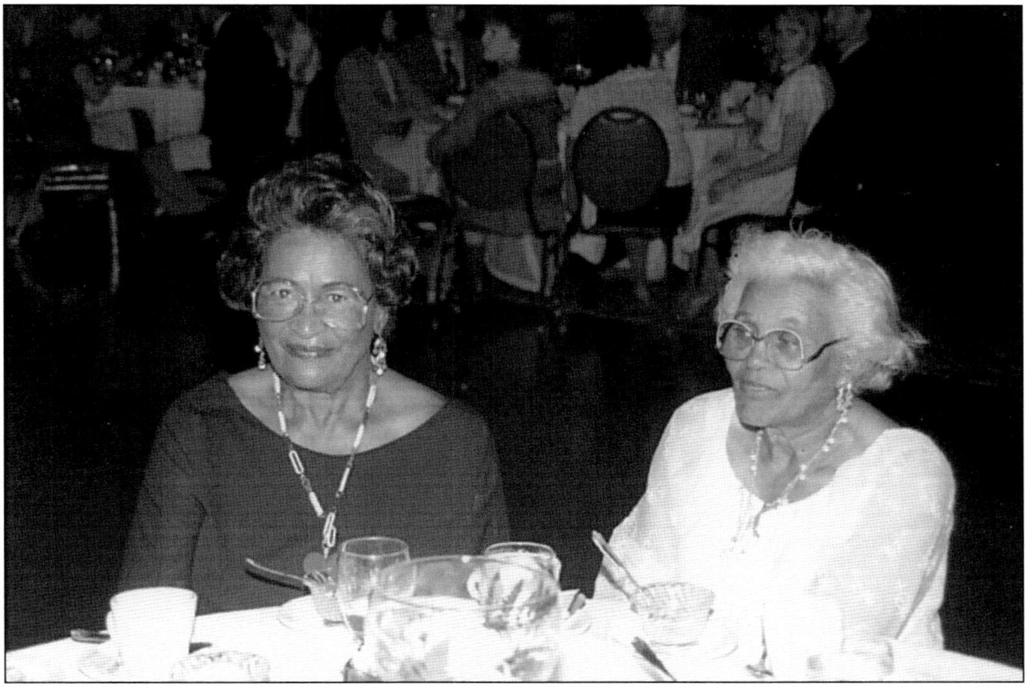

Clealia Jackson dines at a local restaurant with Evelyn Rooks.

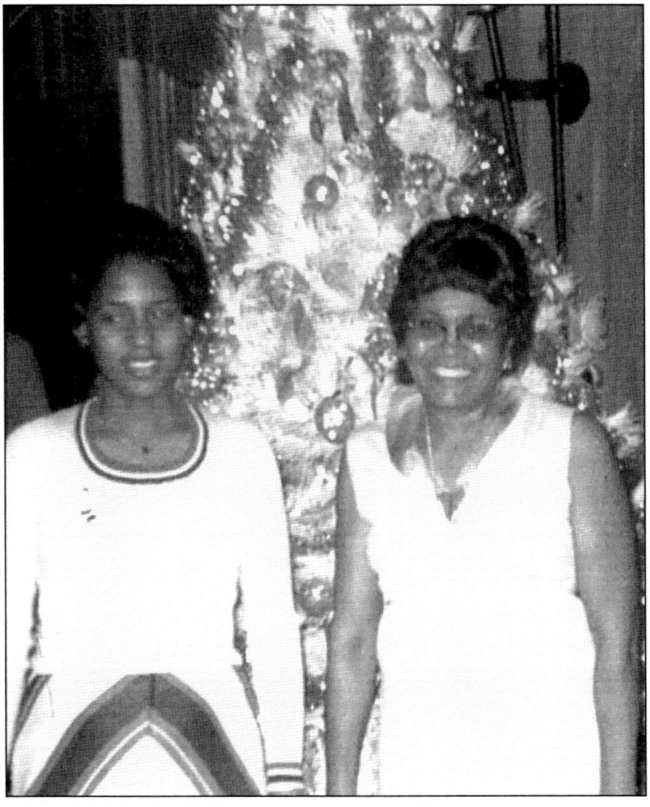

Evelyn Rooks and her daughter-in-law, Sandra Rooks, pose by a Christmas tree at the Sheraton Sand Key Hotel during the holiday season.

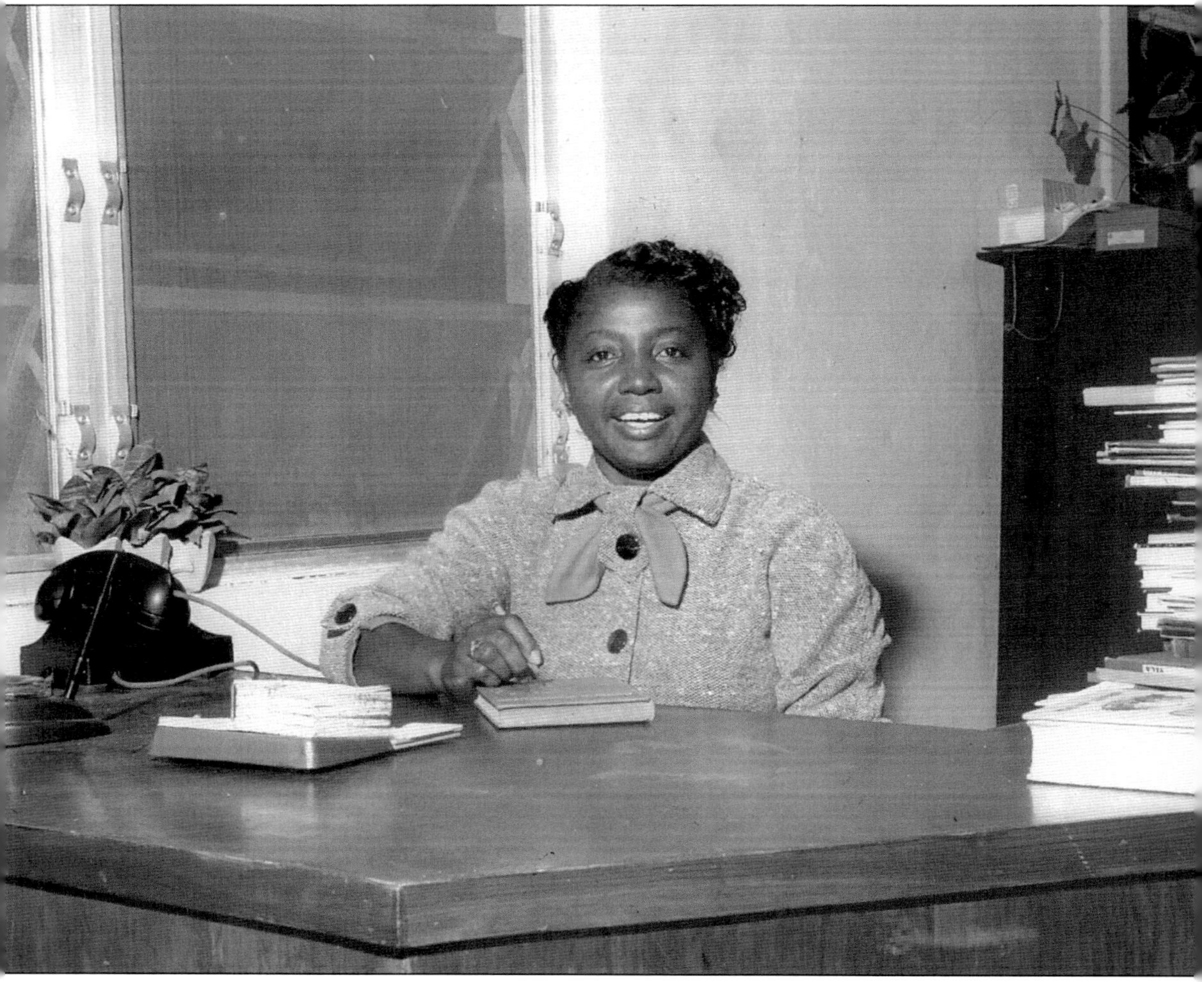

Christine Morris, photographed here in 1950, is best known as a self-styled librarian, friend, community ambassador, and neighbor. She was born in Register, Georgia in 1922. At the age of four, she moved with her family to Clearwater, where her parents, Eddie and Hattie Wigfall, owned and operated their own dry cleaning and alteration business, called Wigfall's Pressing Club. Morris graduated from Pinellas High School in 1941 and attended Bethune-Cookman College, where she was inspired by the head of the college, Mary McLeod Bethune, to dedicate her life to serving others. After college, Morris returned to Clearwater and in July of 1949, was appointed the City of Clearwater's first African-American librarian. Under her guidance, a new era of library service was achieved for Clearwater's African Americans. In April 1950, "the Negro Library," as it was initially known, first opened in a storefront at Palmetto Street and Pennsylvania Avenue. With its growing popularity, the library moved to a new location at the corner of Holt and Palmetto, which is now known as the Clearwater Library's Northeast Branch. Morris retired from the library after 33 years of service to the people of the community. During her years of service, Christine Morris enlightened countless minds, both young and old, whether it was by implementing voter registration programs, tutorial programs, and summer programs for children, or by simply encouraging a reluctant youngster to read.

Eddie Wigfall Sr. poses inside the Eckerd Drug Store on Cleveland Street in the late 1950s or early 1960s.

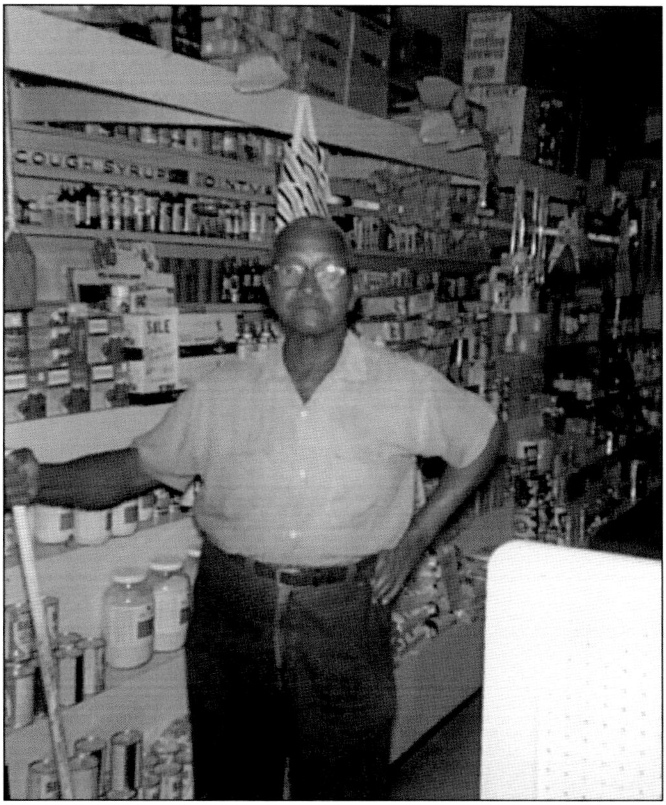

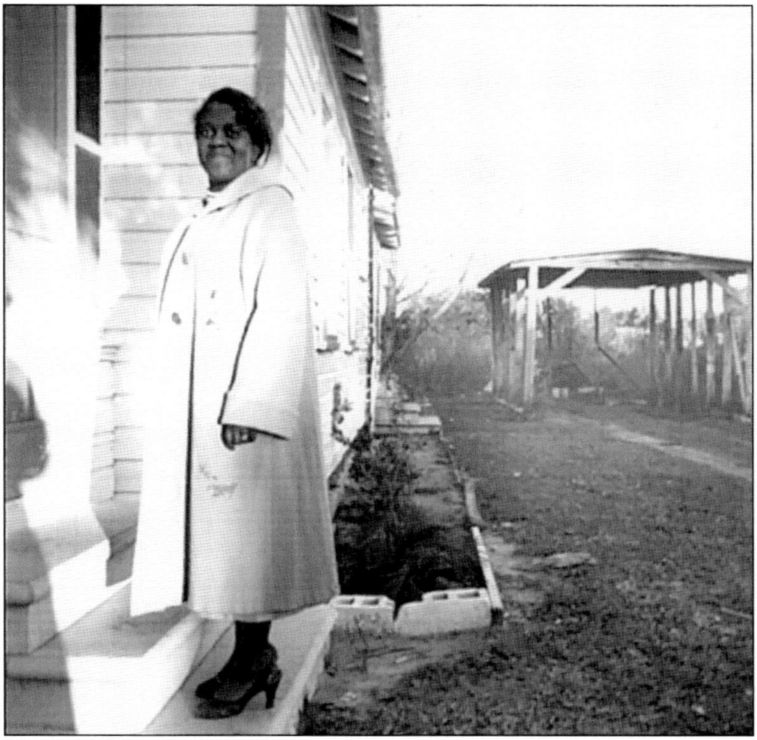

Ethel Bryant enters her home on Roosevelt Avenue in the 1930s. She and her husband Jack "Jake" Bryant were co-founders of the New Deal Taxi Company.

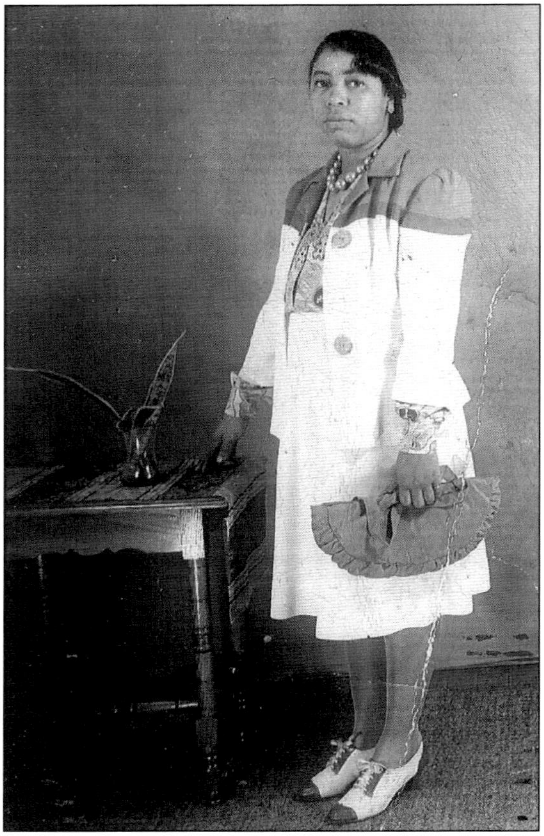

Shown here is Irene Gardner in the 1940s. She is the mother of E.J. Robinson, who constructed the new addition to the Community Pride Nursery, pictured below. Mrs. Gardener worked in a lab at Morton Plant Hospital in the late 1930s.

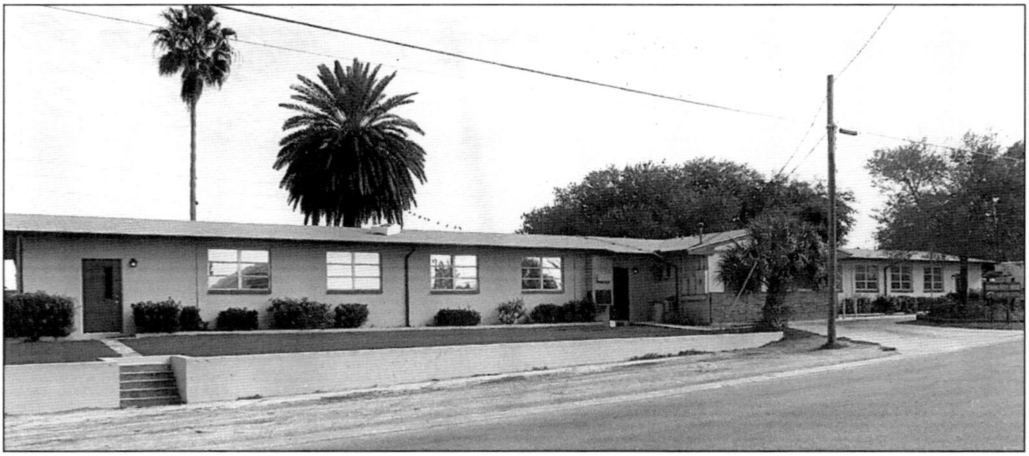

Pictured is the Community Pride Nursery located on Holt Street. It was photographed in the late 1950s.

Shown here is Gertie Ryans in a 1930s photo.

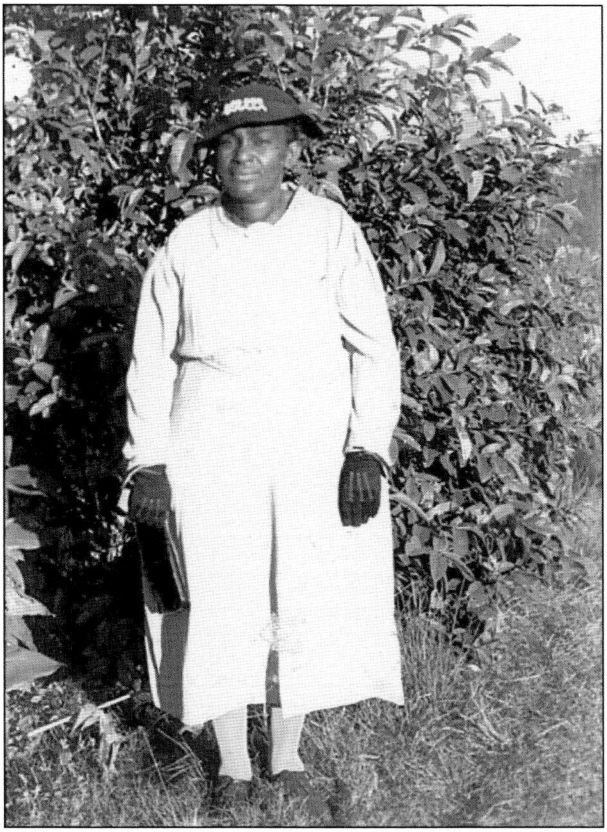

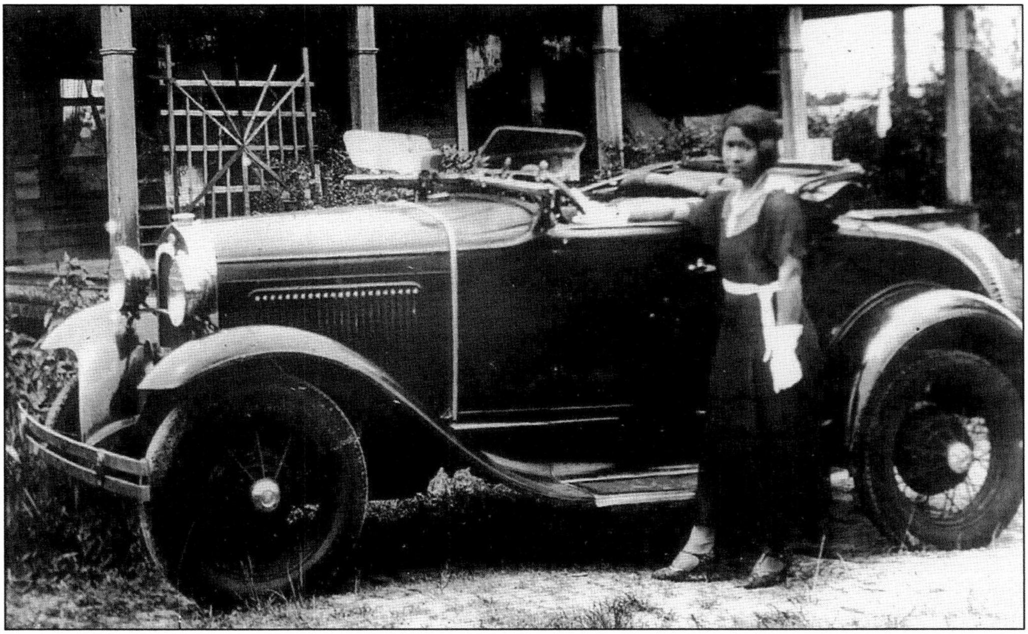

Rosa Jones stands beside her 1927 A-model Ford in this classic photo. Mrs. Jones was skilled in culinary arts and cooked for several prominent citizens at the Clearwater Yacht Club.

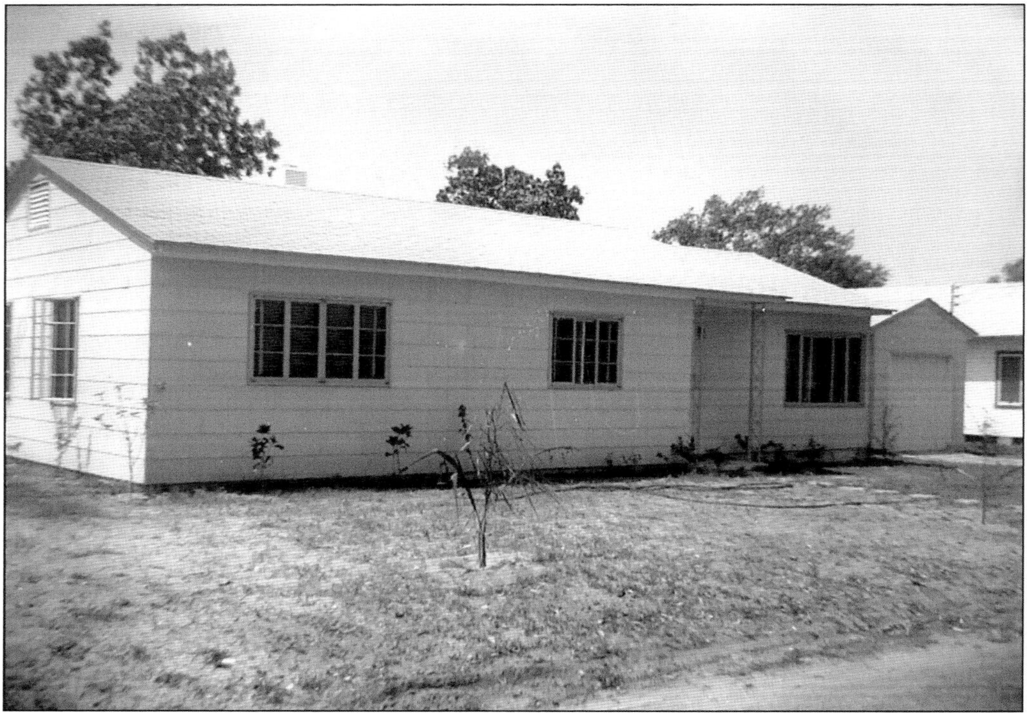

Pictured here is the home of Mr. and Mrs. Milton Rooks Sr., built in 1950.

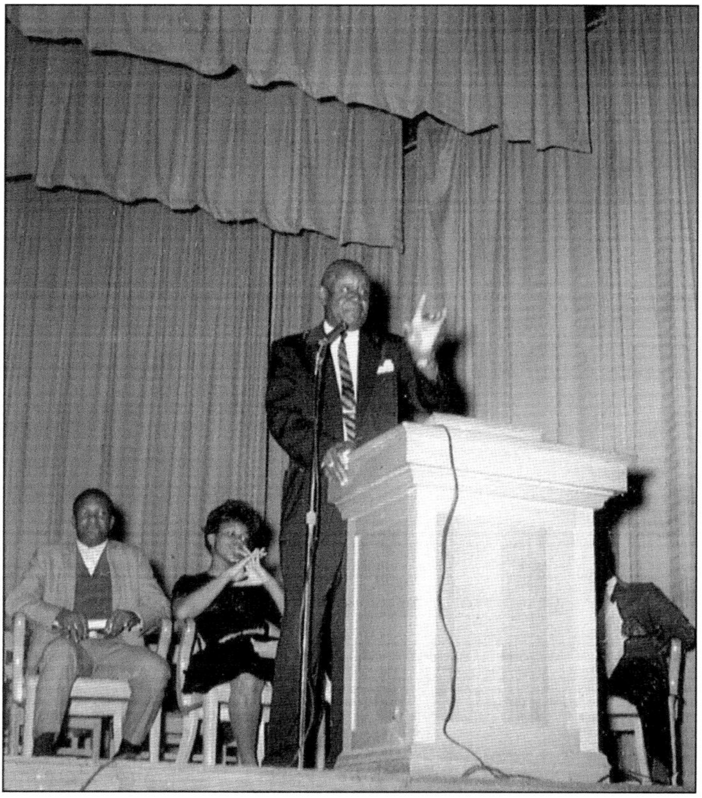

In this photo, the notable Shirley W. Curtis addresses the students and faculty of Pinellas High School in the mid-1960s.

Della Jackson poses with her birthday cake in the late 1940s or early 1950s.

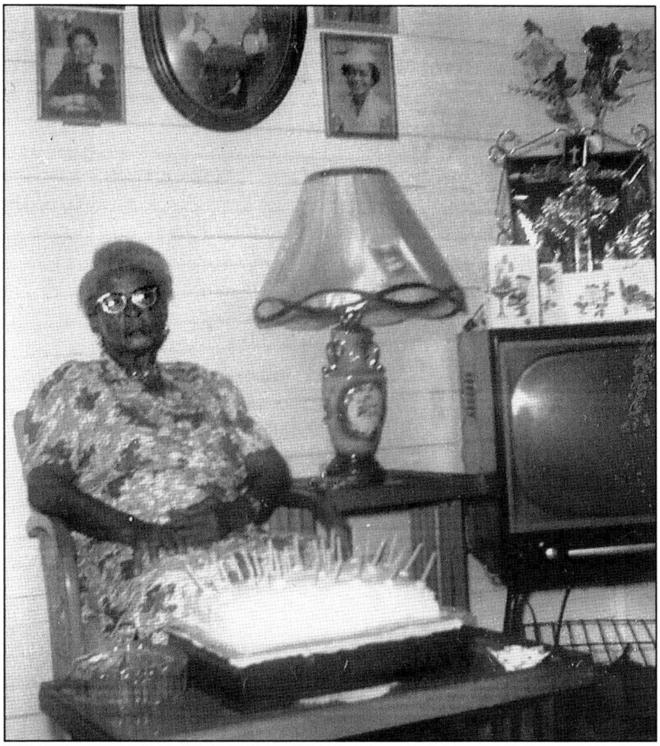

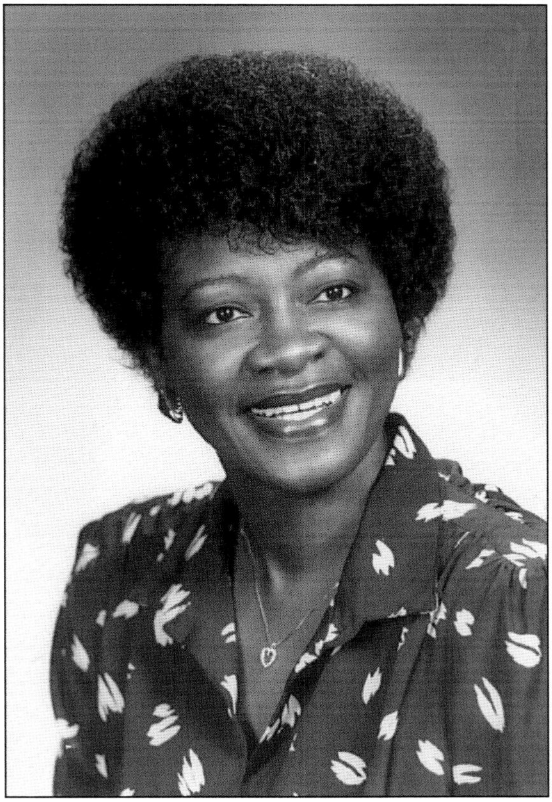

Pearl Mack Johnson was a successful banker. Her father was Loman Mack, one of Clearwater's first African-American police officers.

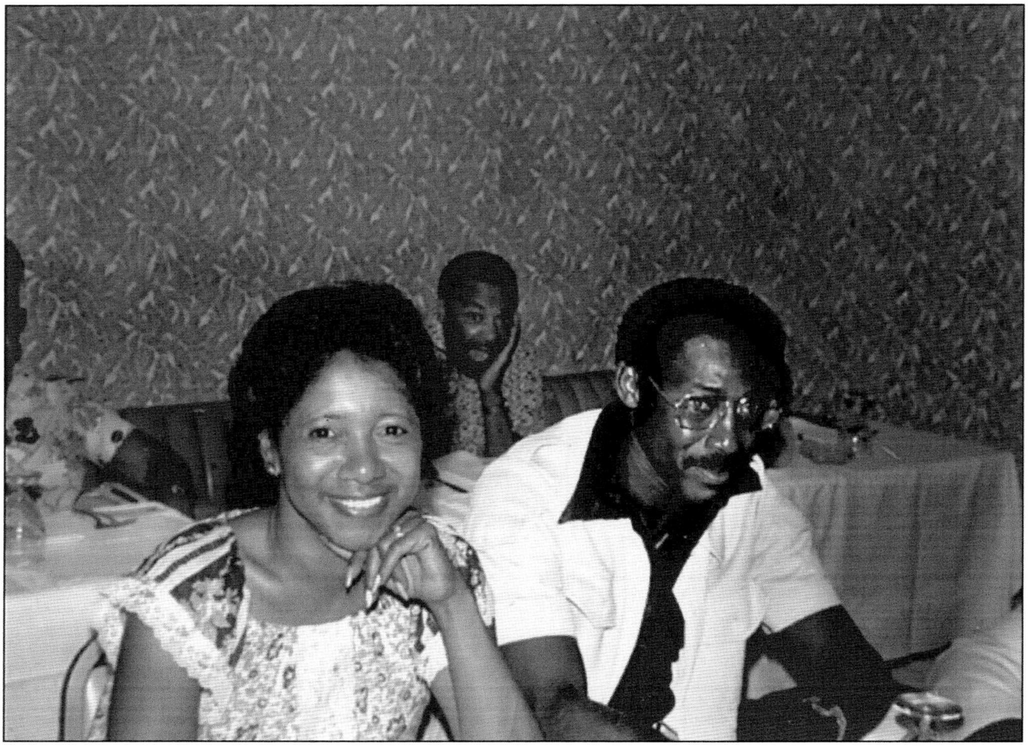

Salathiel Gaiter poses with his wife, Margaret. "Sal" Gaiter was a guidance counselor and coach in several Pinellas County schools.

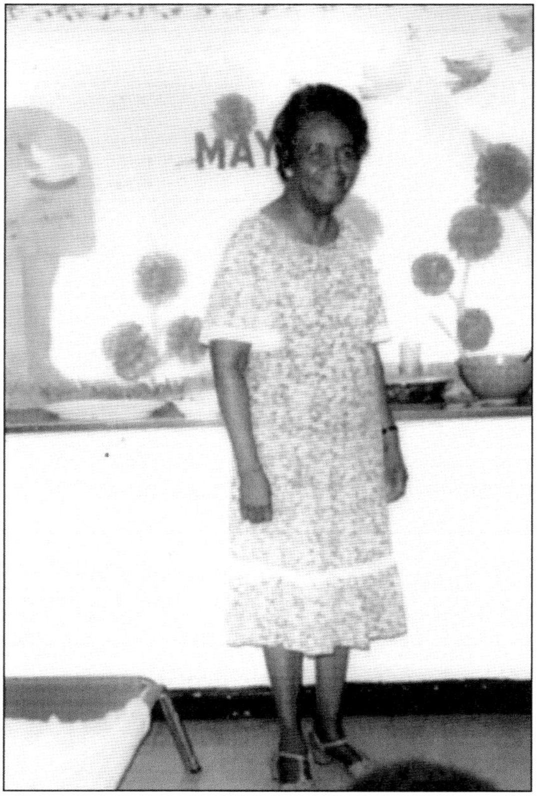

Altamese Bryant is depicted inside her Pinellas County classroom. Mrs. Bryant was a substitute teacher, as well as a teacher at the Reconciler Headstart Center.

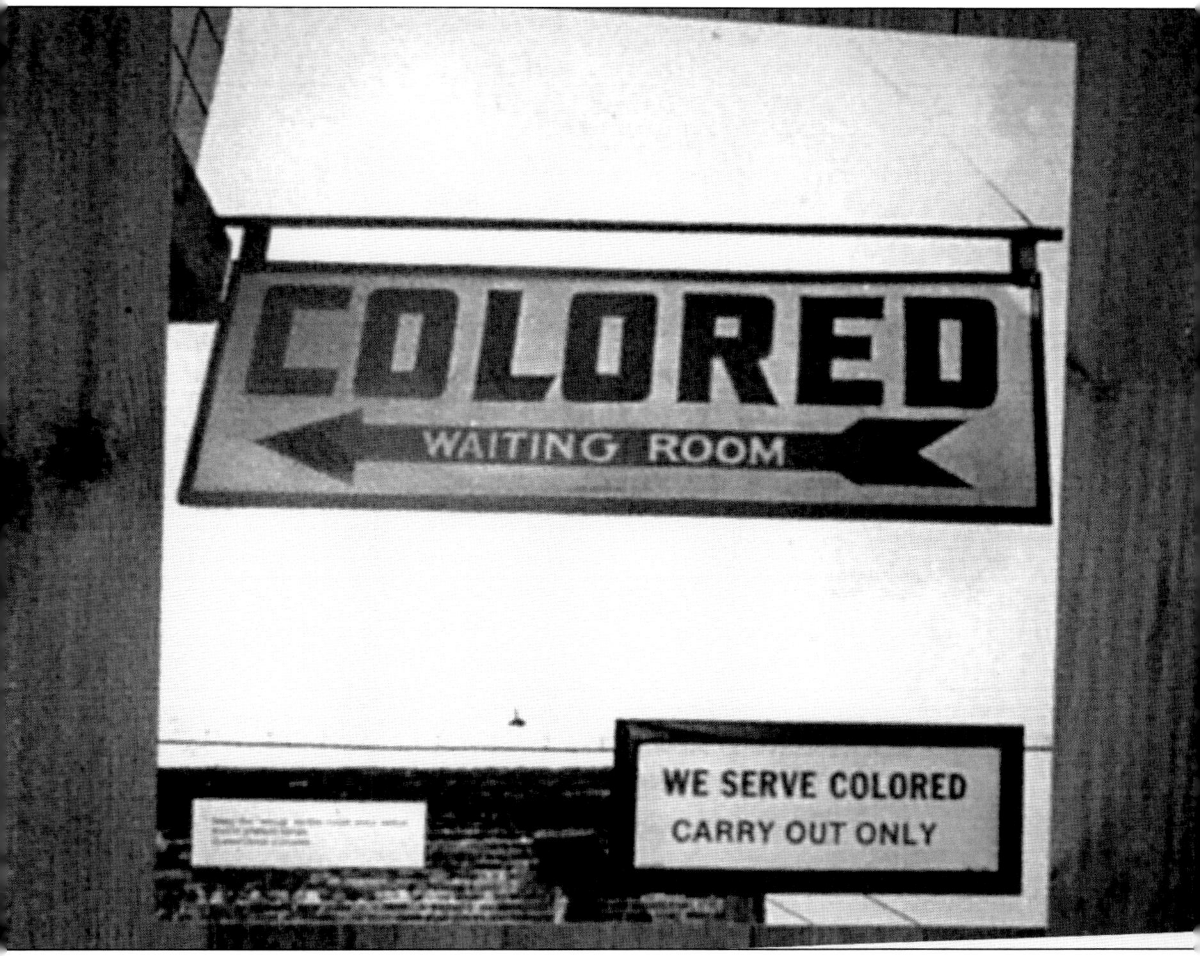

Signs like this were visible throughout Pinellas County. The one shown here was probably at a bus station. Notice the comment, "We serve colored carry out only."

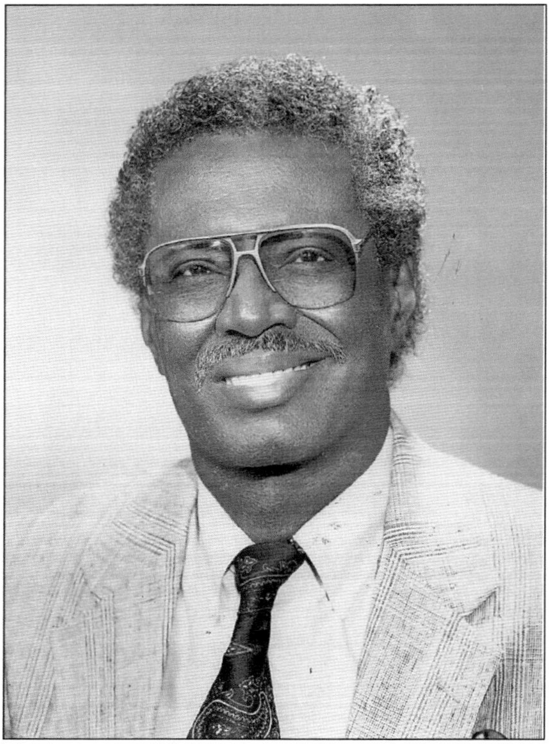

Pictured here is Milton Rooks Jr., who was hired in December 1968 by the City of Clearwater as coordinator of Community Relations.

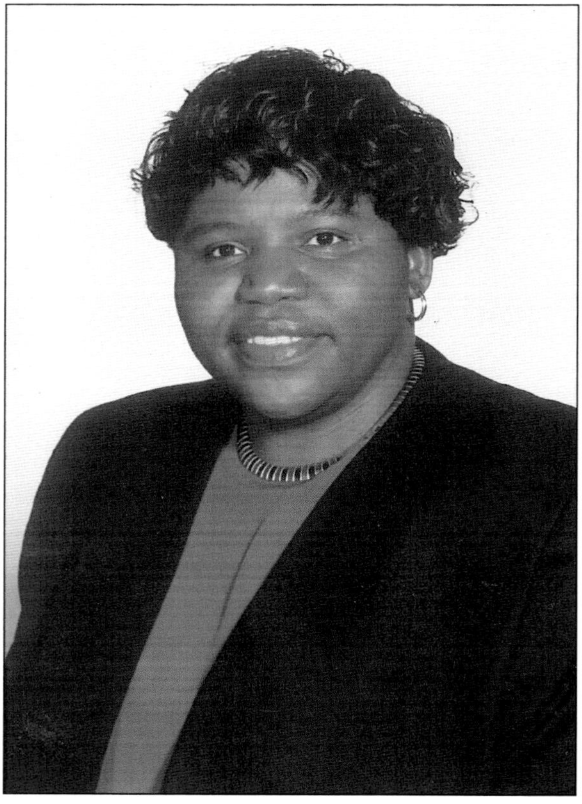

In 1984 Eleanor Breland was hired as Human Relations Director for the City of Clearwater. She still holds this position where she directs, administrates, plans, reviews, and develops programs promoting the value of diversity and equal employment opportunity rights for city employees

Nine

Little Darlings

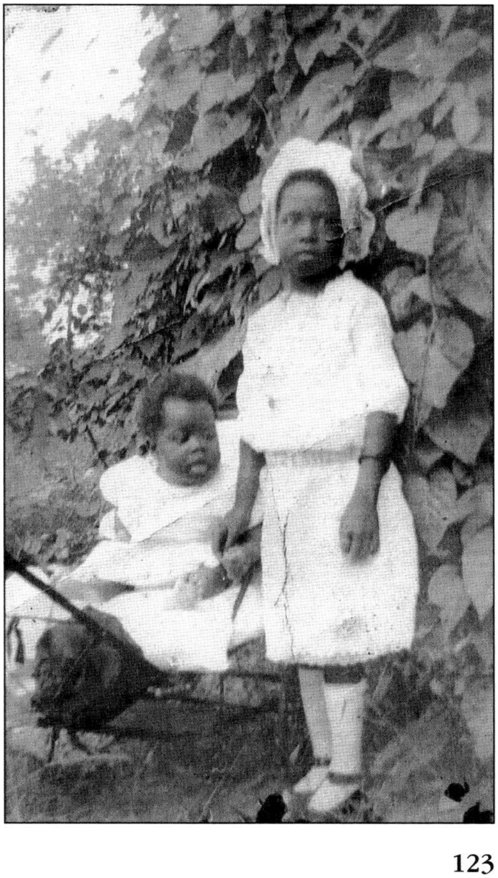

Sister and brother, Heddie and Sampson Hatchett, pose together. Heddie is outfitted in a two-piece dress trimmed in lace and wearing a bonnet. Sampson sits relaxed in the wagon.

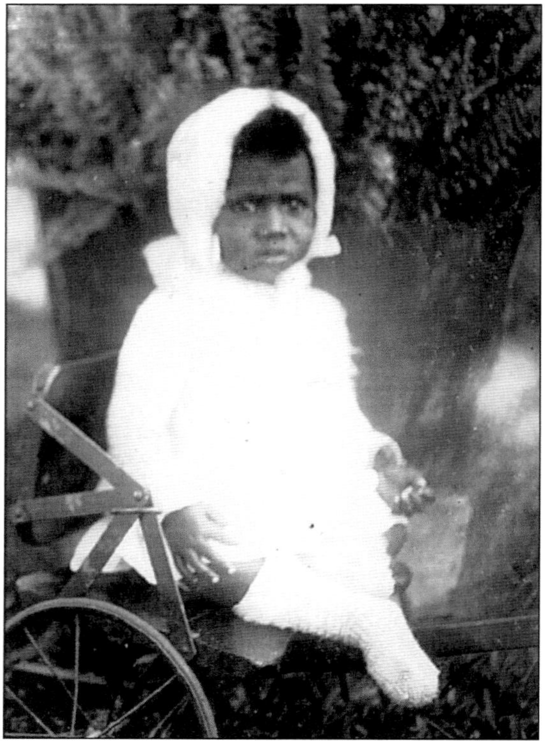

Sam Howard is depicted here in the early 1920s. He is being pulled in an early-style baby buggy. He is fully outfitted in bonnet and booties.

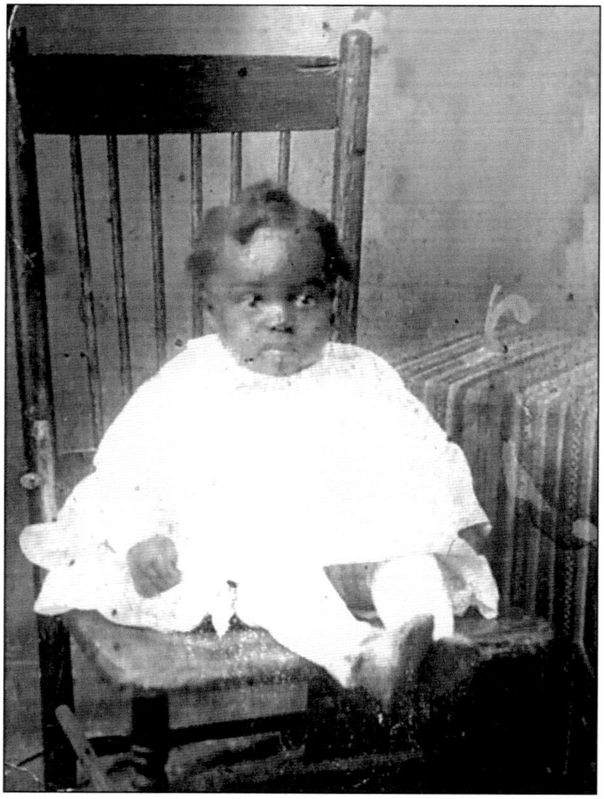

Thelma Young sits obediently in a ribbed-back wooden chair in the early 1900s.

Jacqueline Lewis appears to be celebrating her second birthday in this photo as she stands on top of the table next to her cake.

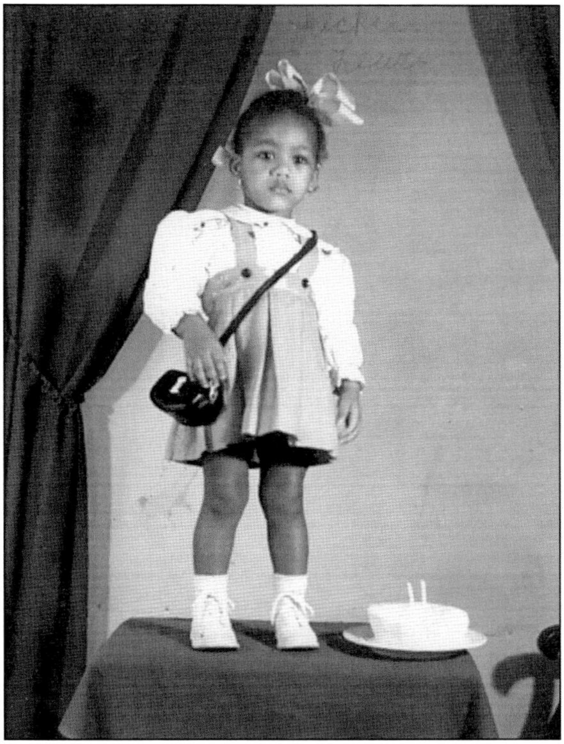

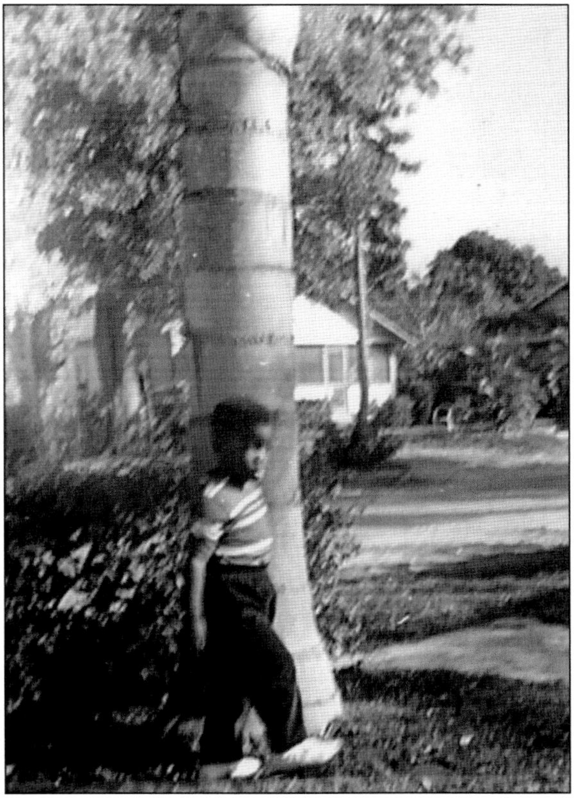

Eddie Wigfall III is shown here at the age of eight. This picture was taken in the early 1960s.

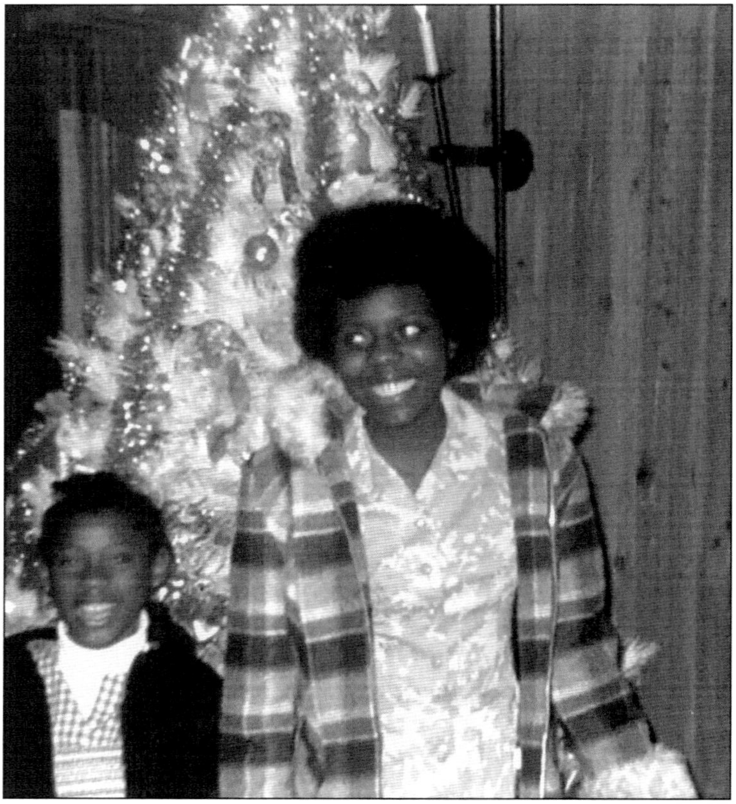

In this picture, Noliwe Rooks, granddaughter of Mr. and Mrs. Milton Rooks Sr. poses with her sister Tarsha after dinner at the Sheraton Sand Key Hotel during the Christmas holidays. Dr. Noliwe Rooks is an instructor of African-American studies at Princeton University. Tarsha Rooks is a Customer Software Administrator with Avaya Communications.

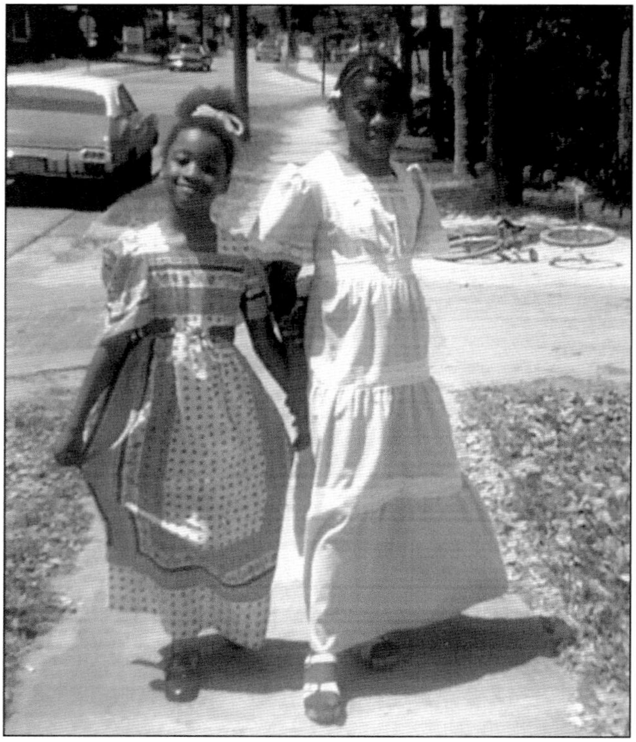

Latriviette Haire, daughter of Mr. and Mrs. Henry Haire, poses with Tarsha Rooks. Both girls wear a long dress purchased for Easter Sunday. Today, Latriviette Haire Jones is a teacher in the Pinellas County School System.

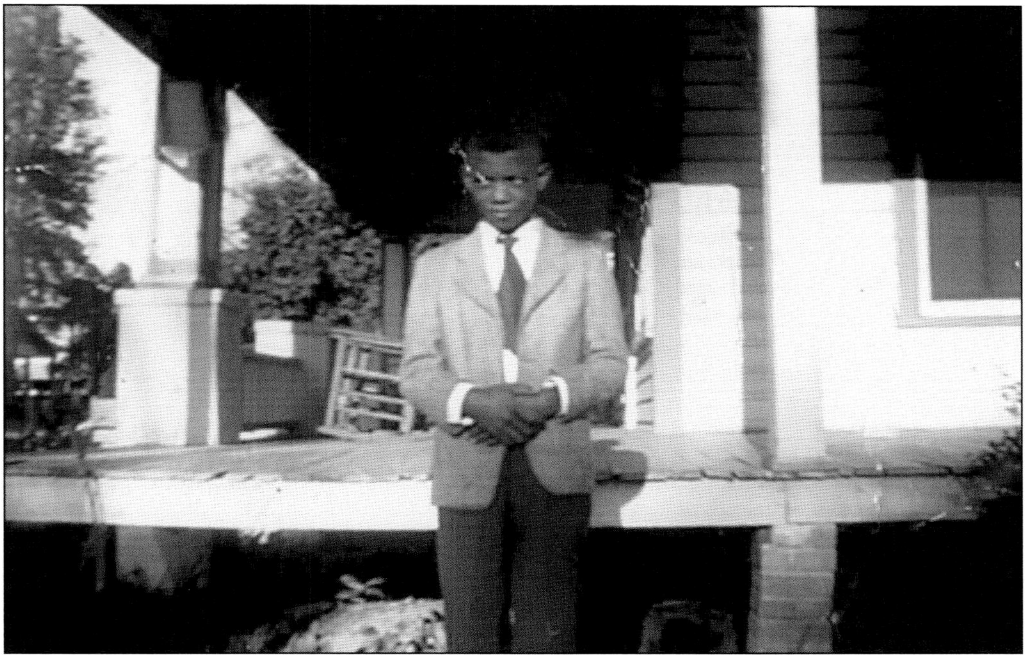

Willard Witherspoon poses outside the Rooks residence on Pierce Street at an early age.

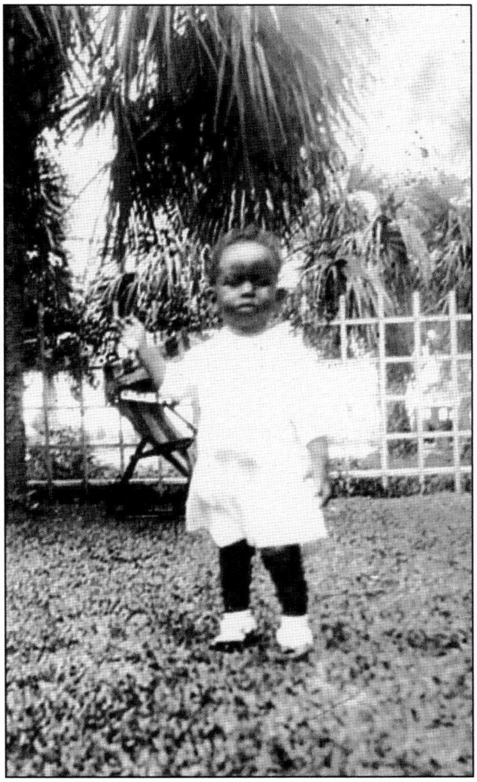

At 17 months, Victor Wigfall stands near a palm tree. He is Christine Morris's brother.

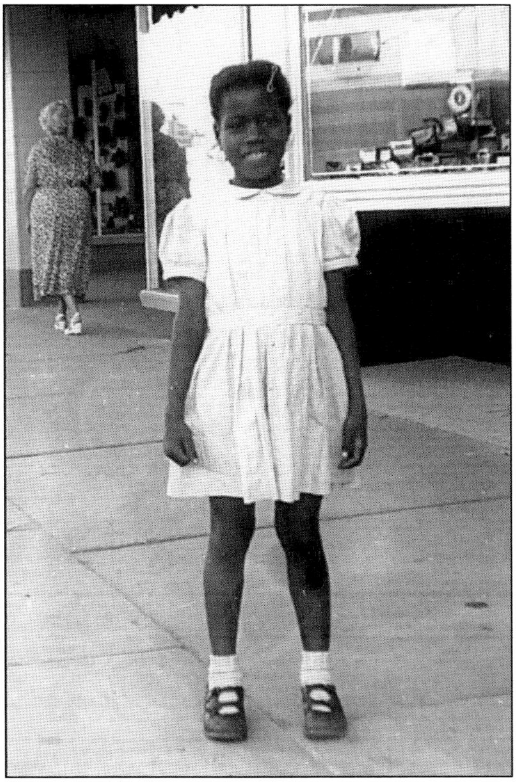

Betty Perry takes a break from shopping in downtown Clearwater in the 1950s.

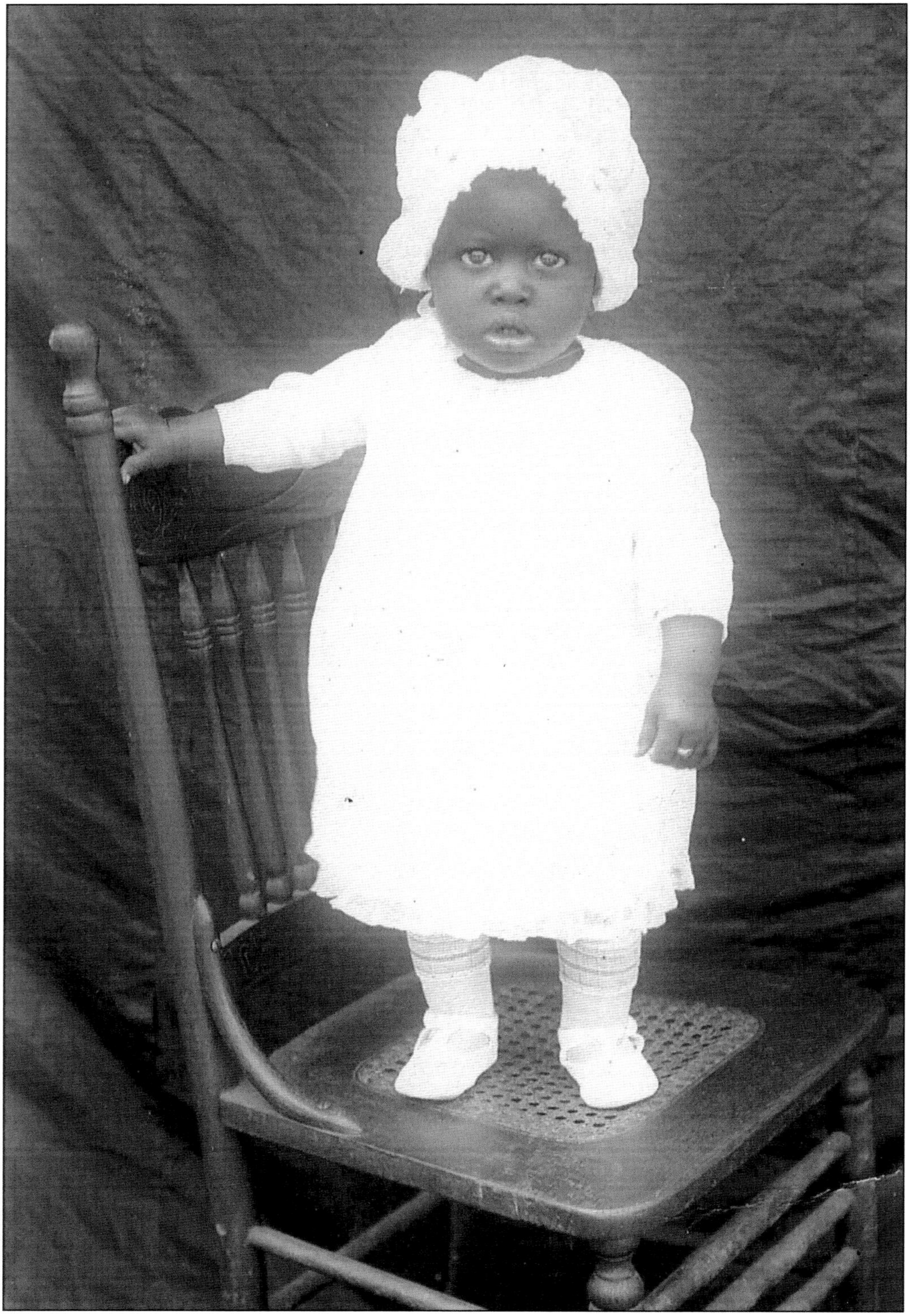

Rosalie Jackson is shown as a young toddler standing proud and holding onto a chair. She, too, is fully outfitted from head to toe. Rosalie's grandparents were pioneers of Clearwater.